Alan Bamberger is a San Francisco-based art appraiser, advisor, consultant and former rare book dealer specialising in fine and decorative arts books. He consults with artists and collectors from all over the world through his much-loved website at artbusiness.com, which has been active since 1998, and which attracts 5,000–6,000 unique visitors a day. Since the beginning, his site has been financially supported by hundreds of donations through collectors, galleries and art sites. Bamberger is the author of two other publications: *Buy Art Smart* and *Art For All*.

artbusiness.com

THE ART OF BUYING ART

How to evaluate and buy art like a professional collector

Alan Bamberger

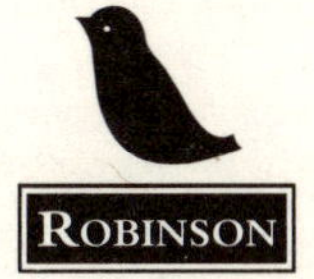

ROBINSON

First published in the USA in 2007 by LTB Gordonsart, Inc.

This edition published in Great Britain in 2018 by Robinson

A CIP catalogue record for this book is available from the British Library

ISBN: 978-1-47214-035-7

Typeset in New Caledonia LT by Hewer Text UK Ltd, Edinburgh
Printed and bound in Great Britain by CPI Group (UK) Ltd, Croydon, CR0 4YY

Papers used by Robinson are from well-managed
forests and other responsible sources

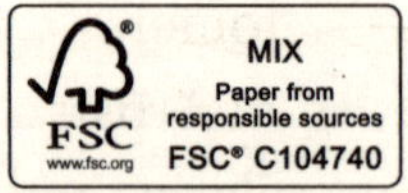

Robinson
An imprint of
Little, Brown Book Group
Carmelite House
50 Victoria Embankment
London EC4Y 0DZ

An Hachette UK Company
www.hachette.co.uk

www.littlebrown.co.uk

CONTENTS

ACKNOWLEDGEMENTS

A substantial number of people aided me in the writing of this book including art experts, art collectors, art dealers, other fine arts professionals, and everyday people who are interested in learning more about art. Much of their help was in the form of discussions, debates, questions and the sharing of beliefs, feelings and opinions about how art should be bought, sold and collected. Their feedback on so many different topics was instrumental in the completion of my task. I would like to thank the following people for contributing to this book.

Special thanks to all the people who responded to my 'Art Talk' column, and more importantly to those from around the world who continually contact me through social media (Facebook, Instagram, LinkedIn and Twitter in particular) as well as my website, www.artbusiness.com, with their emails, phone calls and even letters. You are the one who encouraged me to update, revise and enlarge this book, originally published as *Buy Art Smart* in 1990, and who continue to guide me in my writing with your questions and requests for information about art, artists and art collecting. Thanks also (in no particular order) to all the gallery owners who have so generously shared their experiences and insights with me over the years, including Robert Berman, Catharine Clark, Mat Gleason, Jack Hanley and Brian Gross, to name a few.

Additional thanks to Mark Simpson and Sally Mills of the Fine Arts Museums of San Francisco, Charles Campbell, Stacey Roman, Susan Friedewald, Kevin Mac Donnell, Paul Hertzmann and Susan Hertzig, Scot Levitt, Scott Haskins, Bob Conway, the art librarians at the main branches of the San Francisco and Oakland CA public libraries, the art librarians at the San Francisco Museum of Modern Art, Thomas McKenna, Steve Rubenfaer, Bill Currier, Edan Hughes, Valentine Walsh, Tom Hoepf and Connie Swaim of *AntiqueWeek*, John Garzoli of Garzoli Gallery, Lisa Peters of Montgomery Gallery, Ruth Braunstein, Dr Joseph Baird, Steve Newman, Ray Lewis, Mark and Colleen Hoffman of Maxwell Galleries, Tom Rarick, George Stern and Harris Stewart.

PREFACE

Once upon a time, owning original art was not much more complicated than seeing something you liked, paying for it, taking it home and hanging and enjoying it – no questions asked. But that carefree era is gone. These days, buying art (as well as selling it) is serious business and today's buyers are more concerned than ever about getting good art and good value for their money. Simply put, people want to spend wisely no matter what they buy and that's exactly what *The Art of Buying Art* teaches you when it comes to buying art.

Over the years, the basic principles involved in deciding whether to buy a work of art have stayed pretty much the same. Evaluation techniques and procedures remain more or less constant. What has changed dramatically is access to information. On the whole, today's art buyers are (or can be) more informed than ever about what they buy. The internet is in large part responsible for these changes, especially with the proliferation of online art, artists, art galleries, and art-price and art-research databases. In that regard, you'll find the entirely revised, enlarged and updated appendices more than helpful.

While knowledge is far more accessible overall, so is misinformation – sometimes unintentional, other times deliberate. This means that wending your way around the art world to find art that's right for you can get tricky every now and again.

In response to this, you'll find plenty of tips, instructions, precautions and recommendations to make sure your art-buying experience in today's marketplace is a rewarding one. So, prepare to become an educated, informed consumer and to learn *The Art of Buying Art*.

PART I: DEFINE

The Art of Buying Art is a book for everyone who appreciates original art and would like to own some. You or anyone else can learn to locate quality works of art that you love and pay fair prices for them; no previous knowledge about art or the art business is necessary. In order to accomplish this goal, however, realise at the outset that the art business has become increasingly complex in recent years, and figuring out what you like in art and how to find it are not quite as straightforward as they used to be. These introductory chapters contain basic information that will help orient you as you begin your search for those special works of art that will provide you with a lifetime of enjoyment.

CHAPTER 1

Anyone Can Master the Art of Buying Art

There is no right or wrong art, there is no right or wrong reason for wanting to own art, and there is no right or wrong way to go about buying art. With these thoughts in mind, you are about to begin a book that deals not in rights and wrongs, but rather in suggestions and recommendations that stem from two basic assumptions about people who buy art:

- People prefer to buy good-quality art.
- People prefer to pay fair prices for the art they buy.

All techniques and methods described in this book follow directly from these assumptions as a starting point. If you are like the great majority of art buyers, you too want good quality at fair prices – you want to master the art of buying art.

Unfortunately, most beginner buyers and collectors feel anywhere from inadequate to totally helpless about the prospect of buying art 'intelligently'. Worse yet, they have little faith in their abilities to ever accomplish this goal. To them, art is a mysterious and incomprehensible commodity, the secrets of which are understood only by art dealers, scholars, critics and other educated experts.

As a result, uninformed beginners tend to buy art in pretty much the same way – impulsively. They buy what they like, or what they think they like, wherever they happen to see it for sale, the first time they lay eyes on it. Any questions they might have are put to the sellers; whatever answers they get are instantly accepted. No further efforts are involved. They buy this way because they aren't aware that alternative methods exist and that they can actually control their art-buying destinies.

Here's the truth: *You – or anyone else – can research and evaluate any work of art you see for sale entirely on your own and determine whether you are spending your money wisely if you decide to buy it.* No previous knowledge about art or the art business is necessary. Everything you need to know is laid out right here in an easy-to-understand, easy-to-follow and logical progression.

FACTS ABOUT THIS BOOK

This book is a beginning. However involved with art you decide to get, what you are about to learn will serve as an introduction. You can spend a lifetime mastering the skills necessary to build a substantive art collection, but first you need a good solid foundation – and this book happens to be a great place to get it.

This book is a consumer guide to buying art. It approaches art from a product standpoint and it approaches the buying and selling of art from a business standpoint. As in any other consumer situation, when you buy art, you deserve to be treated fairly, you deserve to know what you're buying, you deserve to know how to protect yourself from advantage-takers and you deserve a quality product for your money.

This is a generic art book. It is specially designed to guide you through the intricacies of the art world regardless of your tastes. No matter what type of art you are thinking about buying, the procedures for familiarising yourself with its peculiarities, learning about the artists who create it and learning how to buy it effectively are remarkably similar in many ways.

The term 'art' as used in this book is whatever you want it to be. Whether your interest centres on Old Master paintings, sporting-scene lithographs, abstract sculptures, conceptual photography, art that moves, technological art or _______ (you fill in the blank with what you like the most), this book will serve you equally well. The only requirement for our purposes here is that the art be original and artist-created, not mass-produced by mechanical means in factory-type settings. (See Chapter 2 for more information on how to distinguish original works of art from reproductions and copies.)

This book favours no artists and it favours no art. In order to keep you from becoming biased or unduly influenced in the direction of your art buying, artist names you see in the text are fabricated, and facts about artist careers are fabricated. Only occasionally, in examples at the ends of chapters, are actual artists' names mentioned and only then to make points about how the art business works, not about those artists. Words describing different types of art (paintings, lithographs, sculptures, etchings, watercolours, etc.) are also used interchangeably throughout the book. All are treated equally, the point being that the entire text is applicable to all art and that no one medium is better to buy than any other.

This book applies to art in all price ranges. Whether you are chasing after multimillion-dollar masterworks or have a per-piece budget of $200, the ways you learn about and ultimately buy your art are essentially the same.

This book introduces you to how the art world works. It teaches you general truths about art, the art community, and the business of buying, selling and collecting. Wherever you go to buy art, whoever you meet in the process and whatever you hear, the great majority of what you read here will apply to your experiences.

This book is about safe, sensible, low-risk ways to begin buying art. A conservative approach is necessary because when you don't have much experience, you can get taken advantage of in too many ways. You can overpay, get stuck with forgeries, buy inferior pieces, be fooled by get-rich-quick schemes, buy art with serious condition problems, buy copies or reproductions when you think you're buying originals, and so on. Once you build yourself a good solid base of knowledge from which to operate – once you master the fundamentals – you can branch out, take risks and experiment with more advanced methods of buying art.

This book is primarily about buying art from established art galleries, including from gallery websites or other established retail online resources. Galleries or similar online resources are generally the safest places for novices to begin buying because they provide personal attention, offer ample learning opportunities, and offer protections and guarantees that may not be available elsewhere. You will also find several chapters throughout the book about alternative sources for buying such as directly from artists, over the internet, at auction, flea markets, garage and estate sales, resale outlets and so on. You're welcome to explore whatever buying opportunities whenever you want, but waiting until you gain some experience and get more comfortable around art before you patronise them is recommended. You can use what you learn here to buy art anywhere, but when you're just starting out, established galleries are great places to learn the basics.

This book is about *buying* art for your own personal enjoyment, not 'investing' in it. It is not about making money. If anything, it's about keeping you from losing money. Those of you who don't have a fundamental love, appreciation, fascination and passion for art to begin with – feelings that are totally unrelated to money – should get out now because in the long run you'll lose. Although financial aspects of art are important and will be discussed at length, they should never be the primary consideration in deciding whether or not to buy art.

THE FOUR STEPS TO THE ART OF BUYING ART

A lot can happen in the time interval between the moment you get the inclination to buy art and the moment you leave an art gallery with your first purchase in tow. Two approaches you may take are 1) you can buy at random and hope for the best, or 2) you can order your activities, logically proceed from one step to the next, and assure yourself the best possible outcome. This second approach is also known as the art of buying art. If you happen to be of the art-of-buying-art persuasion, the way to accomplish this goal involves your following four important steps exemplified by four key words, as described below.

Define: The first step to follow once you get the urge to buy art is to *define* those types of art that attract you the most. You need concrete ideas of what your tastes are and of what in art really affects you in a deep and meaningful way. Part I of this book shows you how to define the characteristics of the art that's right for you.

Select: Your next step is to locate and *select* specific works of art for possible purchase, art that appeals to you according to the guidelines laid out in Part I. In order to accomplish this, you need a working knowledge of how the art business operates. Familiarising yourself with the art community, art personalities, art dealers, art galleries and artists, and learning your responsibilities as an art buyer, are all parts of the selection process. Part II of this book teaches you how to understand and navigate the art world in a way that maximises your chances for selecting those works of art that are best for you.

Research: Once you make your selections, you have to learn more about them by *researching* them. In order to make informed decisions about whether or not you really want to own these works of art, you need to acquire specific information related to the art itself, the artists who created it and any other background information relevant to that art. Part III of this book teaches you basic art research techniques.

Buy: All works of art that survive the research process and still appeal to you at this final stage in your acquisition adventures become subject to one last consideration: price. Before you make that ultimate determination, *to buy or not to buy*, you need to understand general monetary aspects of the art business and, in particular, the financial implications of your potential purchases. You also need instruction in how to effectively complete whatever purchases you end up making – that is, how to conclude them to your best advantage. Part IV, the final part of this book, teaches you how to evaluate art prices and how to buy art advantageously.

Define, select, research, and buy – that's what the art of buying art is all about. This book will not transform you into an instant art expert – that takes time, effort and plenty of practice. It will, however, transform you into an informed consumer, protect you from making bad buys and help you to locate the best art for your money. So, take some time to read this book, follow the instructions and learn the art-business basics. Most importantly, take your time and resist the urge to rush out and spend money until you have a handle on how to spend it wisely.

Seasoned collectors will tell you that the 'work' involved in defining, selecting, researching and buying the right art for their collections is not really work at all, but more like pleasure, adventure, mystery, detective work and discovery all rolled up into one. In fact, nearly everyone will go on to say that the final act of buying is almost anticlimactic to the events leading up to those moments. Collectors across the board further agree that the learning process is self-perpetuating – the more they learn, the better they get at collecting, the greater their rewards and the more they want to keep on learning in the future.

A LOOK AHEAD

The Art of Buying Art is about how to buy original art, but if you have little or no experience of looking at art, how do you know whether what you're looking at is an original work of art or a reproduction or copy of that art? Unfortunately, the fine art marketplace is full of 'fine art reproductions' that may look like original art, but are no more original than newspaper or magazine illustrations. The next chapter teaches you how to tell the difference between original works of art and reproductions or copies of original works of art.

CHAPTER 2

ORIGINAL WORKS OF ART VERSUS REPRODUCTIONS

Once upon a time in the not-too-distant past, Adam Adams, the owner of the Three Star Printing Company, went to a fancy art opening at an established art gallery. The gallery was showing paintings by a well-known artist. Adam looked at one of the paintings, saw the selling price and was amazed at how expensive it was. He walked around the entire gallery, looked at all the other paintings and saw that they were equally expensive. He got to wondering whether other art galleries sold expensive paintings just like this gallery did.

The next day, Adam went out to see more art at more galleries and find out how much the paintings cost that they had for sale. He saw all kinds of paintings and they all cost a lot of money. On the way home from his day of gallery-hopping, Adam had a fantastic idea!

'Instead of printing travel brochures with beautiful little colour illustrations of faraway places and selling them for a few pennies each like I do now, maybe I can make beautiful big colour prints of paintings like the ones I've been looking at in the art galleries. Each print will cost not much more money to produce than a travel brochure, but I'll sell them for hundreds of dollars each or maybe even more. That sounds expensive, but compared to the prices of the paintings

I've been looking at, the prints will seem like bargains. I'll sell them to people who like the paintings but can't afford them. These people will think they're getting great deals and I'll make tons of money!'

There was one slight problem with Adam's idea, however. His prints were not original works of art like paintings or watercolours are. They were copies or reproductions of paintings that were printed the same way the illustrations in his travel brochures were printed. His prints were no different than calendar prints, posters, newspaper or magazine illustrations, or any other images printed with inkjet printers like the kinds that were selling at frame shops and poster stores for only a few dollars each. Paying hundreds of dollars apiece for his prints made no sense.

'I can get around this price issue,' Adam thought. 'I'll change the name of my business to the Three Star Fine Art Publishing Company instead of the Three Star Printing Company. I'll print my prints in finite quantities that I'll call *limited editions*, print them on heavy papers like the kinds of papers artists use, and have the artists who paint the originals sign and number the prints. Instead of marketing them as copies or reproductions, I'll call them *artist-signed and numbered, limited edition digital fine art images*. That's technically what they are anyway, so I'm not misrepresenting anything. They'll sound important and people will think they're getting original works of art just like paintings. My costs will be a few dollars more per print than if I print them on regular paper and don't have the artists sign them, but that's nothing compared to the amount of money I'll make when I sell them.'

So, the commercial printer became a 'fine art publisher' and began producing his prints and advertising them in full-page colour advertisements on art websites and in art magazines. He designed his advertisements to look and read just like the ones the art galleries used to sell their expensive original paintings. He even started calling his inkjet prints giclées (from the French verb *gicler* meaning to squirt, spurt or splatter). People saw his advertisements and, sure enough, they believed his prints were original works of art. They also believed they were saving huge amounts of money compared to what the original paintings cost, so they bought without having the slightest idea that what they were really buying were only reproductions or copies made from high-resolution scans or photographs of the original works of art. Meanwhile, the Three Star Fine Art Publishing Company made tons of money, Adam Adams never had to print another travel brochure again, and he lived happily ever after in a great big house on a hill.

This may or may not be how the 'limited edition fine art print industry', or, as I prefer to call it, the reproduction print business, got started, but it's probably not far from the truth. Today, reproduction print sales represent a significant percentage of all art business transactions, with the larger publishing companies having annual operating budgets up to millions of dollars.

Here are the facts: *These limited edition prints are not original works of art. They are not made by the artists who conceive and create the originals. They are copies of original works of art produced and printed by printing companies. You do not get original works of art when you buy them; you get signatures of artists on digitally produced copies of original works of art.*

The distinction must be made here between original artist-made prints and reproduction prints. Unlike reproduction prints, handmade prints like etchings or lithographs are entirely conceived, created and produced by hand by fine artists known as 'printmakers'. Many artists also create original digital images on computers or by manipulating existing images to create entirely new and original ones. The key difference is that these are original images produced by artists, whereas reproductions or copy-prints are simply photographic or scanned copies of works of art that already exist in other mediums like painting, watercolour, etc.

Reproduction print processes do involve a degree of skill and technical knowledge and ability, but the publishers and not the artists are almost always the ones who do that work. Advertisements sometimes claim that the artists 'oversee' or 'closely cooperate' in the process, but those who actually do participate are in the small minority. Their participation is rarely hands-on and it usually involves little more than making sure the colours and finished reproductions are accurate copies of the originals. The overwhelming majority of artists play little or no part in the reproduction process – all they do is sign and number the finished copies.

Publishing companies use a variety of techniques to obscure this minimal artist involvement and also to obscure the fact that the prints are copies and not originals. The most obvious two techniques have already been mentioned – they print the copies in limited quantities and then have the artists sign and number them.

To enhance the illusion that reproduction prints are no different from original works of art, marketers create names for the prints like giclées, pigment prints, archival ink print and so on. Those names are used in combination with a bewildering array of ambiguous words and phrases like 'hand-signed', 'consecutively numbered', 'acid-free paper', 'no-fade inks', 'certificate of authenticity', '100 per cent rag paper', 'limited edition art', 'subscription edition', 'commission offering', 'authentic', 'original', 'produced in close cooperation with the artist', 'hand-accented', 'blind embossed', 'deluxe embellished edition' and so on. For example, an *authentic, original, limited edition, giclée pigment print* sounds important and accurately describes a substantial percentage of limited edition prints, but it also accurately describes most mass-market publication illustrations!

To complete the illusion, copy-prints are marketed and sold just like original art is sold. The prints are advertised on art websites, in art magazines, sold out of stores that look just like art galleries, professionally hung and lit, beautifully framed, and treated like original art by the people who sell them. The big publishing companies thoroughly accomplish their objective – laypersons have great difficulty telling the difference between original art and copy-prints.

More facts about copy-prints:

- *Original prints made by artists are usually printed in editions of fewer than 100 (usually far fewer).* Reproductions or copy-prints are usually printed in editions of at least 300–500 and occasionally into the thousands! (For purposes of comparison, a book with sales exceeding 50,000 copies is considered a bestseller.)
- *The financial values of copy-prints have no relation to the values of the original works of art they reproduce even though the people who sell them would like you to think they do.* Suppose, for example, that a fine art publishing company makes a limited edition print of the *Mona Lisa*. Granted, they can't get Leonardo da Vinci to sign it, but let's say that the chief printer and an important museum curator sign it. Do you believe for one moment that the print's value has any relation to the value of the priceless *Mona Lisa*? Of course it doesn't!
- *The great majority of copy-prints cost less than $100 each to produce and sometimes as little as a few dollars each.*

The great majority of copy-prints sell for hundreds and even thousands of dollars each. They're advertised as affordable when, in truth, they're overpriced for what they are!

- *Publishing companies, not artists, often receive the bulk of the revenues generated by sales of copy-prints.* The artists usually receive modest percentages, assuming they don't sell the reproduction rights to the original works of art (and sometimes even the original works themselves) outright.
- *The bottom line is that copy-prints are not art.* Every time a publishing company sells a copy-print, one less artist sells one less original work of art.

Now that's out of my system, let me add that the great majority of reproduction prints are beautifully produced, highly decorative and perfectly acceptable to buy and collect. If you love a particular image and buying a reproduction print is the only way you can afford to own it, go ahead and buy it. Have no illusions, though, about either the originality or the financial prospects of what you're buying. At best, copy-prints are not much more than collectibles relating to the artists who sign them, in much the same way that an art book or gallery exhibit catalogue would be if it was signed by an artist.

HOW TO RECOGNISE LIMITED EDITION COPY-PRINTS

Until the onset of digital printing, recognising limited edition copy-prints was not that difficult. Since they were printed in ways that were very similar to how most commercial illustrations are printed, all you had to do was look closely at their surfaces, with magnification if necessary, for dot-matrix patterns – the same types of patterns you would see if you looked closely at newspaper or magazine illustrations. Unfortunately, today's digital printing techniques are far more sophisticated.

Inkjet printer patterns are often so fine that you need a jeweller's loupe or hand-held microscope to see them (you can buy good 60–100X pocket microscope online for $10–$20). Special textured papers can obscure these patterns further and make them even more difficult to detect. Some of the more advanced digital reproduction processes practically eliminate dot patterns altogether. In other words, simple identification tests no longer work across the board.

One identification technique, however, has always worked and will continue to work for as long as copy-prints are produced. If you ever have doubts about whether what you are looking at is an original work of art or a reproduction print, ask the seller the following question: *Is this print a copy or reproduction of an original work of art?* If the seller is not sure or is unable to give a satisfactory answer, have them contact the publisher. Better yet, ask both the seller and the publisher and get their answers in writing along with a money-back guarantee that their representations are correct.

OTHER TYPES OF 'ART' THAT ARE NOT ORIGINAL

Variations on limited edition copy-prints can be found in nearly all segments of the art trade. Although the following items are often advertised and marketed as affordable 'art', once again, they're copies of originals, not original works of art, and should be priced as commercially available or mass-market prints or posters, not as original artworks. If you want to buy original works of art, several such products to avoid are listed below.

Reproductions of famous works of art. Any type of art from any time period can be reproduced including bronzes, paintings, prints, antiquities, metalwork, ceramics and porcelains. Contemporary recasts of Remington bronzes, reissues of Currier & Ives or Audubon prints and other reproductions of famous works of art are occasionally marketed using words and phrases like 'limited', 'authorised', 'collector editions', 'precision-crafted using the finest materials and techniques', 'unique', 'special' and so on.

No matter how these are marketed, they are copies. They have no connection to the originals other than being similar in the way they look. The original artists are not involved in their production – most died many decades ago.

Textured reproductions of paintings. These items also tend to be copies of famous works of art, but they deserve special mention because of how they are marketed. Potential buyers are told that these copy-prints look just like the originals, that their surfaces are textured just like the paint on the originals, that they're framed just like the originals, that some art experts may even think they're originals, and that owning these copies is like owning the originals.

These claims are nonsense. First of all, anyone who knows art can instantly tell the difference between these copies and the original works of art they represent. Second, they are produced by machines and not by artists. Third, they may seem cheap when compared to the originals, but they often cost little to produce compared to the prices they're marketed at, and in that sense are often overpriced.

Limited edition reproduction prints with small amounts of hand highlighting. This is a relatively recent arrival on the copy-print scene. The printing processes are the same, but small amounts of paint are then added by hand to the surfaces of the finished prints. Highlighted prints can sell for hundreds of dollars more than what their counterparts with no added paint sell for.

The truth is that the few added brush strokes typically take a few minutes at most to apply. Furthermore, the highlighting might not even be added by the original artists, but rather by people who are hired to do it for them. Dollar for dollar, these prints can be even more overpriced than ordinary copy-prints. If you have any doubts about what you are looking at, ask the seller the following question: *Is this a copy or reproduction of an original work of art that has been retouched by an artist?*

Remarqued limited edition reproduction prints. These are also copy-prints with handwork. Instead of altering the images, though, the artists add small sketches, usually in pencil and along the bottom margins, where the prints are also signed and numbered. These sketches are rarely much larger than a square inch or two and usually take a few minutes to complete. Nevertheless, they increase per-print prices by at least several hundred dollars, and often more, in the great majority of cases. For you maths fans in the crowd, an artist who charges $200 for a sketch that takes five minutes to finish is making $40 per minute or $2,400 per hour or $4,992,000 per year (assuming a 40-hour working week).

Contemporary printings of vintage photographs, especially digital reproduction prints of photographs originally taken with film cameras. These recent additions to the copy-print market are often enlarged from the originals and are occasionally signed, titled, numbered or accompanied by certificates of authenticity. The original photographers are often famous and may or may not still be alive. The original photographs themselves are often valuable or collectible, and their subject matters are often historical or significant in other ways. Images of famous sports figures, rock-and-roll stars, and early panoramas of cities, for example, are among the more popular subject matters currently being sold by copy-photograph dealers.

Copy-photographs can be made from any existing photographic image including negatives, positives, digital files and moving-picture film. As is the case with other forms of copy-art, marketers use ambiguous-sounding terms and phrases to sell contemporary prints of old photographs, such as 'from the original glass negatives', 'never before published', 'certificate of authenticity', 'archival printing', 'hand titled', 'numbered', 'exclusive limited edition', 'original prints' and so on. Selling prices can range into the thousands of dollars per image and, as with other limited edition copy-prints, copy-photographs are presented as affordable when compared to what the originals would cost.

The truth is that copy-photographs are relatively cheap to produce and can be produced whenever more prints are needed. If the original photographers are still alive and can sign reproductions, that at least gives them some value. When photographers are no longer living, the reproductions have no connection to either them or to the financial values or the collectability of the originals. From a collectible, historical or archival perspective, they're worth about as much as they cost to print and not much more. They have a certain amount of value as decorative images, but the ones that have the real value are the originals. If you have doubts about what you're looking at, ask the sellers: *Is this a recent copy or a reproduction of an original vintage photograph?*

Copies of well-known photographic images can make great decorative additions to collections, especially when the originals are either in museums or are prohibitively expensive. In case you're interested in certain photographers or images, many museums and institutions with photography collections or archives, including the Library of Congress, offer what are called 'photo-duplication services'. Anyone can contact these institutions directly and buy copies of famous photographs in their collections for prices starting under $50 each. The Library of Congress, for example, has over *ten million images* in its archives.

MORE ABOUT GICLÉES

A 'giclée' or digital print is a print-out of a digital file located on a computer's hard drive and printed by a digital printer. As mentioned above, the word 'giclée' is derived from the French verb *'gicler'*, which means 'to squirt, spurt or splatter'. Collectors like giclée prints because of the way they look. Digitally produced prints have a unique appearance about them that is difficult to achieve by using conventional printing processes. Colours can be strikingly vibrant, details can be crystal clear and the overall visual impact of a digital image can be highly dramatic.

From an art standpoint, there are two types of giclée prints. The first type exists only as a computer file, that is, it is created by a digital artist on a computer. These giclées are considered original works of art and are usually sold by the artists themselves or by galleries specialising in original digital art. The second type is a digital reproduction or copy-print of a work of art that is in another medium. That is, it is made by either photographing or scanning a piece of art like a painting or a watercolour, converting it to a digital file on a computer and then printing that file out with a digital printer. These giclées are basically equivalent to photocopies and are usually marketed by commercial printing companies. Many artists also offer digital prints for buyers on a budget or who can't afford their originals.

If you love the look of giclées and want to buy them, make sure you understand the difference between original digital images and reproduction prints. When you're not sure about what you're looking at, ask the seller: *Is this an original digital print created by a digital artist on a computer or is it a reproduction or copy of a work of art like a painting or a watercolour?* Reviewing the artist's career accomplishments is another good way to check for originality. Résumés or CVs of digital artists usually include their experience and accomplishments creating computer images and graphics; résumés of conventional artists usually talk about their paintings or watercolours.

A LOOK AHEAD

Now that you have some instruction in how to tell the difference between originals and copies, you're ready to go out, start looking at art, figure out what you like and define the types of art you would most enjoy buying. The next chapter talks about how to set aside any preconceived notions you might have about art so you can approach the art world with an open mind.

CHAPTER 3

DISCOVER THE ART WORLD

The great majority of people who decide to buy art are relatively unaware of the incredible variety that's available for purchase. Their tastes are often the products of happenstance, their upbringings, past experiences and limited arbitrary encounters with art. They operate according to preconceived notions about art collecting, art buying and what the art they want to own looks like – notions they've held for perhaps years or even decades. This is best illustrated with an example.

Suppose you're back in kindergarten and your art-class assignment one day is to draw an apple. You eagerly take out your purple, green and black crayons and draw a green form shaped like a figure of eight with black and purple lines coming out of it. Then you make purple, black and green dots all over the back of the paper, crush the whole thing up and confidently place it on the desk in front of you. For whatever reasons you have at that moment, this is an apple. More importantly, it's your apple, you're proud of it and you believe you did a great job making it.

When the art teacher comes by to critique your work, you find out differently. You are gently but firmly informed that you don't crush up your paper and that an apple is round and red with a place on top for the stem and maybe a leaf or two. You sadly accept this fact, throw away your apple, take out a new sheet of paper and draw the art teacher's apple in place of yours.

The combined effect of this and similar experiences you have while growing up is that your definition of art becomes narrower and narrower and narrower. You are told that art should look a certain way, be made a certain way, mean certain things, be this size and that shape, these colours, have this texture and so forth. If it fails to satisfy any of these criteria, it's bad, incompetent, a bunch of scribbles, trash, junk, stupid and, of course, it's not art.

Take a few moments here and jot down *your* preconceived notions. Include what you think the art you're interested in buying looks like, who the artists are, where you might go to buy it, how much it costs and any other relevant specifics. Be as thoughtful and detailed as possible and *save these notes*. They define your official starting point and will serve as a reminder of where you were when you began this book.

Done writing? Good. Now take your piece of paper, fold it up, put it in a drawer and forget about it. While you're at it, imagine putting everything else you know about art into that same drawer and forgetting about it, too. Your current knowledge may well come in handy later but, for the time being, let's start with a blank slate. Approach your quest to define what you like as though you've never read or heard a thing about art before in your life, as though you have no opinions about it whatsoever.

Whatever you think, forget it for now. Don't let your brain get in the way. With your brain in full gear, you look at a painting, print or sculpture and hear little voices in your head saying things like 'My friends will stop speaking to me if I buy this', or 'This thing will never increase in value', or 'I have no idea who this artist is – his art can't be any good.' Screening out all this interference allows you to begin at the very beginning and survey your most basic gut reactions to art.

An empty mind permits you to see, feel and experience pure emotion, to let the art control you. Don't filter your response to the art through a belief system that may or may not have a basis in fact. By letting your raw feelings guide you, you take the first major step in defining what you really like. After all is said and done, of course, you may find that you are attracted to the exact same art you were before you started, but then again, you may discover that your true tastes are for art that you never imagined you could appreciate.

LOOK, LOOK, LOOK

Now that your mind is out of the picture, let's get art into the picture. You've got to familiarise yourself with the product you intend to purchase. *Your first assignment is to begin the definition process by getting out there and seeing as much art and as many different kinds of art as you possibly can.*

Either you can take a systematic approach to your looking and see one particular type of art at a time or you can see many different types in no particular order. Whatever you feel comfortable doing is fine, but remember, don't be selective in your viewing – look at everything everywhere.

The best way to start is by looking at art up close and in person like at museums, art fairs, art galleries, arts organisations, artist associations, art walks or open studios, historical societies (if you like older art) and corporate collections. But don't stop there. Wherever your day-to-day activities take you – shopping malls, banks, the doctor's, hotel lobbies, restaurants – keep a constant eye on the walls, the pedestals and the display areas. At this early stage, the art you see in a shopping mall is just as important to look at as what you see at a museum.

Another great place to look at art is the internet. Looking at art online is nothing like seeing it in person, but the good thing about the internet is that you can see far greater varieties by all kinds of artists from every corner of the earth in a far shorter period of time than you can by physically travelling from place to place. You can browse museum collections, scroll through gallery websites, visit artist web pages and much more. Social networking sites like Instagram and Facebook in particular are great places to search for art and follow your favourite artists.

See old art, new art, abstract art, big art, little art, bright art and dark art. Look at paintings, sculptures, etchings, prints and watercolours. Look at 'works of art' that you're not even sure are art. Once again – *look at everything*. Don't try to understand it, analyse it, read about it, find out who the artists are, figure out what it is or how it's made, or ask other people what they think about it. Just plop yourself down in front of it and look. Monitor your reactions to it – that's all.

Do you like it or not? Does it make you feel happy, sad, calm, angry, exhilarated? Do you love it or hate it or have no reaction to it at all? Does it make you think about certain issues? Does it transport you to other realities or to faraway places? Does it change the way you think? Show you new ways of looking at things? These are the internal reactions you are looking to define.

Two additional pointers:

- *Pay attention to art you hate as well as art you like.* Recognising what you want to avoid is just as important as recognising what you love.

- *Don't ignore certain types of art you are already familiar with because you think you know what your reactions will be and believe that nothing about them will ever change.* That's your brain getting in the way again. View it as though you are seeing it for the very first time.

HOW TO LOOK

Looking at art means more than giving casual glances as you pass it by. You've got to spend time studying individual pieces.

Stand up close and focus on small areas of the art. Stand back and look at the whole thing. Stick your nose right up to the canvas or wood or paper or bronze and study the minutest details. Back away slowly and watch how the art changes. Move so far away that the art practically disappears into its surroundings.

Look at the colours, subject matters, sizes, styles, frames, pedestals. Look at single brush strokes on a painting, single lines on an etching, single details on a sculpture. Look at the materials making up the art; see how it's put together.

If you happen to see something you really like, note what it is, where you saw it, how it looks and why it attracts you – nothing more. You'll have plenty of opportunity to return and learn more about it later.

Resist the temptation to speak with people about whatever you're looking at. Start asking questions and you'll be right back in that rut of letting your mind or the minds of others control your responses. Avoid exposing yourself too early in your explorations to opinions on what's good, what's bad, what to buy or what to avoid. At this formative stage, no one has the inside track on what's best for you better than yourself.

Don't read literature or brochures about the art you are looking at. Don't look at explanations, titles or prices. Pay no attention to the names of artists or how famous they are. All this information interferes with your gut feelings. Suppose, for example, you see a painting and hate the way it looks. Then you come closer, read the label and find out that Pablo Picasso painted it, and it's selling for $14 million. Do you change your mind all of a sudden and decide you really like it? Of course not!

Remember, all you're doing here is looking and feeling. You are not committing yourself in any way; you can change your mind about what you like at any time. You are simply getting in touch with how you feel when you look at various types of art. *The goal of 'looking without thinking' is this: By experiencing a little bit of everything that's out there and taking some time to study it in detail, you begin to acquire strength of conviction and begin to define what really thrills you.*

Out of all the millions of art pieces that have ever been and have yet to be created, you will choose to own maybe one, maybe five, maybe one hundred. And you'll choose them because they mean something special to you and you alone. Now is the time to acquire a feel for where that special meaning lies, and to identify what qualities in art attract you the most.

Example 1

The most sophisticated collectors I know are the ones who spend the most time looking at art. Some focus only on the art they collect, while others are more adventurous and are constantly on the lookout for new and exciting pieces to add to their collections. One collector I know makes a point of looking at and studying a far greater amount and wider range of art than he collects. He stays in shape, so to speak, and, as a result, is able to evaluate many different types of art on a variety of levels, whether he collects them or not.

This person began by collecting nineteenth-century art, moved on to abstract and conceptual art and artists from the second half of the twentieth century, and eventually focused on collecting contemporary art. By keeping informed about a wide range of current events in the art world and considering whatever art was brought to his attention – whether he knew anything about it or not – he developed an uncanny ability to spot and act on trends in the marketplace before most other collectors. Two big benefits of his buying ahead of the market were that he had a larger selection of pieces from which to choose and the prices he paid were often reasonable due to the fact that not that many other collectors were buying in his chosen areas.

Example 2

An incredible amount of art is bought by people who buy more or less at random. They buy because someone tells them to, because their friends own one, because they think they're going to make a bundle of money when they resell, because they think the artists are 'famous' or 'hot' and that they'll impress their friends, and so on. Buying art this way has little upside:

- The buyers themselves suffer because they are being controlled by outside forces. Rather than buying what they love, they're buying what they think they should buy.
- Artists suffer. Rather than select from the great variety of quality art that artists produce, inexperienced buyers put their money into those few names that they already recognise, that happen to be trendy, are hyped the most, get the

best news coverage and so on. Many outstanding artists who are not that publicity-oriented have difficulty selling their art because so many people are blinded by glitz and glamour and buy like sheep.

- Dealers who deal in quality art suffer. The market gets flooded with art that is not that good, but rather satisfies whatever mass tastes happen to be – whatever buyers think is the thing to buy at the moment. At worst, money goes to slick business people who know more about marketing what's hot than they do about art.

What's important here is that you come to understand the incredible variety of art that's available in the marketplace, pinpoint your tastes, develop a sense of independence and purpose, stay true to what you love and avoid jumping into the market before you have a good solid footing. Develop confidence in yourself and your preferences. Then start buying.

A LOOK AHEAD

As you begin to get an idea of what qualities in art attract you the most, the time comes to start getting practical – to let your brain back into the picture. Putting thoughts to your feelings once again becomes necessary because that is the only way you'll be able to communicate your needs, acquire information and, in the end, buy art. Your next step in defining what you like, therefore, is to identify and describe the art you really want to buy.

CHAPTER 4

DEFINE WHAT YOU LIKE

So far, you have experienced art on a purely emotional level, evaluating how it looks and feels to you with no interference from the brain, that is, the intellectual or cognitive components of whatever you're looking at. You have seen and noted particular works of art that possess a certain magic for you, that impress you in ways you find appealing. Defining what you like means putting the characteristics and qualities of this special art into words.

Not only do you have to define it, but you have to be specific. The better you are able to pinpoint your preferences, the better the art community is able to understand and serve you.

Begin this procedure by reviewing any notes you took during your Chapter 3 adventures. Return to locations where you saw art you liked. Look at that art again and find out basic information about it. If you have questions about specific works of art, have gallery personnel or other art professionals such as curators, consultants or experienced collectors explain and clarify whatever details you're unsure of. Record all relevant data for future reference. Avoid getting involved in any serious discussions about art at this point (it's a little premature for that), and confine your fact-gathering mission to the basics:

- Find out the names of the artists.
- Find out where the art originates. Is it American, European, South American, Japanese? Is it from London, from Tokyo, from New York City?
- Note when the art dates from. Is it contemporary, from the twentieth century, nineteenth century or some other period?
- Note the style or styles of the individual works of art. Are they abstract? Realistic? Impressionistic? Conceptual? Pop Art? Surreal?
- Identify the mediums that the art is created in. Are they watercolours, bronzes, oil paintings on canvas, etchings, colour woodcuts, mixed media and so on?
- Identify the subject matters. Are they representations of anything in particular? Landscapes? Seascapes? Still lifes? City scenes? Busts of famous people? Geometric abstracts?
- Find out the financial values of any works of art that are for sale or, when possible, art you like that's in private collections (as opposed to art on permanent display in museums or other institutions).
- Note any other relevant physical characteristics that are consistent from one piece to the next such as what sizes, shapes and colours they are.

Once you have assembled this information, combine it into a concise opening statement that you can make to anyone who is interested in knowing what you prefer in your art. As conversations progress, you can fill in the additional details as required. Here are some examples of good opening statements:

'I'm interested in contemporary oil paintings of spring scenes in the French countryside.'

'I love contemporary folk art by Louisiana artists.'

'I'm looking for abstract sculptures by New York City artists created between 1970 and the present.'

'I want to buy etchings and lithographs of sporting scenes that have waterfowl in them, preferably ducks.'

Make sure your statement provides adequate introductory information about your needs. Suppose you are in an art gallery and the owner asks what you are interested in buying. You answer: 'Seascapes.' You feel perfectly comfortable with that answer because the central feature of every work of art you like is a large body of water. But if you think for a moment, 'Seascapes' happens to cover a huge amount of territory. Your statement is too general – the dealer has virtually no information to work with. He could show you hundreds of seascapes, none of which you would find acceptable.

The dealer has no idea whether you want coastal scenes, clipper ships tossing about on stormy seas or peaceful sunsets over tropical beaches; large pictures or small ones; bright pictures or dark ones; contemporary examples or ones painted decades ago. You can only carry on a constructive conversation about your tastes in art when you have a good opener and plenty of specifics with which to follow it up.

Don't worry that defining your preferences too narrowly at this early stage will eliminate huge amounts of art from consideration before you even get going. This is not the case and, in fact, the opposite often occurs. Once you begin focusing on specifics, you realise that a lot more is available within that particular realm of collecting than you ever imagined existed. And remember, just because you define your interests now doesn't mean that you must stick to them for the rest of your life. You can modify your opening statement or change your preferences at any time.

The general rules for buying art are pretty much the same no matter what you decide to collect. By setting an initial direction now and following through to the point of purchase, you acquire the basic skills necessary to form a quality collection of whatever type of art you eventually choose to focus on.

BE REALISTIC

An important part of defining your likes is making them workable in the real world of buying art. By setting realistic, reachable goals for yourself, you maximise the chances of your being able to find exactly the art you are looking for. If your preferences in art are great in theory, but impractical in terms of buying, you've got to adjust them appropriately. Below are some factors you should take into consideration.

Make sure you can afford what you want to buy. As soon as possible, figure out your budget; decide approximately how much money you are willing to spend per work of art. If the art that thrills you the most is too expensive, look for something more affordable that has similar characteristics to those favourites.

Suppose, for example, that you love French Impressionist paintings, but that your per-piece budget is only $5,000. Decent-quality French Impressionist works start in the tens of thousands of dollars each and proceed rapidly upward from there. For your $5,000, you can barely even buy a decent sketch on a small scrap of paper. You could solve this problem by looking instead for Impressionist-style pictures by contemporary artists that approximate the look of those you like and that sell in the $5,000 range. Your opening statement would be, 'I want to collect paintings by contemporary artists done in the manner of the French Impressionists that cost between $3,000 and $5,000 each.'

Whatever your budget, make sure you can buy a reasonably good piece of art. If you can't afford better-quality examples of what you like the most, lower your sights accordingly. Collectors across the board will tell you that regardless of your budget, buy as close to the top of your chosen area of focus as you can.

For instance, if good-quality examples of the art you like the most cost $8,000 to $10,000 each and you only have $2,000 to spend, you won't be able to get very much for your money. You'll be forced to buy closer to the bottom of the market for this art than the top. The solution is to find more affordable art you like just as much where $2,000 buys the best or at least a better example of what's available, not a mediocre one.

Make sure what you like is readily available and that you have a good selection to choose from. You won't find anything to buy if the type of art you're looking for is so rare that it hardly ever comes onto the market.

Make sure you choose your art for art reasons, not money reasons. Buy because you love the way the art looks, you are fascinated by the history behind it, you're impressed by the artist and so on. If you like specific works of art mainly because you think they'll go up in value, think again. For one thing, only a small percentage of art increases in value over time (as you will see in Chapters 19 and 20). Additionally, getting all caught up in money matters can destroy the fun of buying art.

Keep your preferences conservative at first. Focus on art that dealers and collectors generally accept as being collectible. The more you learn and the more experienced you become, the more experimental you can afford to be in your buying.

BE THOROUGH

Be complete and thorough when defining your likes; don't overlook any important details. You must be fully aware of the qualities you want in your art and of the basic principles that will guide your buying. The truth is that some art buyers are not aware of these things and, consequently, the art they end up owning is quite different from the art that they originally set out to buy.

Suppose you meet a collector who tells you, 'I love to collect paintings of Florida coastal scenes by established Miami artists.' You visit him at his home, he gives you a tour of his collection and, at first glance, all his pictures seem to be exactly what he told you they were. But as he presents each piece and describes it, he finishes with statements like, 'Paintings by this artist sell for $1,250 and up – I paid only $150 for mine at a small local auction,' or 'I got this one on sale for a quarter of what it's worth.'

Whether or not this collector originally intended it, a guiding principle behind his collecting – one that belongs in his opening statement – is that he purchases only coastal scenes he can buy cheaply enough to brag to his friends and acquaintances about what great bargains he got. A more appropriate statement about his collecting would be, 'I love to buy Florida coastal scenes by established Miami artists that I can get for much less than they're really worth,' or 'I collect bargain paintings that happen to be Florida coastal scenes done by established Miami artists.' He cannot really title his collection 'Florida Coastal Scenes Painted by Established Miami Artists.'

The bargain factor clearly influences his choices. By limiting his purchases to 'bargain' paintings, he automatically eliminates all non-bargains from consideration. This could possibly result in his compromising quality for price or in depriving himself of important coastal scenes or art by significant artists that simply can't be found at bargain prices. His obsession with bargains may adversely affect his collecting.

Here are examples of two other constraints that can and do significantly alter the intended courses of many a collection:

1 Only purchasing works of art that a particular person – wife, mother-in-law, best friend, employer, etc. – approves of. The resulting selection is more indicative of the tastes of the third parties than of the buyer.
2 Buying all art from a single gallery, website or artist. A buyer who patronises only one resource does not really buy what he or she likes; they buy what the resource likes.

A LOOK AHEAD

Defining what you like, tempering it with the realities of your budget and buying situation, and explaining it in ways the art community understands completes the first step in the process of buying art. The next step – which is the goal of Part II – involves your selecting specific works of art for possible purchase according to your requirements. In order to make the best choices, however, you need basic training; that is, you need an introduction to how the art world works.

Part II: Select

Selecting a work of art for possible purchase is easy. Since you are now able to identify what you like, all you have to do is walk into a gallery or browse its website, take a look at what's available, see something interesting, and say to yourself, 'I wouldn't mind owning that.' Selection process completed.

The hard part is locating relevant galleries in the first place; knowing what to do once you get there; being able to tell whether you have encountered a good dealer or a bad one; effectively interacting with anyone you meet before, during and after your visit; and knowing how to behave in order to maximise the quality of each visit. Consequently, the goal of Part II is not to teach you how to select art – you can do that already – but rather to provide you with the information you need in order to ensure that your selection process has a positive outcome. Part II is a basic course in understanding and navigating your way through the art community. The truth is that you can't come face to face with and select the art that's right for you until you know how to get around.

CHAPTER 5

WHO SAYS IT, WHAT THEY SAY, HOW TO TAKE IT

So far, you've kept pretty quiet about your art interests and intent to buy. Everything you've done, you've done pretty much on your own. Keeping your contacts brief has allowed you to wander from place to place, both in person and online, make initial observations about what you like and acquire basic information about it with little or no interference from outsiders. Sooner or later, though, you must deepen your contacts, make your intentions known in greater detail and progress towards buying art.

Once you begin to do this, the way the art world relates to you changes. You are no longer a looker – you are now a participant. Art people start taking vested interests in how you should think, feel and react to art. They declare, expound, criticise, hold court, pass judgements, share beliefs, emote, foretell the future and say whatever else comes to mind regarding your particular situation. They want a say in your selection process.

Speaking with others about art can be quite difficult at first. You hear many different things from many different people, and you're never quite sure how to respond. You don't really know who's right and who's wrong, who knows what they're talking about and who doesn't. You have little choice but to take whatever you hear at face value because you don't yet have the knowledge to analyse and digest.

So what do you do? You jump right in and start talking or calling or emailing. You tell people exactly what you know and exactly what you're looking for. That's the best practice you can get and the only sensible way to begin. By participating in conversation after conversation, you eventually figure out how to evaluate what you are hearing, extract the information you need, formulate your own opinions and determine whether the art that you've selected is really right for you.

When you don't know much about art, however, and the people you are talking or corresponding with do, you are at a continual disadvantage. They find out more about you faster than you do about them. They control the conversations and have a variety of options in responding to whatever you say, while you have very few.

Imagine putting on a pair of boxing gloves and stepping into the ring with a professional fighter. He can give you a painless and highly educational lesson in how to box, he can exit the ring without saying a word and leave you standing there, he can pound you to a pulp, and so on. You can listen, run, plead for mercy or put up your gloves and see how long you last – and that's about it. Depending on his response to your situation, you can leave the ring knowing more than when you stepped into it, you can leave learning nothing or you can end up staring at the ceiling.

This is similar to what you encounter as you begin to speak with people about art. You step into the art ring with professional after professional, tell them about your situation and listen to their responses. Some help you, others tell you nothing, a few take the opportunity to hinder or manipulate you to their own ends.

Your task is to separate the helpers from the hinderers as quickly as possible, filter what you hear and use the best information to locate the art you want to buy. Sooner or later, you acquire the necessary skills to assess accurately all that people tell you. This chapter is about how to make it sooner.

WHO SAYS IT

Figuring out whose views to accept and how much to accept them is difficult at first. Anyone can sound like they know what they're talking about as long as they present themselves in a reasonably competent and trustworthy manner. You can't really apply any quick and easy rules to diagnosing a situation, but you don't have to operate blind, either. Knowing a little about the structure of art interactions comes in handy here.

To begin with, be aware of conflicts of interest. In any conversation, know when another person stands to benefit from having you see things their way and having you focus on the art they want you to select. The greater the profit potential is for a person – monetarily, psychologically or otherwise – the more inclined that person is to give you a biased view of art.

Art scholars, professors, museum curators and others who are not involved with the art business, but rather with the academic, scholarly and critical side of art, can usually be relied upon for accurate, unbiased information. They do not profit from having you believe their views about art, do not ordinarily take sides and purposely steer clear of the business side of art. When you read what they write, listen to them speak or ask their advice, they generally attempt to present issues fairly and allow you to make the necessary decisions for yourself.

Individuals involved with the art business are different. People who sell art for a living such as art dealers, gallery employees, auction house staff or websites selling art profit directly by having you see things their way and believe what they believe. With such people, you have to be a little more careful about who and what you listen to and believe. Most sellers represent their art fairly and tell you exactly what you need to know. But remember that the possibility of their making sales always looms on the horizon. If they see they can influence your selection process, there's a good chance they will.

Much of what sellers tell you relates specifically to the art they sell. Even when you speak with them casually, outside of direct selling situations, be aware that they believe very strongly in what they sell or the artists they represent and present consistently positive cases for owning their type of art and less positive cases for owning other types of art. They want you to like what they like, whether you buy it or not.

Keep in mind also that sellers don't always know that much about types of art outside their areas of speciality or the artists they represent. They know plenty about what they sell, but are not necessarily well informed about what other people sell. When you ask sellers about art they don't deal in, you won't always get accurate answers. But you will get answers, answers you should always corroborate with other knowledgeable sources before accepting.

Sellers are most helpful in educating you about the art and artists they represent. When you speak or email with them, keep conversations focused on their specialities. Whether or not their types of art turn out to be the right art for you, they can tell you just about everything you need to know about it.

Art collectors are much like sellers in that they also prefer having you see art the way they do. Suppose, for instance, that a private collector is giving you a tour of his collection. He believes certain things about the art he has purchased, and it's in his best interest that you believe him too.

Let's say you agree with his views on collecting (that is, you like and appreciate what's in his collection) and decide to select and buy similar art for yourself. In doing so, you indirectly increase the value of his art by increasing the demand for that art in the marketplace. The more people agree with this collector's views on collecting and buy what he buys, the greater the demand for that type of art becomes.

This collector also benefits from your support in a psychological sense – you make him feel good about himself and his collection when you agree with him. If you don't see eye to eye on a particular point, he'll most likely attempt to convince you he's right. Knowing that you disagree with him about the art he has chosen to buy may make him feel uncomfortable because he may feel that perhaps he has not spent his money wisely.

Collectors feel strongly about what they collect and that's fine; but once again, you've got to decide whether believing them works as well for you as it does for them. They may have quality collections and know what they're talking about – in which case you're safe following their leads. On the other hand, they may think they have bought wisely when, in fact, they haven't. They may think their art is worth a lot more than it actually is, or they may think it's a lot more significant than it actually is. You certainly don't want to follow any leads in either of those circumstances.

Be careful when speaking with collectors for the simple reason that they frequently do not know as much about art as full-time art professionals. They tend to buy in their spare time and not spend their lives amassing knowledge about art the way that people in the business or museum curators, critics and art scholars do. Furthermore, their focus is much narrower than that of most experts. Although some may speak with strong conviction and sound like they know everything there is to know, be cautious and double-check what they tell you before accepting it as fact.

Artists are somewhat like dealers and collectors rolled up into one in that every artist is both a major collector and dealer of his or her own work. As with collectors, artists tend to focus on their own art to the exclusion of all else. As with dealers, they have an obvious conflict of interest when advising you on what to buy. They want you to understand, appreciate and buy *their* art. When you collect a particular artist's work, it is important to know that artist for purposes of better understanding her art. If, however, you are speaking casually or in generalities with an artist whose art you do not collect, keep in mind that she is heavily invested in converting you into a fan of her art.

Speak with as many dealers, collectors, artists, auction house and art gallery personnel, museum curators and other professionals as possible. And visit as many relevant websites as you can. By listening to everyone, you acquire a well-balanced picture and overall understanding of what you want to select and eventually buy. Accumulating information from a diverse variety of sources protects you from coming under the influence of any one or two in particular. Weigh all points of view on a continuing basis so you can progressively strengthen your convictions.

WHAT THEY SAY

You hear and read plenty about art as you wend your way through the art world from one person to the next. What you hear can be broken down into three basic categories:

- Facts about artists or works of art.
- Emotional reactions to artists or works of art.
- Market information about artists or works of art.

Facts are easy to evaluate. They are either true or false and can almost always be verified simply and directly. Sometimes the people who state the facts offer that verification themselves. Other times, you have to corroborate what you hear by independently contacting art experts or researching at museums, libraries, online and other resources.

The operative word here is *verify*. Any time you are presented with new or unfamiliar information, check it out – do not automatically accept it as gospel. Make sure that whatever you are told is true and generally accepted by the art community. Unfortunately, you can't automatically believe everything you hear.

For example, an art dealer tells you an artist she represents is famous. You speak with four collectors, two independent art experts, several art dealers, search the artist online and contact several art museums to see whether you can corroborate this information. You come up with the following results: no expert or collector has ever heard of the artist, one art dealer thinks he recognises the name but isn't sure, no museum can provide any information about the artist and you can find little information about the artist online. You have to conclude that, at best, the artist is not quite as famous as the initial dealer would have you believe.

Emotional reactions to art are a little more difficult to evaluate than facts. You will hear everything from raw, spontaneous reactions to the most highly informed and educated reactions (commonly referred to as art criticism). Just as you verify facts, you have to learn to verify – or more accurately, qualify – emotional reactions in order to determine how they might influence your selection-making process. This qualifying may seem difficult, but it's really not. It just involves a little reading between the lines.

Basically, you have to figure out how qualified the people doing the reacting are. Are they knowledgeable professionals who are having informed, educated responses, or are they casual observers who just happen to be passing by and have no idea what they are looking at? How much do the reactors know about the art they are reacting to? That's the key.

Suppose, for instance, you are attending an art opening at Triple-A Fine Arts Gallery and overhear a man remark that the abstract paintings on display are terrible and don't even deserve to be hung in a monkey cage. You politely tap him on the shoulder, introduce yourself and ask him to explain why he feels this way. He tells you he hates bright colours and that his six-year-old daughter brings home better pictures from her art class.

This is probably not an explanation you should take too seriously. It shouldn't affect your decision about whether or not to consider one of these abstracts for purchase. If, however, this fellow goes on to say that in all his years of curating shows at the Municipal Art Museum he has never seen such amateurish work, you could have an entirely different situation on your hands. Suddenly you realise you're speaking with someone who could well know what he's talking about. Not necessarily, though.

As a curator, he certainly qualifies as having experience in the art world, but before you can take him too seriously, you have to find out exactly where his expertise lies. If he turns out to be a curator of Greek and Roman antiquities, for instance, he may not be qualified to criticise the contemporary abstracts on display at this opening. An expert in one field of art is not automatically qualified to judge art unrelated to that field.

If, however, he's an expert on contemporary abstracts and curates contemporary art exhibitions, you listen. But don't blindly accept what he has to say. Politely request that he support his initial reactions with facts. This is how you learn. Perhaps he'll mention a book you should read or name several other artists who work in similar styles much more skilfully, or he may tell you where you can go to see what he considers to be really good abstracts.

When evaluating emotional reactions, always find out the answers to these three questions:

- How qualified is the person doing the talking?
- Can the reactions be supported with concrete proof that they are valid?
- What is that proof?

Market-related information is the toughest of all to evaluate. A primary reason for this is that many people who give you price data have vested interests in what they tell you. Another problem is that you can easily be misled by people who think they know about prices, but actually don't. And if that's not enough, many people are reluctant to give you price information in the first place. They want to keep what they know to themselves and use it to their advantage. As for the internet, that can be an incredibly confusing mass of facts as well as fictions. Part IV of this book treats money matters in depth, but a brief summary is appropriate here.

As in evaluating emotional or critical reactions to art, you must qualify the sources of any market-related information you get. Ask people who talk prices to back up everything they say with facts. Figure out whether they have any vested interests in telling you what art is good to buy, what art isn't and what art is worth how much. Find out the extent of the experience they've had dealing with the monetary aspects of art. For example, a private collector who buys but never sells may not give you as reliable information about the art market as will someone who sells or appraises art for a living. You will also see in Part IV that standard art-price references which place specific monetary values on works of art are available to the public and that you can use them to substantiate what people tell you.

HOW TO TAKE IT

At present, digesting what you hear about art is not easy. You probably don't know that much, you haven't met that many people, you're not sure whom to trust and you haven't established any long-term relationships. You're still operating pretty much in the dark, and you never quite know how to take what people tell you.

And you hear what you hear or read what you read in so many different formats. Some people seem completely trustworthy, congenial and sincere (making you inclined to accept anything they tell you, true or not). Others have strong feelings and no qualms about imposing them on you, whether you're interested in hearing them or not. The more adamant among them can literally attempt to steamroll you into submission (making you inclined *not* to accept anything they tell you, true or not). Most people happen to be helpful and supportive, but not everyone is going to treat you with respect. Be prepared for anything.

Never take what people tell you personally. No one is out to get you. Getting all caught up in why someone treats you disrespectfully is a monumental waste of time. Sure, you'll meet a few people who have to make your life difficult in order to feel good about themselves or prove how much they know. Consider that their problem, not yours.

Listen to and reflect on *everything* people tell you. Get a well-rounded art education from a variety of sources. Most people happily soak up any information that already supports their beliefs but pay little, if any, attention to divergent points of view. This is fine if you subscribe to the 'ignorance is bliss' philosophy, but ignorance does not come in handy if you expect to master the art of buying art. Resisting or discounting opposing viewpoints before checking them out is not a healthy practice.

You don't have to believe everything you hear or read, follow every bit of advice that anyone gives you or change direction at the slightest provocation. You do, however, have to catalogue the data. No matter whether it seems right or wrong, makes sense or not, sounds sincere or condescending, assume at the outset that it has value and deserves your attention.

Let's say you are interested in the artist John Doeman and are in the process of learning as much as you can about him. In your art travels and online searches, you come across people who have heard of Doeman, people who claim to be authorities on Doeman, people who have never heard of Doeman, and people who think they have heard of Doeman and will gladly comment on the artist if you would just refresh their memories as to who he is. Everyone has something to say.

So, what do you do when the subject of Doeman comes up? You listen. That's the best way to go. Even if you know more about the artist than the person who is speaking, listen. Even if someone insults you, listen. The more you listen, the more complete your picture of Doeman and his art becomes. You get an idea of where he stands as an artist, where his strengths and weaknesses lie, and what the prognosis on his future is. You learn why people like him, why they hate him and why they don't care one way or the other.

Whenever someone gives you information about any art or artist, you also learn just as much about the person giving you the information (or opinion) as you do about the art. You learn whom to trust and whom to avoid, who knows what they're talking about and who doesn't. Mastering the art of buying art means knowing how to evaluate art people as well as knowing how to evaluate art.

Example 1

Some sellers say anything to sell art, and sometimes what they say is not necessarily true. One way they occasionally distort the facts is by comparing the art they have for sale to art by more famous artists. Imagine hearing any of the following reasonings from an art dealer:

'The painting you are thinking about buying is just as good as a Jonathan Johnson painting. Johnson's paintings sell for between $25,000 and $30,000 each. At only $3,000, that makes this painting an absolute bargain.'

'If Jonathan Johnson had painted this, it would be worth $30,000. I'm only asking $3,000 for it.'

'You can't touch a Jonathan Johnson at this price.'

None of these statements are valid. Jonathan Johnson did not paint the painting you like, and his price structure has nothing to do with the value of that painting. Though the two may look alike, they are totally unrelated and the dealer is attempting to establish a dubious connection in order to increase the painting's attractiveness and make the asking price seem more like a bargain. Even if the painting happens to be as good as a Jonathan Johnson, the dealer's arguments still hold no water. Much more goes into determining value than how one piece of art compares in quality to another from a visual standpoint alone. The dealer is making a frivolous and irrelevant value comparison for the sole purpose of selling you this piece of art.

Carry this argument to extremes and imagine a seller telling you the following: 'If Vincent van Gogh had painted this, it would be worth $25 million. I'm only asking $3,000 for it.' Does van Gogh have anything to do with this seller's painting? Are you getting an incredible bargain if you buy it? Of course not!

Example 2

Over time, you learn whom you can and cannot trust in the art business. One dealer I know does not always tell the truth. She sometimes tells me several conflicting stories about the same work of art; other times she gives me information that cannot be confirmed by other sources. I can never be sure about what I'm hearing, and experience has taught me to accept nothing she says until I verify it independently.

She sounds like someone I should terminate relations with, but I don't. I continue to work with her from time to time because she happens to be a competent dealer, and she happens to sell good-quality, interesting and worthwhile art.

Aside from the fact that I can accept nothing she tells me at face value, she's great. If I am interested in a work of art she has for sale, I find out the price and that's it. I listen to every-thing else she says – I don't want to be rude – but then I do the necessary research entirely on my own.

Unfortunately, if you were to meet this dealer for the first time, you would have no idea what to believe and what not to believe. She's entertaining and knowledgeable, speaks with great conviction and always sounds sincere. Other art dealers won't warn you about her unless they know and trust you – you have to learn by yourself (dealers rarely gossip casually in public about fellow dealers). If you buy art based on her advice alone, you might end up with a great piece of art at a fair price. But you might also significantly overpay for a lesser example. She makes everything she sells sound equally appetising.

A LOOK AHEAD

Now that you've had an introduction to art people, you're ready to go out and meet some of them – particularly those who are involved with types of art that relate to your buying interests. The majority of these people happen to be art dealers or gallery personnel, and you will meet them as you shop from gallery to gallery or from website to website comparing the selections they have to offer.

As you have seen, the more people you meet and the more sites you visit, the more you learn about art and the better balanced your art education becomes. In the same vein, the more galleries and websites you visit, the better able you are to select just the right art to purchase and the better balanced your art buying becomes. Naturally, you need instruction in how to locate as many of the right galleries and websites and meet as many of the most qualified dealers as possible, and these topics are covered in the next chapter.

CHAPTER 6

COMPARISON SHOPPING FOR ART

Knowing what types of art you want to buy and being able to select specific pieces that suit your lifestyle do not necessarily go hand in hand. So far, you have seen art you like at certain galleries and museums, online and in other public places. But you have only seen that art as a result of random exposures, not organised, systematic visits. What you have seen to this point is only the beginning.

Shopping for art is like shopping for anything else. Now that you have defined your likes, you need to find out who sells that type of art, call or email or speak with them, see what they have to offer, and learn how to make gallery-to-gallery, website-to-website and dealer-to-dealer comparisons. You have to survey what's available in the marketplace. In order to select worthwhile works of art – ones that are priced fairly and that you won't get tired of looking at – you've got to stifle every impulse to buy immediately and instead make a point to comparison-shop first.

Think about how gallery owners and other art professionals select art or artists they want to sell or represent. Out of all the millions of artworks available for sale, they have to decide what to show and which artists to exhibit. Passion, feeling and visual impact, of course, play significant roles in their selection processes, but there's more. When they see art they like, they research it, assess and evaluate its quality, see what else is available in that category, compare prices, and ultimately determine whether they can remain competitive with other galleries and websites by buying or otherwise acquiring and then selling it. They comparison-shop for art that has the most value from business, aesthetic and quality standpoints. Shouldn't you?

WHY EVERYONE DOESN'T COMPARISON-SHOP

Many inexperienced buyers make the mistake of buying art without comparison shopping first. They do so primarily because of a misconception they have that I call the 'uniqueness myth'. They believe that since every work of art is 'unique' – one-of-a-kind – they might as well buy what they like when they see it because they'll never find anything else exactly like it.

This myth is only partially true. Any original work of art is unique in the sense that no other work of art looks *exactly* like it, but that's about as far as you can go with this line of reasoning. In spite of its 'uniqueness', that work of art also happens to be similar to plenty of other works of art. Let's say, for example, that you see a painting of a Paris street scene. Even though no other Paris street scene painting is a precise duplicate of the one you are looking at, hundreds of artists have produced countless thousands of Paris street scenes over the years and continue to do so today. And, if you take the time to look, you can find any number of street scenes that are similar to that one particular scene.

No matter what types of art you're attracted to, you can *always* find a number of other pieces out there that look approximately (and often remarkably) similar. The more art you see, the more you will come to realise how true this is.

Related to the uniqueness myth is another reason why beginners tend not to comparison-shop; they mistake initial attraction for everlasting love. They believe in love at first sight; they believe they can find 'perfect' art, and no other art can ever provide them with as much satisfaction and enjoyment. This rarely happens with anything else people buy, so why should it happen with art? Veteran art buyers will tell you it doesn't.

Whenever you see art that attracts you, know that you are being attracted only in the moment, that you are experiencing the love-at-first-sight phenomenon. For this reason, you should avoid the impulse to buy and instead test that attraction by comparison shopping. Compare the art to similar pieces at other galleries; compare it to totally different pieces at other galleries. Go online, search the artists or subject matters or styles of art and see what types of images match your queries. You may find art that attracts you just as much; you may find art that attracts you more. You'll discover this once you begin looking.

Lastly, some art buyers don't comparison-shop because the galleries, websites or sellers they patronise discourage it. These establishments don't want their clients to know that worthwhile art can also be found elsewhere. They manipulate by saying things like, 'Buy this now because you'll never find another one like it,' or 'This is the best one you'll ever see,' or 'This is the last one of these we have,' and on and on and on. They use the 'uniqueness myth', the love-at-first-sight phenomenon, and whatever additional ploys they have at their disposal, to keep you inside their galleries or on their websites and sell you art. These sellers prefer buyers who ask few questions, blindly accept what they are told, and are convinced that the best art can only be found at certain galleries or websites (namely theirs). We're getting a little ahead of ourselves, though. You'll read more about these sorts of tactics in Chapter 7, 'Dealer Dealings', and Chapter 12, 'How Not to Buy Art'.

ESTABLISHED VERSUS OFFBEAT RESOURCES

The number-one rule to follow when learning how to comparison-shop for your selections is this: *Stick with established galleries or online options when you're just starting out*. You need all the protection you can get at this early stage, and you will see in the next chapter why established galleries and gallery or retail websites are among the best and safest places to begin buying art.

Beating the bushes for art, as so many collectors love to do, can be hazardous to your wallet. When you're just starting out, the best procedure is to avoid art liquidations, private sellers, estate sales, yard sales, flea markets, online resources where you're not sure who's doing the selling, and auctions of all types. Stay away from second-hand or resale or consignment stores, places that sell art on the side but really specialise in other types of merchandise, and so on. Don't shop from online classifieds or at the homes of private collectors. These are all high-risk ventures, and you need plenty of experience buying art before you start to shop wherever you happen to see art for sale.

LOCATING GALLERIES THAT SELL WHAT YOU WANT

Comparison shopping for art does not mean you have to spend months contacting galleries, searching the internet or trying to meet dealers around the world. Your search depends on the type of art you have chosen to buy. For example, if you want to buy art by local or regional artists who are active only in your area, you certainly don't have to make national or international efforts to find out who sells it.

As for how exhaustive or comprehensive you want to make your search, that's up to you. You can go out and locate every gallery that sells your type of art or you can approach the assignment more casually and locate only a few. Know, however, that the amount of effort you put into familiarising yourself with the marketplace is directly proportional to the amount of knowledge you will acquire about your art, its availability, the market for that art and the ability to evaluate the quality of any selections you will eventually make. In any event, do whatever feels most comfortable. You'll learn a variety of gallery-locating techniques here. Choose and follow whichever ones apply to your particular situation.

A good place to begin any art gallery search is by looking at advertisements in major national or international art periodicals and publications, both online and hard copy. See Appendix III for a partial listing of major art-related periodicals and websites with brief comments about each. Many city or regional art-related periodicals and websites are also available. Check with galleries or other art venues to see whether any exist in your locale. These resources often contain comprehensive gallery listings or advertisements and provide the best coverage of local and regional art scenes.

You can subscribe to whatever art publications are most relevant to your needs or find them at main branches of major public libraries. You can also subscribe to their email lists to receive regular newsletters or bulletins (some send them out daily). Or pick them up at major book or magazine stores where you live.

Focus your attention primarily on art gallery advertisements. The articles won't help you all that much at this early stage, but if you happen to see one that catches your eye, either read it or note what magazine it appeared in and save it for later. The articles are much more helpful once you know your way around the art business and understand art-world lingo a little better.

Some periodicals will appeal to you more than others. Your best tactic is to sample them all at first, and eventually subscribe to the ones you enjoy the most and find most helpful to your art buying. In the meantime, browse to your heart's content.

Here are several resources for locating galleries:

- Search online by the name of whatever city or area you're interested in along with keywords like 'art galleries', 'galleries' and 'art openings'. Depending on the size of the area, you should come up with at least one or two relevant websites.
- If you are starting locally or regionally, try exploring entertainment and events sections of major area newspapers or news sites, and city or regional magazines. These publications often contain gallery advertisements, notices of upcoming art openings and ongoing shows, art-related events and so on. Look for special sections where art galleries list current offerings or exhibits.
- If you are interested in seeing art for sale from a broader range of national or international galleries, attending art

fairs is a great way to see large amounts of quality art from a variety of sources first-hand. Art fairs are unquestionably the art world's best option for one-stop-shopping. Appendix I lists some of the major international art fairs; however, national and regional fairs can be equally diverse in terms of exhibitors and selections of art on display – there are many quality regional art fairs around the world so always check your local area. The one-stop-shopping nature of art fairs has made them very popular with the art-buying public. If you can't attend a fair in person, you can also browse the list of exhibiting galleries on the fair's website.

- If you are interested in art from foreign countries, locate and look through a copy of the *International Directory of Arts*. This extensive annual publication is a worldwide guide to museums, art-related institutions, dealers, galleries and much more. You can find it at most major libraries. The *International Directory of Arts* is published by De Gruyter, Berlin, Germany (https://www.degruyter.com).

- Membership lists of regional, national and international art dealer organisations. The major national and international ones can be found in the *International Directory of Arts*, the *American Art Directory* (http://www.americanartdir.com/AAD/home) and also in the annual directories published by magazines like *Art in America* (also see Appendices II and V). Check local galleries and regional art sites and publications for names and addresses of city and regional gallery associations.

- Additional online searches. General online searches can be pretty daunting, but typing in 'Art Dealers Association' on Google gives good results. Searching specific dealer art sites like Art Dealers Association of America (artdealers.org) or all-purpose art sites with large databases like artnet (artnet.com) and Blouin Artinfo (blouinartinfo.com) can be even more productive. A number of larger art websites provide a variety of search options such as by artist, medium, dealer and subject matter. See Appendix II for a partial listing of online art resources.

- Referrals from collectors, curators and other knowledge-able members of the art community. Referrals from museum curators and other unbiased professionals are especially helpful. You may not know many experts or authorities yet, but the more involved you become with collecting, the more you will be introduced to these people. Much of your most valuable information will eventually come by word of mouth.

MAKING CONTACT

As you research, make a working list of all galleries that seem to offer art or artists similar to what you are interested in. Write down full names, addresses, phone numbers, emails and website addresses, and include any other relevant details such as where you read the ads, why the ads attracted you, who referred you and so on. Include the following types of galleries on your list:

- Galleries or websites that represent particular artists whose work you have already seen and like.
- Galleries or websites that offer the look you like by what-ever artists happen to be creating it, whether you recognise the names of the artists or not.
- Galleries or websites that sell art you find appealing, even though you may never have heard of the artists.
- Galleries or websites that sell art you like in your price range.

- Galleries or websites selling what you like that have been in business for long periods of time.

Next, contact these places. The three main ways to reach them are by phone, email or personal visit. Tell everyone you meet where or how you heard about them and what interested or attracted you, and ask how or where you can learn more. Your primary objective here is to view the art for sale by the galleries – personally, in brochures or catalogues, or online – and see how much you like it. If you happen to see a selection of art you really like, get basic facts about it and nothing more – the in-depth research and decisions about whether to buy come later.

With first contacts like these, keep interactions simple; find out what each gallery sells and about how much it costs, and get an idea of whether it's right for you. Don't get involved in long discussions about art. Don't let anyone start selling to you. If you prefer making contacts by phone or email, don't let anyone pressure you to come in for personal visits – ask them to send or direct you to whatever materials will tell you more about the gallery's art, and that's that. Personal visits are best, but if you're not comfortable with that, you can do pretty much everything online. The best procedure, though, is to visit all galleries that appear to have what you want. Nothing beats seeing art up close and in person.

If you're curious about how much a particular work of art costs and the asking price is not readily apparent, ask. This is a good time to begin getting a basic feel for prices. Don't immediately eliminate a gallery if a quoted price is way over your budget. They may also sell art with a comparable look and feel that is more in your price range. Keep price discussions simple, though. Advise gallery personnel that you are just beginning your quest, are curious about what sells for how much, are gathering basic knowledge, but are not yet ready to buy and don't want to get much more involved than that.

Comparison shopping for art is the process that exposes you to a variety of dealers, a variety of galleries and websites, and a variety of ways of doing business. It gives you an overall understanding of how the marketplace operates and what it has to offer. Comparison shopping provides you with ample opportunities to make intelligent selections and informed buys.

You may never do business with many of the galleries or websites you locate and visit. You may decide to buy your art from only two or three or four resources after all is said and done. No matter how many you eventually patronise, at least you will have made the contacts and had the experiences of meeting them and seeing their places of business or perusing their selections. All this gives you a significant advantage over other collectors who never bother to broaden their horizons beyond one or two sellers.

Example 1

The best art is the hardest to find; plenty of people are looking for it. When a desirable work of art comes onto the market, many people may want to own it, but only one lucky person ends up with it. That person is usually a serious collector and comparison shopper – one who stays in contact with a wide range of galleries and online resources. Good art sells fast, and you want to be first in line when it comes onto the market.

One very thorough collector I know maintains constant contact with many galleries and online sellers. He stays on top of the market by sending out periodic want lists of the art and artists he is looking for to anyone he thinks could possibly come across artworks that might interest him. When new dealers open their galleries, his list is one of the first things to arrive in their email. He follows every such contact with a phone call or a personal visit when appropriate, introduces himself to the gallery owner, and clearly restates what he is looking for. He is able to point out a number of fine examples in his collection that he has acquired as a result of his diligence.

Example 2

You can actually save money on art by comparison shopping, keeping a wide range of contacts and knowing many dealers who sell what you like. A significant amount of art is bought, sold, consigned or traded between dealers before it ends up in private collections. One reason for these gallery-to-gallery or seller-to-seller transactions is that dealers are constantly on the lookout for art they know their customers will buy. Dealers scour the market and buy or otherwise acquire the rights to represent this art wherever they happen to find it.

Let's say that Dealer A knows what you like to buy. He sees a good example of that art at Dealer B's gallery, a gallery you have never visited. Depending on how sure Dealer A is that you will buy the art, he either buys it outright, trades for it or asks to have it on consignment so he can offer it to you.

When Dealer A gets the art from Dealer B he will, in the great majority of cases, raise the price and offer it to you for more than Dealer B is selling it for. If you buy the art from Dealer A, you pay that difference in price for never having met Dealer B. If Dealer B had already known you and was aware of your interests, she would have offered you the art before passing it on to Dealer A. You could have paid Dealer B's lower asking price rather than Dealer A's more expensive one.

In this example, the art passed through only two sellers before being offered to you. Sometimes art passes through four, five or even more before it finally ends up in private hands. And the more sellers that handle an art piece along the way to its final destination, the more expensive it gets. Each seller adds on a profit margin in the form of a percentage mark-up, a commission, or a referral or brokering fee. If you can keep that dealer-to-dealer chain short, you can save money.

A LOOK AHEAD

The first stages of comparison shopping for art involve locating places that offer selections you like and cataloguing the most likely of these resources for return visits. Initial contacts are brief, but as you move closer and closer to buying, interactions become increasingly complex and involved. For your more serious encounters, you need basic information about art dealers, galleries and websites, the similarities or differences you will find between one and the next, and how to interpret those findings. This information, which is discussed in the next chapter, will protect you from advantage-takers and help you make the most of your gallery contacts.

CHAPTER 7

DEALER DEALINGS

Art dealers and art galleries are a fact of the art business. The art business cannot exist without them. You have to shop at their establishments, and you have to interact, communicate and negotiate with them at various points in the process of buying art, whether in person or online.

Unfortunately, some art buyers, especially those who are not that knowledgeable about the art business, believe dealers are a necessary inconvenience that must be tolerated. They think all dealers do is buy art cheaply, mark the price way up or display it in their galleries on consignment, take huge commissions and sell it expensively. To them, dealers are nothing more than merchants who always want their piece of the action, doing little more than acting as middlemen between one owner and another.

The truth: art dealers are experts at what they do. Art dealers are professionals who provide a structure to the art business and are eminently qualified to assess, evaluate, buy, sell, represent and otherwise transact in art in the marketplace. They know how to present and sell art from artists or private sellers to other art buyers and then do the same thing again if those buyers ever decide to resell. Without them, buying or selling all kinds of art in any structured, organised manner would be extremely difficult. The art-buying public would have far fewer professionals to evaluate and select the best art from the rest; to educate, inform and advise them in their buying and collecting; and no formalised settings in which art transactions could take place, either at physical locations or online.

In many ways, art dealers are similar to stockbrokers, real estate agents and other merchandise agents or brokers. All keep abreast of their respective markets, know how to place fair and reasonable monetary values on art they deal in, know how to locate quality art and make it available to interested buyers, and are qualified to advise buyers as to what best suits their needs. The best among them spot trends and even dictate tastes well ahead of the rest of us.

A word of caution: art dealers are not oracles to be obeyed without question. As in any business, a few dealers make their living by taking advantage of unsuspecting clients. Sooner or later you find out who these dealers are and learn to avoid them. The majority, however, are respected professionals who attend to your particular situation as it relates to the art market in general.

'But buying art from established art dealers, galleries or gallery websites is expensive,' you say. 'I know what I'm looking for, and I'm going to see whether I can find it elsewhere for less.'

Be extremely careful if you're new to the art world and this is what you're thinking. Art is not necessarily cheaper outside of galleries. Yes, prices may seem lower at resale websites, online auctions, places like second-hand stores, frame shops, artists' websites or studios, resale outlets, antique shops and so on, but look a little closer. What you frequently see are inferior works that art dealers have already passed on or would never consider selling in the first place, not to mention the possibilities of them having condition problems or being outright forgeries.

This is not to say that all art outside of galleries is damaged, inferior or fake. Quality art *is* out there, but it's not easy to find, plenty of savvy dealers and collectors chase after it, and if you're just starting out, it's not that easy to distinguish from lesser works. What happens all too often, unfortunately, is that when amateur art buffs invite art dealers to comment on their backwater bargains, the standard dealer response is some version of 'I hope you can get your money back.'

Of course, if you buy from galleries, you won't be able to impress your friends with what a super bargain you found in a for-sale ad online, nor will you realise instant appreciation on your purchases by paying full gallery retail. But just in case you're interested, the great majority of gallery art fares *much better* financially over time than 'wherever you happen to find it' art. So, in the end, you usually get the most for your money anyway.

'But art is a matter of personal choice,' you say. 'What I like is my business and no one else's. I don't need any art dealers to tell me what I should be buying.'

Not true. Recognising quality in art and selecting and eventually buying worthwhile pieces is a learned, not an innate, ability. You must learn how to tell the difference between good, better and best quality in art you like in order to make intelligent buys. Art dealers come in mighty handy here for a number of reasons:

- Art dealers see countless thousands of works of art. All they do is look at art, and when they take a break from looking, they talk about art. Their recommendations come from a broad-based knowledge of the art market.
- Art dealers are qualified to give you in-depth price information or explanations about whatever art you are considering buying.

- Art dealers screen all art that is offered to them and sell or resell only the best.
- Art dealers educate you. They answer your questions, discuss specific art and artists in depth, recommend online resources or books to read, and share other important specialised knowledge. They want you to gain experience.
- The best dealers offer money-back guarantees of authenticity, full condition reports, trade-back arrangements, free updated appraisals, consultations on the scope and direction of your buying or collecting, and other amenities. Try getting *those* from private sellers, at online auctions or resale sites.

Now, supposing that some years after you start buying art, you decide to sell some of it. Your tastes have changed, you're moving into smaller quarters, you're upgrading your collection, or whatever. Dealers, galleries or websites with which you have good, solid established working relationships come in mighty handy in these instances, too. This book is about buying art, not selling it, but nevertheless, you should know at least a little about how dealers help you sell as well as buy.

'But I know how much my art is worth,' you say. 'I can sell it on my own without any outside help.' Believing this is a big mistake – in fact, it's three big mistakes.

First mistake: Private sellers think that with no professional help, they can accurately determine how much their art is worth. They go online and think they can price it when, in truth, the internet is such a morass of misinformation that it's almost impossible for inexperienced sellers to find the accurate facts and interpret whatever they're looking at. The monetary values they come up with are generally inaccurate (usually too high) and almost always based on inadequate and arbitrary research. *The facts*: You have to know an artist and his or her market inside and out in order to value their art accurately.

Second mistake: Sellers believe they can locate the perfect private buyers or collectors for their art. They take out online classifieds, search the internet for names of collectors, hang out at art galleries, fairs or auctions trying to find out who the big buyers are, read articles about collectors and then email them, and so on. *The facts*: Contacting private collectors personally is difficult; private collectors prefer to remain private.

Third mistake: Sellers believe they can sell their art to collectors at full retail price or, what's even more absurd, to dealers at full retail. *The facts*: Selling to private collectors is harder than finding them. Collectors pay retail to long-established galleries or professional sellers they know and trust. They pay retail for the amenities that galleries provide, and they are not inclined to buy art with no guarantees from total strangers. Dealers, on the other hand, buy at wholesale and sell at retail – they obviously do not buy art at the same price they sell it for, or they wouldn't be in business.

Dealers help you resell your art in ways you can't manage yourself, assuming they're interested in selling it or assisting you with selling it yourself (the more established your working relationship is, the better the chances of this happening). They know the market for your art, they know detailed information about the artists, and they know who collects those artists and how to make contact with them. And there's more:

- Dealers recognise how important your art is, how that art fits into the artists' careers, whether it is high or low end in terms of quality, and so on.
- Dealers recognise the strengths and weaknesses in your art and the strengths and weaknesses in the markets for that art.

- Dealers know which collectors would like to own your art. They understand the individual needs of those collectors and know how to present your art properly. Dealers stand a much better chance of selling your art to those collectors than you do.
- Dealers give you a realistic idea of how much money you can expect to sell your art for.
- Dealers often net you more for your art than you can by selling it to 'private collectors' on your own. Believe it or not!

Art dealers are in business to help you whenever your situation involves a transaction in art. Whether you're buying, selling, trading or collecting, take advantage of the services dealers offer and the insight and amenities they provide.

All is not wonderful in art-dealer-land, however. In a perfect world where everything was fair, buying art would be easy. You could visit any art gallery, present your situation, state what you wanted to buy and how much you wished to spend on it, make your selection, write out the cheque and take your new acquisition home with you. Unfortunately, we do not live in a perfect world, and buying art is not quite that straightforward. Not every dealer is fair.

The art business, like any other business, is populated with great dealers, good dealers, average dealers, worse-than-average dealers and a few terrible dealers. The art they sell ranges, like fashion, from excellent to awful (most of it being closer to excellent than it is to awful, of course). Prices range, too. Most of their prices are fair and reasonable, but a small percentage of them are ridiculously inflated. Major goals of your comparison shopping are to meet, understand and communicate with dealers, and, ultimately, to differentiate between who sells good-quality art at fair prices and who doesn't – and who has the best (and worst) selections for you.

CHARACTERISTICS OF GOOD ART DEALERS

Good dealers listen to what you have to say. They allow you to lead the discussion about what you are interested in buying. They want to know what you are looking for. They show you any art they have in stock that could possibly interest you. When they don't have anything in your field, they refer you to galleries that do.

Good dealers want you to learn. They determine how much you know, offer advice where it is needed and suggest where you need help. They either tell you who has the knowledge and experience to help you or they educate you themselves.

Good dealers discuss options. They offer you a variety of alternatives as to which direction you can take with your art buying. They discuss the good and bad points of each option. They never make you feel pressured to move in any particular direction.

Good dealers give you plenty of facts. They discuss the visual, scholarly, aesthetic and historical aspects of the art you are interested in. They compare and contrast artists, quality levels, works of art and art prices. All your questions are answered in a direct and straightforward fashion.

Good dealers provide you with outside tools and resources for continuing your education on your own. They recommend websites, books to read, museums to visit, experts and collectors you should follow or familiarise yourself with, and collections to see. They present you with information not only from their own galleries but also from other resources. They do not try and convince you that their galleries are the only ones you should ever patronise.

Good dealers speak your language and work with you at your own pace. You never feel compelled to buy. You are always free to make your own decisions. You leave their galleries knowing more than when you arrive, and feel that they are genuinely concerned about your success as an art buyer.

DEALERS TO AVOID

Unfortunately, not all art dealers have your best interests in mind when they attempt to sell you art. These sorts of dealers can be avoided, though. Certain tell-tale signs almost always mean you should exit the gallery you're in and move on to another.

Avoid dealers whose sales presentations focus primarily on the emotional as opposed to the facts. These dealers speak only about the way the art looks – the beauty, the drama, the colour, the intensity, the feeling. If you listen carefully, however, you notice that important details are conspicuously absent from the presentation, namely facts about the art, the artist and the market for the art.

Watch out for dealers who avoid price talk. They're usually evasive for a reason, most likely because what they sell is priced pretty high in comparison to similar art available elsewhere and they prefer not talking about it. They would rather invite you into their private viewing rooms and tell you how their art transports you into unique and marvellous worlds (the financial world not being one of them). Interrupt the travelogue with price questions and you can get some rather strange and occasionally ugly responses. Any time you hear phrases like, 'If you have to ask the price . . .' or 'It's worth many times that in beauty alone . . .' or 'How you feel is what's important, not how much it costs,' you're in trouble.

Dealers, of course, have a right to say whatever they want about the price of the art they sell. No law forbids them from believing that price is irrelevant and what counts is the mystical, cosmic interplay between you and the essence of the artist as embodied in the art, or whatever else they might say to divert you. But the facts are that any art piece has a corresponding fair and reasonable monetary value, one that anyone familiar with that artist's market will agree on, give or take a little.

Watch out for dealers who focus their sales presentations *only* on money. These are the exact opposite of those who avoid price talk. All these dealers do is talk money. The worst offenders go so far as to totally ignore the way the art looks and sell artwork as if it were stocks or bonds. In extreme instances, galleries tell prospective clients the art will increase in value-specific amounts over specific periods of time – which is a ridiculous, misleading and borderline fraudulent way of selling art. No one knows what the future holds in terms of how a work of art's price might fluctuate over time.

In a way, the people who buy art based on financial reasons alone are as much to blame as the dealers for the proliferation of cost-oriented selling. A good percentage of buyers, especially first-time buyers, are attracted to art by the possibilities of financial gain, and such buyers make easy marks for investment-style selling. Dealers simply play into their fantasies about buying art now and cashing it in for big profits later.

Typical statements you hear during the course of a make-big-bucks-fast sales presentation are:

'Who cares whether or not you like it. In eighteen months it'll be worth twice what you're paying for it.'

'As soon as this artist has a show at the Municipal Art Museum, you won't be able to touch one for this price.'

'Buy one now while you can still afford it.'

'This piece has a retail value of $10,000 on the open market, but I'm going to let you have it for only $3,500.

'This artist isn't going to be around for much longer. As soon as he dies, his prices are going through the roof.'

'This edition is almost sold out. Cash in while we still have some left. Once it sells out, prices will skyrocket.'

'This is the only one of its kind. You can either buy it or forget about ever being able to buy one as good for as little money again.'

'This piece will make a great investment.'

'You could buy these for a song ten years ago. Think what they'll be worth ten years from now.'

These types of statements are not only basically untrue, they're also disgusting. To portray a piece of art as nothing more than a speculative commodity or an artist as a person who will hopefully die soon and boost the value of his own art is the basest way to run an art business. Anytime you find yourself in these sorts of situations, no matter how much money you are being told you can make, leave immediately.

Watch out for dealers who attempt to qualify you as a buyer. They decide how much of their time is worth spending on you based on the amount of money they believe that you have to spend with them.

One gallery I know that specialises in selling overpriced art to unsuspecting out-of-town buyers uses a couple of well-placed questions to get to the bottom line. When you visit this gallery, shortly after you enter, a salesperson asks you the question, 'Are you in town for the medical convention?' A medical convention may or may not be taking place, but that's irrelevant. The question is a lead-in to finding out what you do for a living and, therefore, whether or not you can afford this gallery's art. If you answer no, the staff person responds with 'I thought for sure you were a doctor. You certainly look like one. What do you do for a living?' or 'What brings you to the city then?' or 'I've been seeing doctors all week, and I'm ready for a change. What do you do?' If your answers indicate that you've got money, get ready for an aggressive sales presentation.

Avoid dealers who are not sensitive to your needs and who don't listen to you. These dealers often force you to look at art you are not the least bit interested in. Rather than admitting they don't sell what you want and referring you to galleries that do, they try to change your mind and force you to buy what they sell.

Watch out for dealers who focus on one or two artists – ones they represent or have good selections of their works – and avoid all others. No matter what you say, the conversation always returns to these few artists. You get a very one-sided picture of the art market from these dealers. Avoid them unless, of course, they happen to be showing artists you collect.

Avoid dealers who pressure you, who need your sale to make their next commission or who are constantly on top of you to buy. Being victimised by a hard sell is always painful. Galleries that are more concerned about their bottom lines than serving your needs are a sad fact of the art business. When you feel that the art wants you rather than you want the art, just say no.

Watch out for dealers who find out how little you know about certain art or artists and then go to work educating you whether you want to learn or not. Once these dealers realise you're not experienced, anything goes. You may be introduced to a 'world famous' painter, one that the seller can't believe you've never heard of. You may get spoken to in 'secret technical art lingo' that you don't understand, but can have the privilege of learning if you decide to patronise that gallery. Never let anyone bully you with their supposed expertise.

Finally, avoid art dealers who answer any of your questions about their art with the reply 'I don't know.' This answer is *never* acceptable no matter what the question. At the very least, it shows the dealer is uninformed about some aspect of what he or she is selling. It's also a convenient way of dodging a touchy question such as whether the art is worth what you are being asked to pay for it. At worst, 'I don't know' is a great way for a dealer to avoid telling you something he doesn't want you to know.

Example 1

Antique dealers occasionally call me when they meet private individuals who have art for sale. One time, an out-of-town dealer called to tell me about a middle-aged couple who had a group of paintings for sale and asked me to come out and take a look. I wanted to make sure the trip would be worth my while so I asked him to find out some particulars about the art and call me back.

The next day, he called to tell me that the paintings had originally come from an elderly lady who had apparently acquired them over a twenty- or thirty-year period. He then gave me basic information about some of the paintings, such as sizes, subject matters, artists' names and how much the couple was asking for them. Several of the artists were collectible and all asking prices were reasonable. What I heard sounded good, so I decided to make the trip.

I arrived at the couple's home and introduced myself. The husband led me into a rear room and, with a sweep of his hand, directed my attention towards the paintings, all of which were leaning against a wall and stacked one in front of the other. I began looking through them and immediately realised that this trip was going to be a complete waste of time.

The paintings by name artists were either outright forgeries or terrible examples. The rest were by complete unknowns. I had even seen some of these paintings for sale at various shops over the past several years, which meant that on top of everything else, the 'elderly lady' story was a lie.

I looked through the collection, bought nothing, politely thanked the couple for their time and left. The sad part of this story is that several weeks later I was at the home of a relatively inexperienced collector who proudly told me he had beaten the dealers and made a great art purchase from a private home. He showed me his three latest acquisitions and – you guessed it – they had all come from this out-of-town couple. One of the paintings was a forgery, for which he had paid almost $2,000. The other two were junk.

Example 2

Some collectors prefer buying their art directly from the artists to buying it from dealers. They enjoy searching for artists online or meeting them in person in their studios and negotiating purchases without dealer interference. This is fine but, once again, be aware that if you're inexperienced and buy without professional input or assistance, you'd better know what you're doing. While buying directly from artists can be a rewarding experience, there can also be drawbacks.

First of all, artists are not art dealers (with a few exceptions), and artists' studios, websites or social networking pages are not art galleries. Artists are skilled at creating art and not necessarily at selling it. Most are far removed from the business of buying and selling art. They may understand the marketplace and price their art fairly; then again, they may not. You need to know how to tell the difference.

As for the overall marketplace, artists may know plenty about the art and careers of their artist friends, but they do not necessarily stay on top of current art world trends or events, even within their own communities. They do not usually provide amenities that galleries do such as trade-back policies or free updated appraisals, and they cannot provide you with an overview of the market the way galleries can.

Artists focus primarily on their own work. They often give you very biased ideas about what your buying options are. You would not, for instance, expect an artist to suggest that her work is not right for you and then refer you to another artist whose work she thinks would better suit your tastes. In the great majority of cases, her work is what suits you, and that's that. In other words, you'd better be pretty certain you want to buy work from a particular artist before engaging them.

As for you, arbitrarily picking artists whose work you happen to like is not the way to collect. Until you acquire a good overview of the market, and learn how to evaluate and compare, you'll have difficulty recognising which artists might be good to collect, whether or not to pay their asking prices, whether you are getting the best-quality work for your money and so on. Have dealers educate you and help you make these sorts of decisions while you're still in the learning stages. Once you've developed a feel for what you're doing, buying from artists can be a wonderful experience. More and more collectors are doing it, particularly online. You'll learn how to buy directly from artists in Chapter 10.

A LOOK AHEAD

Being able to distinguish between one art dealer and the next is a big step towards selecting the right art, but it's only part of what you need to know. Dealers operate and sell art from their galleries and websites, places where you will be spending significant amounts of time viewing art, learning about art and eventually buying art. Understanding what art galleries are and knowing how to use them and their websites to their full potential is just as important as understanding the dealers who operate them. Chapter 8 will help you to attain this goal.

Insider Tips on Art Galleries and Their Websites

These days, best procedure is to visit gallery websites first, before showing up in person, so you'll at least have some sense of what to expect when you get there. You always want to do a little prep work ahead of time, because when you step into an art gallery, you encounter much more than a space filled with art. You leave the everyday world behind and enter a unique microcosm of reality. The term *art gallery* is almost too mild a description of what confronts you once you are inside. Most galleries could more accurately be described as shrines to art or art temples. They are places where art is hallowed above all else and where devotion to that art is embodied in the ceremony of dealers passing it on to collectors in exchange for money.

Galleries are designed to focus your total attention on the particular art or artists they represent. When they do their job well, you are aware only of what's going on right before your eyes. Your life, for those brief moments, consists of art, art and art.

Whenever you're inside a gallery that displays art you find appealing, you feel compelled to a certain extent to select a piece or two that you might consider buying. A portion of that compulsion may be attributed to your genuine desire to own the art and another portion to the gallery's efforts to convince or induce you to own it. Some of the more intimidating galleries can actually interfere with and alter your normal decision-making process in favour of their art.

Controlling your own destiny inside galleries is not always easy. Meeting art dealers on their home turf can be difficult, especially for beginner buyers. The dealers and their staffs know plenty; you hardly know anything. They have dealt with hundreds or thousands of customers; you've barely had a chance to get your feet wet. They have all their sales tools right there at their fingertips; you have little or nothing in the way of defence. They see certain qualities in you the moment you walk through their doors; you don't have the vaguest idea what these galleries are about and what to expect from them. They have all the advantages.

This is not to say art dealers lie in wait in their galleries, ready to play on your inexperience and manipulate the way you think. The overwhelming majority do nothing of the sort. But they are in the business of selling art, and if they can figure out how to talk you into buying some, that's exactly what they'll do. In order to understand the art of buying art, you have to know how to navigate your way through art galleries; understand what happens within them; know what to look for, what to watch out for, how to interpret it all and end up buying only the art you love.

GALLERY INTERIORS VERSUS THE REST OF THE WORLD

Art gallery interiors present art at its absolute highest level of appeal. The track lighting is perfectly focused, the walls behind the art are plain, and the carpet or flooring is basic and spare. You see little, if any, competition from the surrounding environment. These are important points to keep in mind because under these kinds of circumstances, just about anything looks great. Professionally displayed and lit, even a sack full of trash can look like a masterpiece worthy of a place in any of the world's great art museums.

Another fixture of gallery interiors is the gallery owners and staff. The information they present you with is designed to heighten the beauty of their art even further. They believe in the art they sell, and they know exactly what to say in order to sell it.

Finally, you have the art gallery's viewing room, the place where art looks even better than it does in any other location on the gallery floor. Galleries without viewing rooms also have special spots where their art looks best. When you and an owner or staff member head over to the viewing room or viewing spot, art in tow, for a closer look under these perfectly ideal viewing conditions, you see and hear about that art at its absolute unobstructed finest. At this point, you have to be completely sure whether you want to own it or not, because the deck is definitely stacked in the gallery's favour.

Keep in mind that if you buy the art, you have to remove it from the protective environment of the gallery and take it out into the cold, cruel world where it is no longer the centre of the universe and no longer has a supporting cast telling you how great it is. It gets no special treatment in your environment; it becomes just another thing in a room full of things. Suddenly, it has to stand on its own and prove that it is really as great as the gallery made it look and made you think it is. The truth is that sometimes it is and other times it isn't.

Many inexperienced collectors, unfortunately, do not account for the effects that ideal viewing conditions of art gallery interiors combined with overwhelmingly positive employee input can have on art. They buy art on the spot without ever seeing it outside gallery settings and away from the hype, display it in a totally different setting, and expect it to thrill them just as much as it did in the gallery. In some cases, perhaps several weeks or months later, they begin to wonder why it doesn't look as great as they originally thought it did when they bought it. At worst, they actually regret buying it.

What you have to do in order to prevent this from happening to you is to take any selections you are considering buying out of the viewing rooms, out of the galleries, away from the salespeople, and into your own environment where you can live with them anywhere from a few days to maybe a week or two *before you buy*. You see and hear how great they are from the sellers. Now, let gallery influences fade into the background, let your personal feelings come to the foreground, and decide whether or not the art really means as much to you as the gallery presentation has led you to believe it does.

How do you take a selection out of a gallery without having to buy it? Easy. Art galleries offer a courtesy service, known as 'taking art home on approval', that allows you to keep art and live with it, at no financial risk, for anywhere from several days to a week or two for the sole purpose of deciding whether or not you are sure you want to own it. Some galleries ask you to leave a deposit or even pay for the art in full when you do this, but all will completely refund your money if for any reason you decide not to buy. Getting art on approval is absolutely essential when buying online, for example, as you'll see in Chapter 11, and most websites and artists offer this amenity.

When you're just starting out collecting, always take art you have selected for possible purchase home with you on approval first. You will see for yourself how drastically gallery interiors, websites and sales presentations can sometimes influence the way art looks, and you will discover that some art you initially thought you wanted to buy is really not for you at all. One word of caution: never take art home on approval unless you are serious about buying it.

ART GALLERY BACK ROOMS, STORAGE AREAS AND OFFICES

Almost all art galleries have more art for sale than what you see on display in their public viewing areas. Galleries often have additional works of art stored in stock rooms, back rooms, office areas, separate warehouse storage facilities and so on. Some galleries keep online inventories of art they have in storage, pieces they have access to out of private collections and art they can purchase for you through other dealers or resources. A gallery may have ten additional pieces available or it may have ten thousand.

Whenever you are in a gallery and don't see art that interests you, don't turn around and walk out. Introduce yourself to the owner or a staff person, state exactly what you're looking for and find out whether they have access to any art you might like even though none is currently on display. You do yourself a major disservice every time you browse in silence and then leave, because you miss seeing or hearing about everything for sale that is out of public view.

See back-room selections and actually go into storage areas with dealers whenever possible, but only if invited (it's not appropriate to ask unless you have an established relationship). These experiences add to your knowledge of how galleries operate and to your understanding of the range and variety of art they have to offer. Other advantages to seeing art that is not on display in public viewing areas are as follows:

- A gallery may have significant selections of an artist or type of art you like, but may not currently be showing it.
- A gallery may have a good selection of art by an artist you are not that familiar with, but whose art you might find appealing once you have a chance to see multiple examples.
- You may notice art you like that gallery owners wouldn't have thought you were interested in.
- You may see art you like that is out of place in a particular gallery or that the gallery no longer deals in and that the owner is willing to let you have at an attractive price.
- You are afforded opportunities to learn about art and artists whose work gallery owners keep in stock but don't regularly display in public areas.
- Dealers will better understand from how you respond to the full scope of their art how best they will be able to help you in the future.

As with storage areas, offices can also be interesting and informative. So, whenever you have the opportunity to see and speak with gallery owners or staff members in their offices, do so. But again, wait to be invited; don't invite yourself. Visiting office areas and seeing the centres of operations increases your understanding of what art galleries are all about. It also makes you less intimidated and thus better able to make decisions regarding the substance and direction of your collecting.

Another advantage of access to places other than the main floor is that you sometimes get the chance to see new arrivals and hear about upcoming shows or events before the general public does. When things happen, they happen in offices and back rooms first. Acquiring this sort of inside access takes time and is part of the process of developing long-term working relationships with dealers, but as you get to know certain dealers better, you'll find yourself receiving special attention that ordinary clients do not normally receive.

ART GALLERY LIBRARIES AND WEBSITES

In any gallery, pay attention to all books, exhibition catalogues and other art reference materials out on display for public use. More importantly, look to see whether the gallery even has an art library. A gallery library may consist of five books or it may consist of five thousand. It may be in an office, in a work or storage room, or out on the main floor. Libraries are usually in plain sight, but when you can't find one, ask whether one exists and, if it does, whether you can see what it looks like. As for you computer types who might think libraries no longer matter, they do.

A good solid art gallery library contains art books, exhibition catalogues, art periodicals and other materials that relate directly to what the gallery sells. Art dealers use these references when they have to research particular artists or works of art or when they want to share knowledge with their clients. Access to comprehensive reference materials, both online and in book form, is indispensable to a good art dealer and an excellent indication of how serious that gallery is about knowing the history and details behind the art it sells, and about having the means on hand to convey that information to their customers. In fact, there's a saying in the art business that goes, 'You're only as good as your library.'

Good reference libraries should contain standard references, including access to online databases, like those you will learn about in Part III. The more of those you see, the better. Also, it is an advantage if the gallery refers to them and shares that information with you, the better. The best galleries support any statements or claims they make about their art with documentation from standard reference materials that are recognised and accepted by those in the art community.

Superior gallery libraries also have access to substantial online price information and databases that you will learn about in Part IV. Briefly, galleries use this information to determine sensible selling prices for their art, and the more willing they are to share that information with you, the better.

Get into the habit of asking gallery owners or staff members whether they can provide you with printed or online information about particular art or artists they have on display that you are interested in. Make them use their libraries and reference materials. This gives you the chance to see how they access information and is also a great oppor- tunity to learn what reference materials provide the best answers to your specific questions. Most dealers are skilled at art research; learn from them whenever you get the chance.

One caution, though. Ask for library references only when you're seriously considering buying art. Avoid making frivo- lous requests or forcing dealers to go online or haul out book after book when you're only using them for personal research or are not really interested in learning about or buying the art you're asking questions about.

Beware of galleries that have no libraries to speak of. Galleries with minimal reference materials on hand may be more interested in merchandising art than in educating and cultivating informed collectors. A poor or non-existent gallery reference library or an unwillingness to access information for you online is never a good sign.

TIPS ON RECOGNISING THE BEST (AND WORST) GALLERIES FOR YOU

The goal of all gallery visits is to identify those establishments best able to supply you with the art you want to buy. As you progress from brief initial contacts to more in-depth interactions, you will be choosing those places where you will most likely do business in the future. Here are the two most important characteristics you want those galleries to have:

- Good selections of the work of particular artists or types of art that you find appealing.
- Personnel with a wide range of knowledge about that art, who have experience selling it and who show sensitivity to your collecting needs.

Galleries that do not meet these two conditions are not good places for beginners to shop.

Avoid establishments that offer only isolated examples of art you like; avoid gallery personnel who don't appear informed about what they are selling. While you're in the learning stages, you need to surround yourself with those in the know. You take serious risks if you don't.

Suppose, for example, you walk into a gallery because you see an attractive bronze statue by a sculptor whose work you like on display in the front window. You take a look around and see no other work by this artist. You ask the owner about the sculpture, and during the course of conversation you find out that it's the sole work by this sculptor he has ever had for sale, that he learned most of what he's telling you only since he acquired it and that he has seen just several other pieces by the artist during his entire career. Conclusion: this dealer does not qualify as an authority on the sculptor and, unless you are, you would want to hold off on buying the sculpture without doing further research.

Avoid galleries that have no direction or focus in what they sell. These places are easy to spot because they display many unrelated pieces of art by many different artists, perhaps even spanning many time periods, countries, styles and so on. When the selection gets too general, the amount of knowledge the dealer has about that selection is usually too general as well.

Example 1

A collector once came to me with a 'bargain' painting he had discovered while rummaging through the back room of a local art gallery after being invited to look around. He said the dealer appeared to know little about the artist and was not that familiar with his market or how desirable his art was. That was why the price was so low.

I took one look at it and suspected it might be a fake – a good fake, but a fake nonetheless. I recommended he return it as soon as possible but, just to be on the safe side, I had him contact another dealer first in order to confirm my suspicions. The dealer agreed with my assessment, the collector returned the picture to the gallery and, fortunately, was able to get his money back without any problem.

What happened here was that this collector was not yet experienced enough to be buying odd works of art from uninformed sellers. He knew this particular artist was highly collectible and had seen a few examples of his work, but that was about all, and not enough of an education to buy like a pro. He automatically took the word of the dealer (who didn't know enough about the artist either) and ended up getting fooled by a good-quality forgery.

A big problem with dealers who are not experts in what they sell is that they can inadvertently buy and sell forgeries. These dealers are not necessarily to blame and may well think they are buying and selling authentic art but, in some cases, they do not know enough to tell the difference between the real thing and skilfully executed fakes. Not all gallery owners are experts in everything they sell.

Example 2

A collector once asked me about a sculptor whose work he was interested in purchasing. He had visited a gallery for the first time, seen the work of an artist with whom he was previously unfamiliar and liked it very much. The gallery owner had got the collector all excited by showing him a book that contained an entire chapter mainly about the sculptor and his lifestyle. The collector believed from this presentation that the artist was extremely well known and possibly even famous.

I was familiar with this artist and told the collector he had been given the wrong impression. Although the artist was known and respected, being categorised as 'extremely well known' or 'almost famous' was definitely out of the question. Seeing that much of his excitement seemed to be based on the one chapter that had been written about the artist, I asked what book the dealer had showed him.

He gave me the name of the book and I immediately recognised it as one that was not taken very seriously by people in the know. True, the sculptor did have a chapter in the book, but the artists included were not necessarily there because they were famous. They were included primarily because they had been friends of the author or had travelled in similar social circles. The book contained little scholarly information, but was rather a collection of anecdotes about how various artists and other creative types were living their lives.

Dealers occasionally show only select references in attempts to make certain artists seem more important than they are or in order to make selling the art easier. Read and listen to everything dealers show and tell you, but unless you know and trust them, do not instantly assume they're giving you either a balanced presentation or all the information you need to know.

A LOOK AHEAD

Understanding art dealers and art galleries well enough to choose the best ones for your needs is essential to intelligent buying. You do not, however, simply make your choices, sit back and wait for the art to roll in. In order to assure yourself of getting the best treatment possible in the marketplace and of being shown quality examples of the art you're looking for, you have to know how to be a good customer. Being a good customer pays dividends in many ways.

CHAPTER 9

HOW TO BE A GOOD CUSTOMER

A dealer–customer or seller–customer relationship is a cooperative venture, whether you're buying at galleries or online. You each have obligations to fulfil in order to make it work. Dealers supply you with art, educate you about that art and, through their galleries or websites, provide amenities, guarantees and protections on the art you buy. Throughout this process of locating and selling you art, dealers prefer that you cooperate with them and follow certain guidelines. By doing so, you make their job of serving you so much easier.

In general, dealers and retail art websites like doing business with people who are serious about art and willing to learn. As relationships deepen, sellers offer their clients increasing fringe benefits that average buyers never receive, such as showing or notifying them about newly arrived art first. These sorts of arrangements do not develop overnight – some relationships take months or even years to mature – but once they do, buying art becomes less of an effort and even more of a pleasure.

THINGS DEALERS LIKE

About the most important favour you can do for dealers is to educate yourself about the art you're most interested in. The better you understand the language and the history behind what you buy, the better you are able to communicate your needs. Informed, educated buyers are the easiest ones to work with – it's that simple. Observe the additional directives listed in this section and hasten your attainment of 'most favoured buyer' status among dealers.

Always be as specific as possible about what type of art you are looking for. Specify, for example, that you're looking for figure paintings by contemporary English artists, scenes of the Mississippi River Valley from all time periods, abstract sculptures done by Brazilian artists since the 1970s, American urban or graffiti-based art, or whatever. As you gain experience, you become progressively better able to describe and define your needs. Tell dealers about your favourite artists, subject matters, colours, sizes, shapes and any other characteristics you prefer in your art. Also keep them informed as to any changes or new interests or developments in the direction of your buying.

Respond as quickly and directly as possible to all art that dealers show you or websites notify you about. Keeping them waiting is never a good idea. Tell them whether you like it and why. Be as precise as you can and say everything that comes to mind (as long as you generally keep it positive). Don't feel shy or embarrassed that you don't know enough to converse – you learn by speaking and communicating with experts. For instance, spending half an hour with a seller evaluating the plusses and minuses of a particular painting whether online or in person can be a highly enlightening and educational experience.

Know your budget and never mislead anyone about your ability to buy. Be fair with dealers on this issue and they'll return the favour. For example, if you are in a gallery that has little for sale under $10,000 and your limit is $1,500 per purchase, say so. Nobody's going to throw you out. Most likely, people at the gallery will still be happy to speak with you about their art and artists, and maybe on some future visit you'll be able to afford a piece of their art.

Encourage dealers or websites to call or notify you, to extend special viewing invitations to you or otherwise inform you about new arrivals. You are never under any obligation to buy. Of course, if you don't buy something at least every once in a while, they'll stop contacting you but, by that time, you may have settled on other galleries or websites who you prefer doing business with anyway.

Act quickly when sellers contact you about art they think you might be interested in, whether you are interested or not. Dealers appreciate quick responses because then they can either sell you the art or, if you don't want it, proceed to contact whoever's next in line. If you make dealers wait for days before you respond, you can bet they won't be notifying you much in the future.

Buy art! Buy art from galleries or websites that regularly exhibit and offer what you want, not only in terms of art, but also art education, special invitations, events and other amenities. Sellers that take the time to teach you deserve something in return, namely your patronage. If all you do is take without giving, you'll find that gallery owners and other sellers will eventually reduce communications with you.

Be loyal to the dealers that help you the most. This does not mean you blindly buy from one or two resources and ignore the rest of the art world. Get to know your favourite dealers, visit their galleries or websites regularly, solidify relationships, work together whenever possible, make sure they know how much you appreciate everything they do for you and generally keep in touch. Continue to meet new dealers and search for new resources online, and buy from whoever happens to offer you art you want; but maintain and deepen good relations with those who have been helping you the longest and the most.

Pay for what you buy when you say you are going to pay for it. Whether you are supposed to pay over several months or within three days, pay on time. Sellers need to know when and how much money is coming into their galleries so they can gauge their own purchases and pay their bills on time. Being slow to pay is never good and will eventually begin to compromise the quality of your collecting.

Listen to the advice sellers give you, even when it may not be what you want to hear. This doesn't mean you instantly accept whatever they say, but rather that you show a willingness to consider new input, ideas and perspectives that may diverge from those you already have. Much of what sellers tell you is for your benefit, and by keeping an open mind, you allow yourself to grow as a collector.

THINGS DEALERS DON'T LIKE

You want dealers to like you. When they don't, you and your art buying suffer. Dealers who don't like you behave in ways that are counterproductive to your buying. For example:

- They spend as little time with you as possible.
- They reduce communications.
- They stop educating you.
- They don't care whether they sell you the best art for your needs or not.

- They don't inform you about the latest developments in the art market.
- They don't speak favourably of you when your name comes up in conversations with other dealers or collectors.
- They may even purposely mislead you.

Observing a few specific cautions, as outlined below, will keep you off dealers' 'least-favoured clients' lists.

Don't be a silent customer, a mystery person. When you visit galleries, introduce yourself, ask questions and state what you're looking for. No one appreciates people who are cagey or secretive about their intentions, especially if they're asking for assistance or information.

Don't take whatever help or benefits you're being offered without offering something in return (in other words, buying art). Sellers know when they are being hit up for free advice and they don't like it. You can ask dealers with whom you have established relationships and already do business for informational favours, but make sure that, in the long run, you compensate them comparably for their time.

Don't talk a big game about how much money you have to spend or are willing to spend and then not spend any. Dealers are not interested in listening to how much money you have either before or after you spend it. Even when you do spend it, they are quite capable of figuring out your financial situation all by themselves – they don't need you to tell them. By the way, as far as dealers are concerned, you have no money to spend until you spend it.

Avoid playing dealers, galleries or websites one against the other. Ask them to comment on each other's art or to gossip about their fellow professionals and you'll find yourself in trouble fast.

Don't be cheap. If you know that $5,000 is a fair price to pay for the art you want, don't offer $1,500 for it. First of all, you'll never own any art. Second, you'll waste everyone's time including your own. Third, lowballing prices is often taken as an insult. Fourth, you'll get a reputation as a cheap buyer, and those sellers who continue doing business with you will only offer you cheap art – cheap in quality as well as in price.

Don't try to hide your enthusiasm about art you really like and act like you don't really care. Some collectors think that if they remain totally unemotional, show no feelings and express a take-it-or-leave-it attitude, dealers will drop asking prices and sell for less. First of all, dealers show the greatest consideration to customers who are excited and completely satisfied with what they buy. Second, dealers love to know when they pinpoint tastes exactly. Third, the deadpan poker-faced routine rarely fools anyone. Start playing sneaky games with dealers, and they'll respond with a few of their own.

Avoid bragging about or showing off good buys you make from other sellers. If you score a bargain somewhere, savour the victory in private. Suppress the urge to tell everyone how clever you are. Act like you know so much that you can buy art without professional assistance and guess what? Sellers will stop assisting you. Smart collectors savour their bargain buys quietly.

Don't tell dealers that you can find art just as good as theirs at other galleries or websites for less money. Buy art where you get the best quality for the best price, and that's that. Going public with gallery-to-gallery price comparisons or who's selling what for less is really irritating. Besides that, you probably aren't telling them anything they don't know already.

Don't respond rudely to art that dealers offer you. If you don't like the way it looks, say something like, 'It's not quite my style,' or 'It doesn't have the right feel to it.' Go into graphic detail about how your eyes ache when you look at it or complain that it makes you nauseous, and you'll lose a dealer's support quickly. Insult the art, and you insult the individual who is selling it.

Don't treat dealers like servants or hired help and feel they should pay you homage because you have graciously singled out their galleries or websites with which to do business. Dealers respond to this treatment by either avoiding you altogether or taking your money and returning as little as possible above and beyond what they sell you. You don't do anyone any special favours by buying their art. They can do just as well without you.

Example 1

Gossip is a fact of the art business. The art world is small, and many dealers know each other and often speak among themselves, sometimes about clients. If you buy art on a regular basis, sooner or later the dealers who specialise in the art you like find out who you are. Some of them hear about you before they even meet you.

When I meet potential buyers for the first time, I occasionally ask other dealers about them. I basically want to protect myself from people who could possibly be difficult to deal with, waste my time or try to take advantage in one way or another. Dealers will sometimes warn me when I'm in for a rough time, and I keep that in mind if we have any dealings at all. In the worst cases, I'm warned about problem buyers repeatedly and, based on the strength of those warnings, decide not to do business without ever meeting them!

Dealers also have good things to say about their clients. They talk about those who are eager to learn, easy to work with, who pay their bills on time, who know how to recognise quality art and so on. I look forward to doing business with these people and am inclined to show them special consideration, even when I hardly know them.

Make sure you treat dealers fairly and with respect, because in the art business your reputation often precedes you. Having dealers hear negative things about you before they know you can really compromise your collecting. On the other hand, when people only have good things to say about you, you have an automatic head start in building gratifying and productive working relationships.

Example 2

I know a collector who would rather buy lots of less expensive paintings than a few more expensive ones. Consequently, he ends up sacrificing quality for quantity. Most of his art is mediocre at best and, in spite of how little he spends, it's debatable whether they're even worth the money. Unfortunately, he refuses to listen to constructive advice from dealers who suggest that he buy a handful of better examples instead of many lesser-quality ones.

Dealers have long since stopped trying to educate this collector and, instead, sell him exactly what he wants – cheap, mediocre paintings. They don't waste their time showing him anything that's any good because they know it will always be 'over his budget'. Remember, most dealers want to see you advance as an art buyer, so seriously consider any advice they give you about improving your buying habits and the quality of your collecting.

A LOOK AHEAD

Some people prefer buying their art directly from artists, either in person or online, to shopping at galleries. They like to search for art on websites and at art shows, visit artist studios, meet artists, see artists in action, discover new types of art, socialise with artists and become directly involved in the artist community. However, buying directly from artists is very different than buying art at galleries. Chapter 10 talks about what those differences are and instructs you on how to proceed when the artist is also the dealer.

BUYING ART DIRECTLY FROM ARTISTS

Buying art directly from artists is a great way to collect art. Many artists never show at galleries, due mainly to the fact that there are far more artists than there are galleries to show their work. Any art dealer will tell you that he or she is able to show only a small fraction of the artists who contact them for possible representation, and that many of the artists who they have to turn away have talent. Additionally, increasing numbers of artists are forgoing galleries altogether in favour of selling their art directly online.

Two cautions about buying directly from artists are in order before we get going. First, don't view this option as an opportunity to buy cheaper by eliminating dealers (and their commissions) from your art-buying adventures. As you've read in previous chapters, galleries and dealers play an essential role in the art world's structure and hierarchy. Continue to visit galleries both in person and online, follow what they're doing, interact with them when relevant and learn about art.

To briefly recap, dealers sift through countless works of art in order to bring the most deserving artists and examples to the public's attention. They present art in ways so that the public can more easily understand it – ways that few artists are capable of doing on their own. Dealers educate, inform and provide valuable overviews of art, artists and the art market for the art-buying public. The best among them set trends, build great collections for their clients, advance the careers (and prices) of the artists they represent, and increase the public's overall awareness, appreciation, understanding and demand for quality works of art.

Second, never try to swerve around dealers and buy directly from the artists they represent. Seeing an artist's work on display at a gallery, for example, and deliberately trying to exclude the dealer from a sales transaction by contacting the artist directly on your own is totally inappropriate. It's extremely poor art-business etiquette, and you can easily end up alienating the dealer and the artist, and ruining your reputation as a trustworthy buyer.

MEETING ARTISTS IN GROUP SETTINGS

Meeting artists at group events, as opposed to one at a time, is the best way to begin an artist art search. Check local arts organisations, area art and artist websites, blogs or social networking groups or pages, and weekly calendar or entertainment websites or publications for dates and times of art fairs, group art exhibitions, street fairs and juried shows offering prizes for the best art. These events can be anything from a few artists selling art at a small local street fair to highly competitive shows with strict admissions requirements. Hundreds of major shows and thousands of minor ones take place annually at local, regional and national levels. They are held at locations like museums, community galleries, art associations, community centres, exhibition halls, public parks, malls, state and county fairs, and so on.

For beginning collectors, convenience and anonymity are two plus points of exploring group-show settings. The work of dozens and sometimes hundreds of artists is on display at one location, thereby allowing you to see plenty of art with very little effort. You can compare and contrast specific pieces you like without having to travel from gallery to gallery or artist studio to artist studio. And you don't have to speak with anyone until you're ready – you'll be just another face in the crowd.

The ability to compare prices is another big advantage of group settings. You see what amount of money buys you what amount of art from a variety of different artists. Learning about art and money is far easier when you acquire data from numerous sources all at once than it is when you confine your activities to single galleries or venues showing only one or two artists at a time.

On average, selling prices tend to be lower at group art shows where artists sell direct than they are at retail galleries. This is true not only because so many artists are competing for sales at the same locations, but also because organisers are often groups like non-profit or community-service organisations who have more interest in showing art than they do in making money. As a result, they tend to charge artists modest entrance or exhibition fees and take smaller percentages of final selling prices than galleries do, assuming they take any percentages at all.

Juried shows and awards competitions have an additional advantage. The best pieces in the show are already selected and labelled by panels of art professionals, which makes your job of evaluating what's 'good', 'better' and 'best' a lot easier. If you really want to enhance your art education, talk to show organisers, participants or judges about how prize-winning pieces are selected and what selection criteria are used.

When you see a piece of art you like at a group show, don't buy immediately. Find out what else the artist has to offer. Research them online and see what kind of profile they have. The artist may only be showing a piece or two at a show, but have dozens or even hundreds of pieces online or on display at other locations. Find out, for example, whether you can visit the artist at her studio and see her full range of work. At the studio, you might find pieces you like even more or ones you like just as much at more affordable prices. Studio visits also bring you closer to artists and give you a better understanding of their art.

MEETING ARTISTS AT OPEN STUDIOS

You can make appointments to visit individual artists at their studios or, better yet, you can meet groups of artists at their studios all at once by attending events like 'open studios', 'art walks' and 'art trails'. These events are held in places with significant concentrations of artists like major cities, communities known for their 'artist colonies', districts or buildings where multiple artists have their studios, and so on.

Many such groups of local artists get together anywhere from once or twice a year to monthly and open their studios to the public at the same time. These are special opportunities for you to browse and meet dozens and sometimes hundreds of artists in person, speak with them about their art, tour their studios, see how they live and/or work and see the best selections of their art available anywhere. There's no easier way for artists to sell art than right out of their own studios. Therefore, an additional benefit of these events is that participating artists can afford to be flexible with their selling prices.

Open-studio events allow you to get as close to artists as you can possibly get in brief encounters and, of course, the festive atmosphere makes the events great fun. For those of you who want personal involvement with the artists you patronise, nothing beats the access provided by open studios.

Dealing directly with artists is perhaps the greatest advantage of open studios, but it can also be a drawback when you don't know that much about art. This is because you're pretty much on your own and have no professionals like dealers or other art experts available to provide critical overviews of what you're looking at. If you're not careful, you can end up patronising artists who know how to sell a lot better than they know how to make art. Avoid this problem by attending your first few open studios with people who know the territory and can help you sift through the deluge.

Another occasional problem with open studios is that artists can use the prospect of increased public exposure to mark up their prices over what they normally charge for their art. Others put more reasonably priced pieces out of sight and only show their most expensive work. If you find yourself in a situation where you like the art but can't afford it, state your budget and your preferences. See whether the artist is flexible on prices or can show you additional, more affordably priced selections.

Whenever you visit an artist's studio, whether at open studios or one-on-one, take things slowly and let the artist show you their art the way they like to show it. Pay special attention when they talk about particular pieces. Never be too quick to dismiss art without hearing the story behind it, because a piece you don't find attractive at first may take on a whole new meaning, beauty or significance once you understand what it's all about. Ask for selling prices of artworks that appeal to you and, assuming you really like what you're looking at, have the artist set aside those pieces that you like the most, even if one or two may be a little over your budget. When you're done, sit down with the artist, review your selections and ask any remaining questions you might have. Making final selections will be addressed below in the 'Getting Down to Business' section.

Maybe the art that you're looking at comes close to what you want, but doesn't quite satisfy you and you'd really love to have a particular type of piece that you believe the artist is capable of making for you. You can always ask whether that's possible, but it can also be risky. Commissioning artists to produce particular pieces is not generally a good idea for beginning collectors. But if you insist and the artist says yes, allow her to create the piece on her own terms and without any further coaching on your part once she understands your preferences. Be prepared to accept the final product even if it's not totally to your liking. Remember, you asked for it, and the artist took her time and tried her very best to make it for you.

Open studios are usually highly publicised within local arts communities. Find out if and when they take place in your area by contacting artists, local or regional arts organisations, art schools, college art departments and art galleries that specialise in exhibiting local artists, and by keeping up with art listings on websites or in the arts and entertainment sections of local publications.

BUYING FROM ARTISTS ONLINE

More and more people are buying more and more art online all the time, not only from artist websites or online stores, but perhaps even more so on social networking websites like

Instagram and Facebook. You can tell plenty from locating and researching an artist's online profile these days, including in many cases being able to view a significant selection of their art. In fact, so much information is now available online for so many artists that you can acquire a complete collection without ever having to set foot in a gallery, or ever meet a single artist in person for that matter – not that you would want to do that, but it is an option. Regardless of the level of personal involvement you want to have, here are some helpful guidelines for researching and buying art directly from artists online.

Search, locate and review as much information as possible about artists whose work you're interested in, not just their websites. This includes social networking pages (Instagram, Facebook, LinkedIn, Twitter, etc.), stores or shops or galleries on group art websites, third-party websites that mention the artist or their art and so on. If you're in the preliminary stages of looking, you can do basic image searches on Google for either specific artists, subject matters or types of art you're interested in. Facebook and Instagram each have their own search options as well. Searching Facebook is similar to searching Google. On Instagram, however, you'll be looking more for hashtags that match up with your wants in order to locate and browse relevant selections of art.

Once you have a list of artist names, visiting their personal websites is generally the best way to start. There, you can usually find information like the artist's statement, biographical details, résumé of shows and experience, selections of their art, specialities, descriptions or explanations of their art, what materials or mediums they use, contact information and more. Some artist sites also provide details on pricing, how to buy, how they ship or deliver their art, and other relevant details like whether you can return the art within a set period of time if you're not totally satisfied. The more of this data you can gather before you make contact, the better. Having a pretty good idea of what you're getting yourself into before you get into it is always recommended.

The most important parts of any artist's website are the résumé or CV, and the gallery or portfolio of their art. The résumé gives you a good idea of how active the artist is and how serious they are about their art. Do they regularly participate in shows and exhibitions or are there gaps in time where the artist does not seem to be active? Consistency and regular shows or activities are generally what you want to see in a good solid résumé.

As for an artist's gallery or portfolio of art, look at all the work and not just a little. Get a sense of the artist's range of skills and abilities. See how well they organise and present their art. Is it arranged in ways that make sense? Generally, you want to see the art separated and categorised into specific groups or series or bodies of work that are similar in theme, idea, concept, subject matter or other related criteria. What you don't want to see is a hodgepodge or disjointed presentation where you can't quite figure out what you're looking at or what the artist's focus might be.

On both websites and social networking pages, check to see when the art was made (or ask the artist about dates if no dates are posted and you decide to make contact). Is the artist currently active or is the art on the website older? As with the résumé, you want to see a consistent track record of production, signs that the artist is regularly producing and posting new work, and that there aren't significant gaps between productive periods. If all of the work on the website is older, for example, it might be reasonable to assume that the artist is either no longer active or only producing a small amount of work. Basically, productive artists tend to be more serious about their careers than artists who approach art-making more casually or periodically.

Look for basic explanations or descriptions of the art. Websites that provide guidance are preferable to those that don't. You want to get a sense of what you're looking at, what the work is about, what's important to the artist, an idea of their capabilities, specialities or intentions. Whatever those happen to be, you want to see selections that are extensive enough to give you a visual understanding of where the artist is coming from as well as how they're progressing and evolving with their art. Clear, coherent and well-organised image pages or galleries of art with a basic introductory text are almost always preferable to confusing ones with little or no explanations. In other words, you want an artist who appears to know what they're doing and where they're going rather than one who's still trying to figure things out.

Another critical component of an artist's online presence is their social networking profile and, in fact, it can often provide more useful information than their website in a number of ways. For one thing, you can get a pretty good idea of how conscientious an artist is about making art and being an artist. Look for signs that they're producing art on a regular basis and not just every once in a while. You can tell this from viewing day-to-day postings and image galleries on sites like Facebook or from image feeds on Instagram. Don't forget to scroll back in time to see how long they've been at it; what's happening now might look great, but you also need to see what's happened in the past in order to form a more complete picture.

Look for consistency in postings; that's always better than random unrelated postings. A well-defined narrative or storyline that's easy to understand and follow is almost always preferable to a confusing progression of posts. See how the artist describes their art. Interesting or engaging texts or explanations of art, even brief ones, show that the artist is in touch with what they're doing, that there's a focus, purpose and direction to their art. Explanations like 'My new art' or 'Latest art' or 'Just finished' or a bunch of general hashtags add little or nothing to a viewer's overall understanding of the work, and may be indications that the artist is not really clear on where they're going with their art.

See how many followers an artist has. Is their fanbase local, regional, national, international? How do they interact with their fans? What do followers think of the art? What kinds of comments do people leave on their pages? Does the artist actively participate and respond to their audience? If you're thinking about buying art, you at least want an artist who seems accessible and willing to engage in conversation.

See how active an artist is. Do they show or exhibit their art on a regular basis? Are they involved in the art community? Do they sell on a regular basis? Are buyers satisfied with their art? Does the artist post images of buyers with their art or of newly purchased art on display in owner's homes or offices? Answers to these and similar questions are critical to making final decisions on whether to buy.

In addition to an artist's website and social networking pages, you also want to see who else might be taking notice. Is anybody writing about them? Are there any reviews or articles or interviews or coverage of shows on art websites or blogs? Do people talk about their art? Incidental coverage like this can sometimes provide real insight into where an artist is right now and what might be on tap for their future.

Keep in mind through all this that you can buy whatever you want to buy for whatever reason you want to buy it, but knowing something about what you want to buy and who you want to buy it from is always preferable to taking a more casual approach and hoping for the best. Researching, making contact with and getting to know an artist online can be more fun and rewarding than you ever realised once you learn how to do it. On the way to making those final decisions about whether to buy, be sure all communications with the artist proceed smoothly from beginning to end and that you understand exactly what you're getting. Be sure you completely and fully understand how you'll be paying, how the art will be shipped and delivered, whether you can return it if not satisfied, and basically what the transaction will involve from start to finish. That's how you maximise positive outcomes when buying art online.

ADDITIONAL WAYS TO MEET ARTISTS

Assuming you enjoy meeting artists, prefer personal contact to buying online and feel comfortable buying direct, you can explore more adventurous ways to meet them such as by sending emails or posting wants or requests for art you like on specialised art websites that focus on those types of art, on relevant local or regional art or artist groups on social networking sites, or on websites or social networking pages of local or regional art and artist organisations. If you're really serious, you can even advertise in art publications. Wherever you look or post your wants, include your preferences (size, subject matter, medium, etc.) and appropriate contact information. You might also mention that you're a private party (as opposed to a dealer), although that's not really necessary. You can mention your budget or price range either in the posts themselves or shortly after making contact with artists whose art interests you.

Publicising your wants on targeted community art websites is another good way to meet artists, especially when you're interested in buying within particular geographic regions. Familiarise yourself with area arts councils, art schools, art galleries, art supply stores, and sales and rental galleries of art museums or institutions to find out the best places to locate the types of art you're looking for. For example, many major cities have converted warehouses or warehouse districts where artists live and work. Find out where these are, and get names of local businesses where artists get together or do their shopping. You'll learn about community organisations and networks at many such studio, warehouse and business locations.

PROFILE OF AN ARTIST WITH WHOM YOU CAN WORK

Wherever your art adventures take you, in person or online, sooner or later you'll meet artists who create art you're interested in buying. At that point, begin making more in-depth contact. Introduce yourself, talk to or email the artists about their art and, when appropriate, make appointments to see more work at their studios or have them show you works online. Your goal is not only to locate art you like at prices you want to pay, but also to identify those artists who understand your guidelines or requirements and with whom you'll be able to get along.

Every artist you meet has his or her own ideas about what you deserve and how much they are prepared to give you in terms of art, time, attention and respect once you tell them what you're looking for and about how much you're willing to spend. At one end of the continuum is the artist who sits down with you or communicates well online, answers all of your questions, wants you to have a good piece of art, stays in touch with you after your purchase, keeps you updated on his or her career developments and so on. At the other end of the continuum is the artist who offers you as little as possible, based on your budget, and can only be bothered with you for as long as it takes to sell you art.

If you're like most people, you'd rather do business with the first artist than the second. Not only do you end up with more art for your money when you buy from these types of artists, but a higher percentage of them generally succeed in their careers than do more self-centred artists. Artists who tend to be positive, selfless, generous, flexible, interested in enriching people's lives with their art and not obsessed with making money or getting ahead attract the attention of the art community. Artists who are difficult to deal with, on the other hand, often impede their own progress.

Below are the types of responses that you should look for when speaking with artists:

'For me, an important part of making art is sharing it with others.'

'The more collectors who own my art, the better.'

'I enjoy meeting everyone who likes my work, whether they buy it or not.'

'I have art in all price ranges.'

'Show me the pieces you like the most or tell me more about what you're looking for, and I'll find others you might also like.'

'I love to talk about art and show people what I do and how I do it.'

'If you can't afford that piece, then let me show you some less expensive ones.'

'If you have any questions about what I do or what particular pieces of art mean, I'll be happy to answer them.'

ARTISTS YOU SHOULD AVOID

Some mention has already been made of qualities in artists that make for poor relationships and ill-advised buys. Most are centred on money and ego issues but, to be more specific, avoiding artists who exhibit the characteristics listed below will help keep you out of trouble.

- The artist refuses to be flexible in selling prices.
- The artist talks down to you or makes you feel inferior.
- The artist is only willing to meet with you if he's relatively sure you're going to buy art.
- Money is a central aspect of everything the artist says and does.
- The artist wants to charge you gallery-type prices for her art even though she's just starting out in her career and has no gallery representation.
- You feel pressured to buy something.
- The artist thinks he should be better known than he is.
- The artist compares her work to that of expensive, well-established artists, claims that it's just as good, and bases her asking prices on what those artists charge.
- The artist has bitter or hostile feelings about the way the art world works or the way his career has progressed.
- The artist is critical of fellow artists.
- The artist flat-out refuses to consider making a smaller, less detailed or less expensive version of a piece you really like but can't afford.
- The artist has a take-it-or-leave-it attitude about your interest in any particular piece of his art.

- The artist is willing to sell you something for what you want to pay, but complains or is unhappy about it.
- The artist only offers you the most insignificant pieces in his studio and stresses how little he has to give for what you want to pay.

GETTING DOWN TO BUSINESS

Suppose you get along and communicate well with an artist, you've chosen a piece of art to buy and you're ready to write out the cheque or pay online. Before you proceed, you should make sure you're paying a fair price for a good-quality piece of art. You'll learn how to research and evaluate art, artists and art prices in Part III but, for our purposes here, you want to make sure you have the necessary information, knowledge or experience to research and evaluate the art effectively.

An important part of purchase-oriented interactions is to review the artist's résumé or, better yet, keep a copy in your files. An appropriate résumé should include information about the artist's participation in group and solo shows, reviews or articles, awards or distinctions, grants received, organisational memberships, names of individual collectors and institutions that own the artist's art, and other art-related accomplishments. Education is also nice to see, but keep in mind that many talented artists are self-taught. Make sure the résumé lists names, dates and locations. Also ask to see any articles, publications, blogs or websites that include the artist. An artist's statements regarding her personal philosophies about how and why she creates art and about what she expects to accomplish through her art are always good to know, but when buying time comes around, you want facts.

Using appropriate tact, politely ask the artist to talk about her price structure, how she sets her prices, why particular pieces of art are priced at the levels they are, what types of art are the most popular with collectors and so on. You're looking for indications that the artist regularly sells art comparable to the piece or pieces you're interested in buying for amounts comparable to what you're being asked to pay. You should also look for signs that the artist regularly produces and sells a variety of works of art or, in other words, that she's serious about being an artist.

If you really want to own a specific piece, but would like to pay a little less than the asking price, observe the following guidelines to assure an optimal outcome (read more about negotiating for art in Chapter 22):

- *When you the like the art, say so.* Artists take extremely well to compliments. You may think artists will hold firm in their prices if you show your enthusiasm, but the opposite is much more often the case. They'll be more flexible because they'll want you to own their art.
- *Be truthful about your financial situation.* Artists will work with you. There is nothing they want more than to sell their art to people who really enjoy it.
- *If you can't afford to pay all at once, ask whether you can pay over time.* Most artists are amenable to these sorts of arrangements.
- *Never disparage a work of art to get the price down.*
- *Never criticise an artist's pricing policy or compare it in negative terms to how other artists price their art.*
- *Don't insult with an offer that's far below the asking price.*

BARTER

Barter is one of the better-kept secrets about buying from artists. Art insiders are aware of it, but relatively few novice buyers or people who buy exclusively at galleries are aware of the barter option. Simply put, galleries rarely accept barter for art; artists, on the other hand, are more inclined to do so, especially if they need what you're offering.

Artists love to barter. They barter art among each other and with their friends all the time. Virtually all artists will accept goods or services from anyone in exchange for their art. Barter is a great way to own art that you don't have the money to pay for, assuming you have something worthwhile to offer in return.

While speaking or communicating with artists whose art you like, politely bring up the subject of barter if you think you have access to things they might need. If the artist says no, drop the subject immediately. But if they say they'll consider it, find out what sorts of things they want and tell them about the types of goods or services to which you have special access. The wider the range of options you can offer, the more likely the chances that barter will play a part in your transactions.

When barter appears to be a possibility, don't insist on all-barter, no-cash arrangements unless the artist is really enthusiastic about making a complete trade with no cash. The likelihood of an artist accepting barter increases exponentially when you pay a portion of the purchase price in cash. This way, the artist gets the best of both worlds.

Regardless of how you complete your final transaction, always get a written statement from the artist describing the piece you've bought. Also make sure you get a receipt that describes the art, a copy of the artist's résumé and copies of any additional relevant materials such as reviews, interviews or articles that talk about the artist and his work. You'll learn more about how to document your purchases in Chapter 23.

Example

I once attended an art show where the great majority of the artists were established in their careers. Average painting prices ranged from $5,000 to $20,000 – more than I was willing to spend. I really liked the art, though, and looked closely at every piece. After a while, I came across a very competent and appealing watercolour. I looked at the price and had to do a double take – instead of the $6,000 to $8,000 I thought it would cost, it was priced at only $800!

When I asked about the piece, I found out it was not painted by one of the artists in the show, but rather by the son of one of the artists. He was only eighteen years old, yet his work was comparable in quality to the other art on display. The price was based more on the artist's age and inexperience than it was on the quality of the art – a reasoning that made good sense but, in my opinion, was taken to the extreme in the case of this watercolour. I bought the picture without hesitation and learned, in the process, that you never know what you'll find at a group art show, no matter how good the artists are or how expensive the majority of the art is.

A LOOK AHEAD

We've talked briefly about buying art directly from artists online, but galleries and specialised art websites can also be great places to shop. There are literally thousands of websites selling art, and if you don't know how to get around online or have been buying mainly at physical locations like art galleries or in person from artists, searching for and locating the art you want can be confusing at best and nearly impossible at worst. In this next chapter, we'll cover the basics of how online art buying works.

CHAPTER 11

BUYING FROM ONLINE GALLERIES AND WEBSITES

Buying art over the internet is unquestionably the wave of the future. When you think about how much art you can see online in one day on your computer compared to what you can see by physically going from gallery to gallery in your area, you begin to see why buying art online is increasing at such a rapid rate. A day of gallery-hopping in most American cities won't show you much more than several hundred works of art by a handful of artists while, on the internet, you can see thousands of pieces in all price ranges and in all mediums by hundreds of artists from all corners of the globe with the click of a mouse.

The most basic level of internet art shopping is visiting the websites of galleries in your own hometown or area (practically all established galleries and the very large majority of minor ones now have websites). You can find out what artists they sell or represent, look at selections of their art, get an overall feel for what individual galleries are like, learn about upcoming shows and find out which galleries sell the types of art you buy – all from your computer screen. When you find a gallery's selection appealing, you either go and visit them in person or begin a conversation online.

Perhaps one of the greatest advantages of the online art market is that buyers now have access to all kinds of art from all kinds of galleries in all kinds of places. For the first time ever, even small local or regional galleries or websites can expose their art to people from around the world with minimal effort, at modest out-of-pocket expense, regardless of what their art-world profiles are or what level of success they've attained. What this means is that more galleries and specialised websites than ever before have better chances of selling their art. If their artists have talent, the art is good and the galleries or websites know how to get the word out in social networks and in other ways, the public will decide whether their art has merit and is worth collecting. In much the same way, musicians have learned to use the internet to bypass major music companies and get their music into the public domain so the listeners can decide first-hand whether they like it.

Not all is peaches and cream in online artland, however. Perhaps one of the more confusing aspects of shopping for art over the internet is figuring out what a piece of art on your computer screen actually looks like in person (especially if you haven't seen a lot of art face-to-face or been buying for very long). Another problem is figuring out how to navigate the huge number of commercial and gallery websites offering art for sale and locating those that have the best art at the most reasonable prices in terms of your needs. Once you get a feel for how to shop for art online, though, and you locate those art sites that interest you the most, progressing to the point of purchase is relatively easy.

FIRST STEPS IN LOCATING ART ONLINE

A good way to begin your online art-buying adventures is to make a list of larger, better-known multi-gallery or multi-artist commercial art websites such as those listed in Appendix II. You can get additional names from advertisements and online newsletters from art periodicals such as those listed in Appendix III. All major arts publications not only have ads for websites that sell art, but they also review gallery shows regularly and publish current art news. Institutional or arts organisation websites, attending local art shows, fairs or events and word-of-mouth around your local art community are other good ways to find out the names of better art websites.

Searching for general types of art on major search engines like Google is not a great idea at first unless you know specific descriptive keyword terms or names of artists or galleries you're looking for, the types of art you want to buy and other relevant details. Just about any art search, using general art keywords like landscape painting or limited edition print or bronze sculpture, but without artist names, will net you at least thousands (and sometimes hundreds of thousands) of matching web pages that are often displayed in no particular order other than by popularity. And the popularity of an art website may or may not have any relation to the quality or significance of the art they're representing or selling. If you're not sure what you're looking for or don't know how to parse search results, trying to find general types of art online through major search engines can be frustrating at best and pointless at worst.

THE DIFFERENT TYPES OF ART WEBSITES

The basic types of commercial websites that sell art at fixed prices are vetted or curated multi-gallery sites, non-vetted or non-curated multi-gallery sites, non-profit or community art sites, art websites that are more informational in nature, vetted or curated multi-artist sites, and non-vetted or non-curated multi-artist sites. (Online auction websites are discussed separately in Chapter 25.) Non-profit or community art sites show artwork, often provide resources for artists and collectors in the area, and can have information for anywhere from a few to several thousand artists. Larger all-purpose art websites are just that – places offering a wide variety of goods or services including art, hosted gallery pages, articles, advertisements, consulting, price data and more. An individual art site, of course, is a website dedicated entirely to a single gallery or the work of one artist.

Curated or vetted websites sell art only by artists, dealers and galleries who have applied and been accepted for inclusion on those sites and have had their art and their career credentials reviewed and approved by art professionals or jurors working on behalf of those websites. Jurors are usually composed of respected members of the art community. Most juried sites provide the names and qualifications of all of their jurors. When shopping for art on a juried website, make sure you know who the jurors are, what their qualifications are and how or why they've been selected to evaluate and accept the art or galleries you're looking at.

Art you see for sale on curated or vetted gallery sites is usually by artists who are either emerging (beginning to get recognised) or established (already recognised) and have documented track records of showing and selling art. Some artists may be just starting out and have minimal exhibition records or gallery representations to speak of, but are considered promising or up-and-coming for one reason or another. Curated sites, therefore, are good places to shop for art by artists who either have potential for recognition, are in the process of becoming recognised or are already recognised by certain segments of the art community.

Non-vetted or non-curated commercial websites sell art by any gallery or artist who joins, pays the required fees, signs the necessary agreements and abides by the rules of the site. Non-juried art websites are an integral part of the online art community because they essentially give you the rest of the picture, list galleries or artists regardless of experience or accomplishments, and let you be the judge. Since all art, galleries and artists are allowed on a non-vetted site, the overall quality of the art can at times be choppy or uneven, and the credentials of the artists or galleries can at times be minimal. Though you have to be somewhat more cautious in terms of getting the facts and figuring out who you're doing business with, non-vetted commercial art websites are interesting places to shop for art by all kinds of artists at all stages of their careers, including those who are just starting out, less well known, undiscovered, experimental, unusual, out-of-the-mainstream or may otherwise operate outside the constraints of the established art community.

Non-profit or community art websites often serve both as resources for local or regional artist communities and also as places where artists can show their art or add their names to local or regional artist directories or databases. For artists, non-profit art websites provide information like tips and seminars on how they can market their art, articles about different types of art or art techniques, calendars of local or regional art shows, information about upcoming shows and competitions where they can enter their work, discussion forums about art issues, and classified advertisements about art classes, art supplies, studio space for sale or rent and so on. For art buyers, non-profit art websites are similar to non-juried commercial art websites in that artists, without qualification, can either show selections of their art or a handful of examples along with necessary contact information for interested collectors. As with non-juried commercial art sites, the art on display at non-profit sites can, at times, be uneven in quality and the credentials of the artists who show or list there can at times be minimal.

All-purpose commercial art websites are large databases of art-related information. These sites are similar to traditional art magazines in that they provide news and articles about the art world along with paid advertisements placed by artists, art dealers and galleries. Some also host gallery pages that may or may not be vetted. Galleries or individual artists can place ads directing viewers to websites where they can learn more or shop for art. All-purpose art websites may or may not get directly involved in the actual buying and selling of art.

The most extensive all-purpose art websites offer services like daily news and articles, event notices, researchable artist or price databases, directories of art institutions, upcoming art auction listings, auction-tracking services, on-site art auctions, worldwide calendars of art exhibitions or events, art consulting and more. Some of these services are free while others are fee-based. All-purpose art websites fall somewhere in between vetted and non-vetted or non-curated sites in that the ones with higher fees and advertising rates tend to attract only galleries and artists who can afford it, whereas those charging more reasonable rates tend to attract a wider assortment of advertisers.

Individual artist websites are the true free-for-all of the online art world and have been mentioned somewhat in the previous chapter. Countless artists from every corner of the globe and of every level of artistic accomplishment, from the most famous to the most strange to the totally unknown, display their art and offer it for sale in an astonishing variety of formats. Shopping online at individual artist websites or via social networks is not for the faint of heart and is recommended only for experienced online art buyers or collectors who are already familiar with the artists they're interested in, know how to navigate their websites, and know what they're looking at and how to proceed from there.

ART ON SOCIAL NETWORKS

Social networks are more personal, immediate and interactive than the types of art websites discussed above, and are playing a more and more significant role in the art-buying experience. They offer numerous additional options for buyers, not only for searching, locating and following relevant resources including galleries, organisations, institutions and individual artists, but also for joining groups, getting active and communicating with any individuals or establishments whose offerings interest you.

What's also great about social networks is that by joining or following your favourite artists or businesses, you are able to stay up to date on the latest events, openings, offerings, sales, art topics or discussions, and more. Over time, you can get a good solid sense of who you're dealing with, what they're like and how they relate to their fans, in addition to watching their art and careers evolve. In general, social networks are good for getting a more complete picture of artists or galleries you locate on larger art websites or elsewhere on the internet. You can join or follow their pages, see who follows them, watch how they interact with people and, in general, get a more up-close and personal sense of what they're like and what it might be like to do business with them. Perhaps best of all, especially for those of you who may feel uncomfortable in galleries or around artists, you can learn plenty without ever having to set foot in their establishments or meet anyone in person, and make contact only when you feel confident and ready.

Last but not least, you can locate and buy all kinds of art on social networks. If you're dedicated and serious enough, you can even buy or get offered newly completed or newly arrived art ahead of everyone else. Some artists have 'storefronts' where you can pay for your art; others accept various forms of credit, while some prefer to do business the old-fashioned way with cash or cheques. Of course, you have to communicate with sellers first to make sure you understand your options in terms of purchase, but once you're both clear, go ahead and complete the transaction.

ONLINE ART SHOPPING BASICS

Art websites and social networks are open twenty-four hours a day, seven days a week. You can spend as much time as you like, browse at your own pace, see art to your heart's content and never feel obligated to make a single purchase. You won't ever get on anyone's nerves or take up too much of anyone's time no matter how long you hang out on their websites or pages.

When you first visit a website or social networking page, get a feel for what types of art they have to offer and focus on facts rather than fluff. Whether you're reading the 'About' pages, customer-service policies, descriptions or blog updates, pay particular attention to the facts – verifiable claims or statements you can corroborate. Also pay attention to any comments, references or testimonials from followers, fans or buyers. Entertaining or beautifully written descriptions of art may be fun to read, but what you really want is proof you've come to a place where you can buy good-quality examples by artists with résumés, experience or accomplishments you can verify.

As mentioned above, good places for novices to begin online art adventures are at larger commercial curated or vetted websites. Not only can they show thousands of works of art by hundreds of dealers, galleries and artists, but compared to smaller sites, they offer a wider range of services and information, are usually better organised and easier to navigate, have standard operating policies, provide direct links to their members, sometimes offer payment options, may provide limited guarantees, and are the closest thing to established traditional galleries that the online art world has to offer.

The homepages or main menus of art websites, particularly larger ones, are usually pretty busy places. Like tables of contents in books or magazines, they provide menus or navigation options of what you can see on the sites. For example, you'll find links to galleries, artists, news, terms of agreement or policies, products or databases, museum or institutional shows, events, auctions or sales and more. A good place to start is on the 'About' page. There you can get the basic lie of the land, an introduction to how the site is structured, what the websites purposes are, what types of art or artists they focus on, and so on. The overall goal of an 'About' page is to give visitors a basic understanding of the site, and make them feel less intimidated and more comfortable while navigating around.

Head back to the homepage or main menu when you're ready to get going. Most sites get you started by inviting you to look at particular types of art, spotlighting certain artists or galleries, and pointing you towards news, articles or information buyers might be interested in. Most also provide search options of varying capabilities that allow you to locate art according to your own preferences or specifications using keywords like medium, price, size, colour, subject matter, style, artist's or gallery's name and other characteristics. A few sites offer more sophisticated features like those where you can click directly from specific pieces of art you like to selections of similar art by other artists or at other galleries. These types of features can really streamline your viewing since you would have likely had difficulty locating comparable items on your own. They're also helpful for novices who need to learn their way around.

Take your time and look at plenty of art. Don't try to see too much too fast, and don't be in a huge rush to buy. Looking at art online can be overwhelming at first. You'll find so much that you can easily overdose or get confused, so when you start getting tired, turn off the computer or phone and come back later when you're refreshed and ready to go. Remember to bookmark relevant pages so you can pick up where you left off.

BUYING ART ONLINE

When you see a piece of art you like, you can often enlarge and inspect it in more detail. Some listings include additional detail shots or close-ups. Look at all of these; good close-ups can show details that would be difficult to see even when viewing the art in person. When you see a piece of art you really like, note who the artist or gallery is and save the page so you can return to it later. When you see a piece of art you really, really like, most larger sites allow you to click directly from the art to pages where you can learn more or make contact with the seller. When you see a piece of art you really, really, really like – so much that you think you might want to buy it – evaluate it according to the research and pricing chapters in Parts III and IV of this book.

Assuming the art satisfies all your requirements and you continue to be enthralled, you now confront the great disadvantage of buying art online – so far, you've only been able to see it on your computer screen and have only an approximate idea what it looks like in person. The people who run the websites, or the galleries or artists selling it, are, of course, well aware of this situation and are prepared to work with you in a variety of ways so you can see the art in person with the greatest possible ease. The time has come to review all shipping, money-back guarantee, insurance, payment and return policies. The more information sellers provide, which should include what's listed below, the better you can feel about doing business.

- *Easily verifiable seller credentials.* Make sure you can verify a seller's or website's credentials. You want to be sure you're buying from a reputable source who provides ample contact information, a documented art-business track record and references to prove it. (If you're buying from a traditional gallery or an artist advertising on a website, follow procedures laid out in Chapter 10 and in Part IV.)
- *Good customer support.* The site, gallery or artist should provide phone numbers so you can call, speak to someone in person and ask whatever questions you have, both *before and after* buying the art.
- *Time to live with the art before you decide whether or not to keep it.* Sellers should offer approval periods lasting anywhere from one to three weeks. The minimum acceptable approval period should be one week, and you should

be able to return it for any reason, assuming it's still in its original condition.

- *Payment options.* The seller should accept major credit cards or have mechanisms in place for secure online buying. Many sites also allow buyers to call in with credit card information.

- A *full money-back guarantee (less shipping) if, for whatever reason, you return the art in the condition in which you received it, before the approval period expires.*

- *Ease of shipping.* Sellers should make shipping and returning art as easy and professional as possible. For example, some sites pack their art in special easy-open, easy-close crates and make returning art no more complicated than filling out brief return forms and calling shipping services to pick up the art at your home or place of business.

- *Cost of shipping.* Shipping art, especially larger pieces, can be expensive, so make sure you really like a piece of art and are pretty sure you're going to keep it *before* you have it shipped. Find out what your shipping costs will be and who pays how much.

Additional points to keep in mind when buying art online:

- *Look over a website's membership policies.* Many sites allow you to register and become a member. Depending on the site, membership benefits may include personal art consultation, email announcements or newsletters, special art previews, early buying opportunities, 0 per cent financing, ways to group and view your selections online, and so on.

- *When you see art you like and it's described in art terminology you're not that familiar with, remember those terms and use them in subsequent searches.* Sometimes finding art online that's right for you is merely a matter of learning which keywords or terms to type into search engines.

- *Some art sites allow you to make offers on art you're interested in.* Whether or not a site states that their asking prices are flexible, making an offer never hurts as long as you follow the guidelines laid out in Chapter 22.

- *Some sites let collectors make requests for specific works of art or post wants for the types of art they collect.* Requests may be emailed to the site's artists and dealers either to see whether they have matching pieces at their studios or galleries, or to find out whether certain artists are willing to meet the requirements of those requests and create the art as commissions. When you know what you're looking for, consider emailing websites and allowing them to search for you. As previously mentioned, if you commission an artist to make art for your collection, you're pretty much obligated not only to keep the finished piece, but also to allow the artist to complete it with minimal interference on your part. Best procedure is to gain some experience collecting before you consider commissioning artists.

- *Focus mainly on websites, galleries, dealers or artists who list selling prices of all of the art they have for sale.* Responding to sellers who mark their art with directives like 'please enquire' or 'price on request' instead of with set amounts is a no-win situation for you as a collector. When you enquire about art that is not labelled with a price, you tip off the sellers to the fact that you like that art and the sellers, in turn, often take those opportunities to start high in order to see how much they can make you pay. They have all of the advantages in any negotiations; you have none.

- *Sometimes when looking at an artist's art, you see that much of it is marked sold.* Usually the artist is trying to create the impression that his or her art is really in demand. Experienced collectors are rarely fooled by this tactic. In fact, artists who show large percentages of sold works actually reduce their chances of making sales because when people see that most of the art is already sold, they get the feeling that the good art is gone and all that's left are the crumbs.

- *When you're on a website that offers both auctions and fixed-price art, confine your shopping to art that is priced and avoid the auctions until you become more experienced as a collector.* Read more about buying art at traditional auctions in Chapter 24 and at online auctions in Chapter 25.

THE FUTURE OF BUYING ART ONLINE

More and more people are getting comfortable with the idea of viewing and buying art online, and more and more art is being sold online. Increasing numbers of artists and galleries know they can reach far more people over the internet than they can by showing in more traditional settings. Expect to see substantial increases in online art sales in the years to come.

The larger commercial art sites have already attracted so many artists, galleries and works of art that they've become somewhat difficult to navigate. At the same time, programmers and website designers are hard at work to make buying art online increasingly more efficient and satisfying. Add social networks to the mix and online art buyers are able to pinpoint the art they like faster, with greater ease and with less wandering than ever before. Expect significant advances and improved online art buying over time.

Art sites are constantly experimenting with better ways to display colours, details and even textures of art, and are striving for a level of accuracy that approximates seeing the art in person, from a distance as well as at close range. Some websites are now presenting their art in ways that simulate actual art gallery experiences, like virtual reality walk-throughs, or being able to seamlessly move around works of art and view them from different perspectives. Expect to see innovations for presenting art in greater detail and at higher resolutions as high-speed connections become more commonplace.

Regarding financial issues, online art buyers used to be pretty conservative, not willing to buy art priced more than $2,000. Today, art is offered and bought at pretty much all price levels. People now trust the online buying experience and feel more comfortable buying art in all price ranges. Added to that is the pure convenience of not having to physically travel to galleries or artist studios and deal with all the hassle. Click and ship has become the order of the day.

Example

The evolution of the internet has changed art-buying patterns in many ways. Experienced collectors now comparison-shop online. In the good old days, they shopped mainly in person and relied on a handful of dealers or other resources to supply them with much of the art for their collections. Today, they have access to a far wider range of sellers and selections and, as a result, can buy better-quality pieces for their collections, sometimes at more reasonable prices than they might have paid before. Middlemen and the subsequent mark-ups they charge have been eliminated in many cases as well because collectors can locate primary sellers directly.

Decorators and interior designers can shop online for their clients. In the old days, they would have to visit many resources personally, sometimes with clients in tow. Much of that travel is now done online. Decorators can either locate and select the art themselves or have larger art websites select it for them.

People who have moved away from their birthplaces but still feel connected to their roots use the internet to 'return home' and shop for art that reminds them of where they grew up. Once again, buying online saves travel time and money.

One collector I know collects European prints from the 1940s to the 1960s, particularly by French and Italian artists. Unfortunately, these types of prints have never been very common on the West Coast of the United States where this collector lives, so he couldn't really buy much from local dealers. He had to travel instead or buy from specialised dealer catalogues. He now buys directly from European dealers, saving time as well as money.

A LOOK AHEAD

You now have a basic knowledge of how the art business works. You know about art dealers, art galleries, artists, online art resources and what your responsibilities are in dealer–collector and artist–collector relationships. In order to further guarantee positive results in the marketplace, though, you need some additional instruction in how *not* to select and buy art – that is, how to avoid common pitfalls to which all too many beginner buyers fall victim. Chapter 12 summarises basic art-buying mistakes and explains how to avoid making them.

CHAPTER 12

HOW NOT TO BUY ART

This chapter is about 'don'ts'. Just as you follow certain rules and procedures when buying art, you need to follow other rules and procedures unless you want to end up regretting the day you ever decided to start. Some of the don'ts you are about to read might sound almost too obvious to mention and others are being repeated just to make sure you remember them. Unfortunately, beginner buyers ignore these guidelines all the time and end up buying art they never should have considered in the first place.

The don'ts list is all about how not to buy art. These don'ts are in no particular order. One is just as important as the next. They involve situations you could easily find yourself in as you wend your way through the art world. Keep them in mind wherever you are, and you'll significantly increase your chances of acquiring good-quality art for reasonable prices; ignore them, and there's no telling what you'll end up with.

For starters, don't buy art without thinking the instant you decide you like it. Ask questions and get the facts about whatever catches your eye before you buy. True, buying art should be fun, spontaneous, passionate and so on, but that doesn't mean you forget about asking questions, throw reason to the wind, abandon yourself to whimsy or impulse and hope for the best.

Don't confuse art with the environment in which you see it. The circumstances, surroundings and happenings at a gallery are entirely separate from the art the gallery is selling. Likewise, no matter how slick and polished a gallery or artist website, focus on the art and nothing else. When you buy art, all you get is art; none of that glitz, glamour, brie, champagne, king prawns, sexy sales personnel, web design or appearance or any other fun stuff leaves with you once you make your purchase.

Don't buy art under the influence of drugs or alcohol. Alter your consciousness and you impair your ability to judge the art that's right for you, both in terms of its appearance and the information you are given about it. Ask dealers and collectors about buys they have made under the influence and those who are willing to talk will tell you some real horror stories. Few have more than one incident to relate, however, because once they buy in a condition other than sober and realise what they've done the next day, they never buy that way again. Say no to drugs and alcohol and yes to buying art intelligently.

Don't buy art at night. At night, you tend to be less focused on rational, practical issues and more on entertaining yourself and having a good time. The chances of your buying art impulsively are greater at night than they are during the day. If you see an art piece you like while browsing through a gallery after normal business hours, put it on hold and return the next day to look at it again and research it properly.

Don't buy art while you're on vacation unless you investigate it as thoroughly as you do the art you buy when you're at home. People on vacation are more carefree and unconcerned about how they spend their money than when they're at home. They tend to relax the rules a bit. This is one reason why you see so many art galleries at popular tourist destinations. And guess what? Many of them stay open at night!

Another mistake art buyers make on trips away from home is buying art not necessarily because it's good, but rather to remind themselves of what wonderful times they had while they were away. Once again, remember that when you buy art, all you get is the art, not the destination or setting you bought it in. You have to live with it long after the memories of that fantastic vacation fade.

Don't buy art simply because you're charmed, delighted and entertained by the seller. When you buy art, you do not buy the personality of the gallery owner, the artist or anyone else. Long after the seller is gone or that great time the two of you had together is forgotten, the art must continue to stand on its own as a quality example that's worth what you paid for it. If you're having trouble figuring out whether it's the art or the seller that is fascinating you more, take the art home on approval for anywhere from a few days to a week and study it in peace.

Don't buy art from sellers passing through town, at special clearance sales, at one-shot auctions, websites you've never heard of, online sellers you cannot research or identify, or through any other unverifiable or transient resources or outlets. No matter how attractive or reasonably priced the art for sale at these sites, places or events may sound, confine your buying to respected dealers, galleries or websites that have been in business for years and are known throughout the art community. Established dealers may not sell year-end, clearance, get-it-while-you-can, bargain art, but they do offer stability and amenities that transient or unverifiable sellers lack. Quality art does not change hands like leftover blouses on a sale rack.

Be extremely cautious about buying art on cruise ships unless you are an experienced buyer, know exactly what you're looking at, and have the means onboard or the online access necessary to corroborate all information sellers provide. Otherwise, wait until you're back on land and at home to research art that interests you. In order to convince you to buy onboard, sellers may tell you that art is a bargain or cheaper at sea than it is on land, but regardless of what they say, compare prices at other venues or websites first. You may save taxes or duties, in which case have the seller tell you exactly how much those are above the base price of the art. However, art prices themselves do not fluctuate depending on whether the art is on land or sea. They do not drop in value the moment the art leaves port and then increase in value the moment it arrives back on land.

If you're new to art buying, regardless of how much of a bargain, how important the artist, how rare the art or how great the investment you think you're getting, wait until you're back home on land to confirm all such claims (and get those claims in writing before you disembark). Most importantly, do not allow yourself to be pressured (which includes not pressuring yourself). Verify statements or claims sellers make; THEN buy the art – not before. When you're just starting out, the best procedure is to shop for art on land where you can compare prices and research the market, not at sea where you're presented with only one option or have limited resources available to corroborate what sellers are telling you.

Don't buy art at one-time estate auctions or similar types of sales unless you have complete information and documentation about whose property is being auctioned or sold, the circumstances that led up to the dispersal, and complete verifiable contact information for the auctioneers or sellers including street addresses (not post-office boxes), phone numbers, auction licenses and permits to sell (all of which should be verified before you bid). Unfortunately, some companies that conduct these sales simply rent houses or halls, pack them with new merchandise, present them as antiques or collectibles or as bargains, and sell them to unsuspecting buyers. Often these sales are easy to spot because they contain significantly more furniture and decorations than you would expect to find at a typical house or estate sale (ten dressers, for example).

Don't buy art because it sounds like a great bargain that's almost too good to be true. First of all, this type of art usually is too good to be true. Second, the fact that a work of art is presented to you as a 'super deal' is not adequate justification for purchasing it. Look closer and chances are it's not such a great deal after all. Sellers who offer incredible bargains usually provide somewhat suspect explanations about why their prices are so cheap. Watch out whenever you hear excuses like, 'I need money fast to finance a new art buy,' or 'I have major expenses coming up and have to raise money,' or 'I could sell this for a lot more if only I had the time.'

Don't buy art based on claims from sellers without first verifying those claims. Sellers are obliged to substantiate whatever they tell you about the art they sell. In addition, any representations or claims must be verifiable outside the confines of the circumstance where the art is being sold. If an artist is supposed to be world famous, for example, get specific information (names, dates, places, awards, distinctions, etc.) from the seller to support that claim.

Don't buy art based solely on appraisals or certificates of authenticity unless you know how to read, interpret and understand the information they contain. Chapter 15, 'Certificates of Authenticity and Appraisals', explains the basics in this regard.

Don't buy art through emails from complete strangers. This sounds unbelievable, but it actually happens. In spite of the fact that art is a visual commodity, a significant number of sellers email randomly about art they have for sale and people end up buying it. To begin with, the whole idea of buying an art piece based on the way a seller makes it sound during an email correspondence and from emailed images is absurd. What's more, you have no idea who these sellers are, how reputable they are, what their galleries look like (assuming they even exist), how you would get your money back if you were not completely satisfied (even when they promise full immediate refunds) and so on.

Don't buy art by name only. You buy art because you like it, not because you hear that the artist is hot, that she's popular among investment bankers, that she's about to be featured in a national magazine and so on. The first thing you look at is the art. The last thing you look at is the name of the artist.

Don't buy art based solely on the fact that it's in a beautiful frame, on an expensive pedestal or lavishly lit and displayed. Putting bad art in great frames or on expensive pedestals, or presenting it in other sumptuous surroundings, is a trick some sellers use to fool unsuspecting buyers. Evaluate the art separately from the drama of the presentation.

Don't buy art because you are impressed by the place or website that's selling it. The furnishings, decorations and interior design of a gallery or other venue have no relation to the quality of the art they are selling. Some of the best art dealers operate out of the most modest surroundings or from the most basic websites, and some of the most unscrupulous dealers have beautifully appointed galleries and expensive-looking websites.

Don't buy art when sellers change the price drastically with little or no provocation. Some galleries or websites sell art by radically dropping prices right before your eyes. They appeal to the greed instinct. This procedure is designed to make you think you are getting a great bargain when in reality you often end up with inferior works at inflated prices.

For example, suppose a painting starts out at $10,000 and, within thirty minutes, the price has dropped to $6,500 because, according to the seller, you qualify for various special privileges. You mention that you're a collector, so the seller gives you a collector's discount; you mention that your aunt once worked in a frame shop, so he gives you a dealer discount; you tell him you work with computers, so he gives you the special high-tech Silicon Valley discount; and so on. The focus is off the art and on the plummeting price. Dealers who sell quality art rarely slash prices in this manner.

A corollary to this is don't buy art at an auction where the prices start high and go down. THIS IS NOT AN AUCTION, but rather a sales technique designed to make you think you're getting a bargain. Essentially, the 'auctioneer' is setting the selling prices rather than the bidders (exactly the opposite of what an auction should be). Established auction houses that conduct regular sales start the bidding low and allow bidders to set the final prices by bidding against each other until only the highest bidder is left. None start prices high and go down.

Don't buy art by famous, well-known or collectible artists at online auctions from sellers you don't know unless you're an experienced buyer and know exactly what you're looking at and how to research it. Unfortunately, online auctions are a risky place for novices to buy any kind of art. The exceptions here are if you are buying from reputable, established, bricks-and-mortar auction houses that also sell online, or if you're buying brand-new art directly from artists who are auctioning their own art (self-representing artists are safe to buy from in the overwhelming majority of cases).

Don't buy art for monetary reasons alone. Serious collectors buy art because they love art, not because they think they will be able to cash it in for profit at some later date. True, some art increases in value over time, but this is never adequate justification for deciding to buy or collect fine art. Remember that art increases in value a lot less often than most people think.

Don't buy art under pressure. You should not select art for your collection based on the presence of a salesperson standing over your shoulder bombarding you with reasons why you should own it. When you begin to feel pressure to buy art, leave the gallery or end the online correspondence.

Don't buy any particular art because all your friends happen to own one by that artist. Everyone has his or her own individual tastes and preferences in art. You buy what you like, and your friends buy what they like. When you buy what other people collect or tell you to buy, you deny yourself the joy of exploring, discovering and being true to your own personal tastes.

Don't buy art you see for sale in restaurants, hotels, department stores or in other non-gallery environments unless those venues have reputations for regularly showing and selling art (which many do these days). When you're just starting out, it's best to confine your buying to full-time art dealers or websites whose only business is buying and selling art. Just as you do not rely on art dealers for overnight accommodation, meals or clothing and appliances, do not rely on hotels, restaurants and department stores for art. Consider buying art at non-art venues only if art is a regular part of their business, and only after you've had plenty of experience collecting and know exactly what you're looking for.

Don't buy art based on predictions. Beware when sellers begin talking about what's supposed to happen with art or artists at some point in the future. Base your purchase on past performance, not on conjecture about what may or may not happen in the future. Predictions about how famous an artist will become or how much the art will appreciate in value are almost always designed as appeals to the greed instinct and nothing more. No one can predict what art prices may or may not do in years to come. The only prediction you can make for sure is that if you love it now, you will likely continue to love it for a long time to come.

Don't buy art based only on a spontaneous or immediate emotional response. The initial emotional reaction you have to any art piece is little more than a rough indication of attraction. Temper the emotion with reason, spend some serious time looking at it, and evaluate how you feel about the way it looks and how it impacts on you before you buy. The more time you spend with it, the better the decision you'll be able to make.

Don't buy art unless you're absolutely sure you want to own it. If you have even the slightest doubts, do not buy. You want the love affair you have with your art to last. You don't want that art to end up in your attic several months after you buy it.

Example 1

I know of a case in which an art dealer and an artist, both fascinating and entertaining personalities, combined forces and sold plenty of art. They received a great deal of media attention and appeared at all the right functions. They were extremely popular on the local social circuit and much in demand. People loved to be around them and showed their appreciation by buying the artist's art. Together, this dealer and artist sold hundreds of paintings at prices that at times ranged into the tens of thousands of dollars.

With the passage of time, the artist retired, the art dealer closed up his gallery and both gradually faded from public view. The market for the paintings, which were never that good in the first place, faded right along with the dealer and the artist. Collectors who once paid hefty prices for their art years ago are now lucky if they can sell it for a fraction of those prices.

The moral of the story? Make sure the art is at least as good as the personalities representing or selling it. If it's not, as soon as the personalities are no longer available to regale the public while it is being sold, the market will likely evaporate. Ultimately all art has to stand on its own without any cheerleaders to hype it. Remember, when you buy art, all you get is art.

Example 2

I know an art dealer who tells the story of how he once bought art under the influence of a few drinks – once and only once. This happened while he was attending the opening-night benefit of a regional art fair. While there, he saw a reasonably priced painting of a mountain scene in one dealer's booth that he thought looked great. At that moment, he believed he could tell from looking at it that it was good enough to sell at his gallery. He was sure he'd heard of the artist before and felt no need to check any reference books before buying.

Here is what this dealer discovered the next day:

The artist was basically unknown, had no mentions in any of the dealer's reference books and had no online profile that he could find. He had apparently confused the name with that of a different, more collectible artist. Furthermore, when he saw the painting in a sober state, he realised it was nowhere near as good as he thought it was. He was astonished that he thought it had looked as wonderful as it had in the dealer's booth just a few short hours before.

Example 3

The phenomenon of 'the art opening' deserves special mention because you can be misled by what goes on at these events in so many ways. If you become at all involved with art, sooner or later you will be invited to art openings.

In order to prepare for the real thing, let's attend an imaginary art opening now. You find yourself at a beautifully appointed gallery sipping fine wine, nibbling on long-stemmed strawberries, rubbing shoulders with beautiful people, meeting the artist and experiencing the art. You are in the eye of the storm, the centre of the universe for this artist and his art. Everything about the environment is designed with three purposes in mind: to sell you art, sell you art and sell you art. Nowhere on the face of the earth does this artist's art look more appealing than it does in this gallery at this moment. And you are there.

You notice a stack of beautifully printed full-colour exhibition catalogues on the counter. You pick one up and begin reading:

Milton Mindholm's art transforms fact into fiction into fantasy and back into reality. He captures the highest essences of craftsmanship with techniques that unerringly undulate between brilliance and genius. He is unsurpassed in his ability to communicate direct mental images from his mind through his fingertips and outward onto blank canvas at which point his majestic compositions evolve into unmistakable being.

You are impressed. Mindholm's paintings are priced between $5,000 and $25,000. You are impressed again. Several pieces have little red dots next to them. You ask a staff person what the dots mean and she tells you they show the art has been sold. *People are buying*, you think to yourself.

This looks to you like an exhibition of serious art by a serious artist. Apparently, some pieces are selling for substantial amounts of money to serious collectors. From what you can see, money spent on Mindholm's art could well be money intelligently spent.

Now the facts:

- The long-stemmed strawberries and fine wine served at the opening have no relation to the quality of art that is being exhibited.
- The beauty, glamour, wealth and fame of the people attending the opening have no relation to the quality of art that is being exhibited.
- The language used in the exhibition catalogue is only an indication of how good the writer is, not how good the artist is.
- The asking prices may or may not have any relation to the quality of the art.
- Little red dots are supposed to mean that art has sold; however, that's not always the case. Some dealers place red dots on unsold art in order to make people believe that it is selling. In other words, do the same old due diligence you're reading about here, no matter where you see art for sale or under what circumstances it appears to be selling.

A LOOK AHEAD

You now have all the basic tools necessary to successfully navigate your way around the art business, to protect yourself from those who might take advantage, to comparison-shop and, in the end, to select those works of art you find the most appealing. As far as actually buying that art, however, you're only halfway there. You don't really know anything about the art you are considering other than what the sellers have told you about it – and that you like it. Acquiring additional information – learning the methods of art research – is the next major step in the art of buying art and is the subject of the next five chapters.

PART III: RESEARCH

Research is the cornerstone of intelligent art buying. So far, you have made some specific art selections based primarily on how much you like the way they look. If you go ahead and buy without researching them, however, you have no idea what you're buying and you have no idea what you're getting for your money. Sure, sellers tell you plenty about your selections, but research corroborates what you're being told and can reveal additional information that perhaps sellers overlooked or, in worst-case scenarios, deliberately didn't mention. Art research is all about getting the facts you need to know before you buy.

Research is necessary because facts affect value. Not only do you do yourself a huge favour by researching potential purchases and getting the facts first, but you also do the entire art world a favour. The more people who research their art and buy intelligently, the more difficult it becomes for galleries and websites to stay in business by selling inferior art or thrive on uninformed customers who buy impulsively. Informed buyers breed fair dealers who sell quality art at reasonable prices.

'But research sounds like such a complicated process,' you say. You feel intimidated at the prospect of having to research art. You have no idea how to start, where to go or what to do once you get there. 'Research is only for art scholars, and you need a PhD to do it, right?'

Wrong.

Anyone can learn to research any work of art. Not only that, it's easy. You don't have to spend years training under art professors, museum curators or art historians. All the basic techniques you need to know are explained right here in Part III.

Not only is research easy to learn, but it doesn't take much time either. Once you get the hang of it, you can usually locate most of what you need to know about a particular artist or work of art in less than thirty minutes. Sure, more detailed research is necessary on occasion but, more often than not, a few minutes are all it takes.

Research is also rewarding and even fun. Researching a work of art is kind of like being a detective and putting together the clues. The more you know about art, the more you're able to understand and appreciate it and the more enjoyable collecting becomes. The simple truth is that you experience art more fully and completely when you understand the facts and the history behind what you are looking at.

One more thing: by mastering the techniques of art research, you establish your independence as an informed buyer. You eventually acquire the ability to analyse and evaluate every work of art you buy entirely on your own, with minimal help from galleries or other professionals or authorities. You make your own decisions and do what's right for you. You use effective research to master the art of buying art.

CHAPTER 13

RESEARCH THE ARTIST

Behind any work of art is an artist, a human being. The product of that artist's career is art. Because of facts specific to her and her alone, the art that she creates is unique in ways that distinguish it from all other art. By understanding the progression of events in an artist's life and career, you understand her art. Add these facts to your visual appreciation of the art itself and you achieve a much deeper sense of what her art is all about.

On the practical side, facts about any artist, her career and what she has accomplished relate directly to the monetary value of her art, its collectability and its saleability in the marketplace. This type of information helps you decide whether to buy art you like and find visually appealing.

The great majority of information you need to locate and evaluate is as basic as where an artist was born, where she studied art, how old she is, how long she has been an artist, what exhibitions she has participated in, what awards or distinctions she's received and so on. You can learn plenty about an artist and her art from simple biographical data like that.

This procedure is similar to verifying the qualifications of any professionals you are interested in hiring before they perform services or supply products for you. You might also make the analogy to researching a company before buying their stock. You want to make sure you are getting quality services or products from people who know what they're doing. Just as you hire an attorney to handle your legal affairs or hire an accountant to keep your books, when you buy an art piece, you do, in a sense, hire the artist who created that piece. You pay that artist for services rendered – the product of those services being art. And if you're like most people, you want your art to be created by qualified artists with established track records who charge prices commensurate with their abilities and the quality of the products – or art – they produce.

Buying art based on an artist's credentials is not necessarily a fool-proof method of determining whether you are spending your money wisely; but in the great majority of cases, the more extensive and distinguished the artist's career, the more comfortable you can feel about buying that artist's art. Furthermore, accomplishments in art stand for all time and continue to affect marketability long after the artist has passed on. Below is an example of how even a small amount of biographical data can aid you in a decision-making process.

Suppose you have selected two very similar paintings for possible purchase, both the same size, subject matter, quality and style. You like them both equally well and have decided to choose one to buy. Each is priced at $4,000. One is by an artist named John Doeman, the other by Henrietta Hooper. You find out that Hooper was born in 1950, started painting seriously in 1973 and has been an artist full time since 1979. Doeman was also born in 1950, recently took up painting and is having the first public show of his work at the gallery where you saw the painting you like. What can you assume or conclude from these facts? Plenty!

Conclusions about Henrietta Hooper: she makes her living as an artist. She has been painting for decades and is established in her career. She has proven herself as an artist and survived financially for over forty years by selling her art. Chances are extremely good that she is going to continue painting and not give up art for another career. If she has sold successfully for so many years, she has certainly produced a substantial body of work, most of which is probably pretty good.

Conclusions about John Doeman: he is an unproven commodity. He started painting only recently, and even though the quality of the painting you like is comparable to that of Hooper's, you have no way to tell, due to Doeman's relative inexperience, whether he will be able to maintain that quality level in all his work and eventually be considered equal in stature and accomplishment to Hooper. In addition, you have no idea whether his art is consistently good and sale-able or whether he just happened to get lucky and paint up a nice-looking opening show. You have no idea how many paint-ings Doeman has painted or sold during his short career – certainly fewer than Hooper. You have no way of knowing whether he will produce a sufficient body of work to become recognised as an artist or whether he will stop painting next month and fade into permanent obscurity.

You rarely have so little information to go on as you do in this example, but you see how far you can get on a minimum of facts. Assuming you are concerned about how you spend your $4,000 and don't want to take any unnecessary risks (which is pretty much the way beginners should approach art collecting), buy the Hooper, not the Doeman. You get a work of art by an established and recognised artist if you go with Hooper. With Doeman, you're not quite sure what you get.

How would you decide between these two paintings know-ing nothing about either Hooper or Doeman? You could flip a coin. You could put them side by side and stare at them hoping one might start looking slightly better than the other. No matter what you do, though, you'd be buying blind.

'But,' you argue, 'if I decide I like the Doeman, shouldn't I buy it regardless of what the facts are?' Absolutely. You're perfectly entitled to buy it, no matter how many facts you have and no matter what those facts are. What's important is that you have those facts, know what you are buying before you buy it, and that you have no misconceptions about either Hooper or Doeman or their careers. Informed buyers make intelligent collectors.

HOW TO LOCATE ARTIST BIOGRAPHICAL DATA

The primary source of artist data is printed information found online on websites or in databases, books, artist encyclopaedias, directories, exhibition catalogues, price databases, archives, publications and so on. In addition to accessing information online, all major public or university library art departments, art museums and better art galleries have substantial amounts of reference materials on hand. They often also offer free access to online databases that charge pricey usage or membership fees. The references we are talking about here, the ones you will learn how to use, are standard and accepted by the art community. For specific tips, pointers and instructions for how to research artists online, see Appendix XII.

While most art research is done online these days, it is still important to know the range of references available, particularly in book form. For example, if you are collecting or researching antique or vintage art by minor or less known artists, or more obscure types of art, online data can sometimes be scarce or difficult to locate. Books still come in handy here. Additionally, comprehensive reference books can give instant access to hundreds or even thousands of images, and it's still much easier to thumb through pages of images than go through them one by one online. This is true for younger contemporary artists as well as older ones. Other than viewing images, though, researching younger contemporary artists is generally done online.

For those of you who prefer not to use libraries, Appendix XI contains a list of dealers who specialise in selling art reference books and Appendix II lists some of the major online art reference resources and databases. Art museum bookstores are also a good source of reference materials, but their art books tend to be a little more general in nature than those sold by the dealers in Appendix XI. Dealers in specialised art reference materials are good to know because if you decide to get at all involved in collecting, having quality references within easy reach is essential.

The types of references you will be using are briefly summarised by category here. Many of the more important basic references in each category are listed in Appendix II with brief comments about each following the listings. This appendix by no means covers all art references, but it is reasonably comprehensive and includes more than enough basic resources to get you started no matter what artist you are researching.

By the way, don't be intimidated by the total number of reference books listed in Appendices III–VII. Once you know how to research, you develop a feel for which references in particular will be the most helpful to you on a case-by-case basis. You will rarely have to check dozens of titles, but rather just the few that relate to your specific situation.

Artist Indexes (see Appendix IV). Artist indexes are a good place to begin any research. These references contain names of hundreds of thousands of artists of all time periods and nationalities. They are alphabetised lists of names, usually accompanied by brief basic biographical information such as birth/death dates, nationalities and specialities (painter, sculptor, etcher, etc.). Keep in mind that many younger contemporary artists are not yet included in standard reference books or databases and have to be researched mainly online wherever they happen to be mentioned.

Indexes are important because, along with basic data, some also list titles of additional art reference books that include more detailed information about whatever artist you are researching. You then locate these references and use them to assemble more complete biographical profiles. Be aware that art indexes do not always list every additional reference that contains information, so continue researching even after checking the books to which the indexes refer.

Each index lists artists slightly differently, but an average entry looks something like this:

Quinara, Samaris; 1890–1969, Brazilian painter, EncArtAmer.

From this entry you can see that Samaris Quinara lived from 1890 to 1969, that he was a Brazilian painter and that further information about him can be located in a reference that is abbreviated as 'EncArtAmer'.' Full bibliographical information (title, author, publisher, copyright date, etc.) about abbreviated resources can be located at the beginning or ending of all indexes. In this case, EncArtAmer refers to an artist reference called *Enciclopedia del Arte en América*, which focuses on North, Central and South American artists. Some indexes also contain basic price data in addition to biographical data, but more about that later.

Artist Encyclopaedias (see Appendix V). These multi-volume sets and databases supply information about artists of all time periods and all nationalities. The three most frequently used encyclopaedias, Benezit, Theime–Becker and Theime–Becker's supplement (called Vollmer), are written in English, French and German, respectively, so you may need to have entries translated when you locate them. All of these contain information about artists from around the world, although they are best for researching European artists. They are also all available online by subscription (or at major public or institutional libraries). Other more specialised encyclopaedias, some of which are listed in the appendix, include only artists from specific parts of the world. This is not a complete list, so check with art dealers, art librarians or other experts for the names of additional specialised encyclopaedias if you need them. Some auction-price databases also have biographical information for artists.

Artist Dictionaries (see Appendix VI). These references, which are usually in one to three volumes, are more specific than general encyclopaedias. They might include artists from only one country, one discipline, one time period, one US state, one sex and so on. For example, you can find dictionaries specific to categories such as the following: California artists, Ohio artists, Utah artists, Texas artists, Indiana artists, American Indian artists, nineteenth-century English artists, women artists, New Orleans artists, marine artists, naive artists and so on. Some of the major artist dictionaries are listed in Appendix VI, but once again, this is by no means a conclusive list. As with encyclopaedias, learn which dictionaries are most applicable to your specific needs. Some are available online, but a number of the more obscure ones are not.

Artist Annuals and Directories (see Appendix VII). These references are published regularly and are constantly being revised, updated and enlarged. Some are published annually while others are published every few years or so. Like dictionaries, artist annuals and directories list artists alphabetically and usually according to specific criteria such as the type of art they produce, the state or country they live in, and so on. *Who's Who in American Art*, for instance, is available both in book and database formats, published every other year, and includes only living American and Canadian artists and related visual arts professionals like curators, critics, collectors and educators. Once again, the titles listed in Appendix VII do not constitute a complete list of these types of references.

Art Archives and Files. Art archives and files are collections of documents, news clippings, correspondence, catalogues, writings, oral histories and other miscellaneous information about art and artists. Archives and files often include data that is unpublished and is not available anywhere else. The major British art archives are located in the National Archives. Information about the Royal Society of British Artists can be found here: http://discovery.nationalarchives.gov.uk/details/c/F117612. British art and artists' records held by other archives can be found here: http://www.nationalarchives.gov.uk/help-with-your-research/research-guides/art-and-artists-records-held-by-other-archives. The major American art archives, called the Archives of American Art, is headquartered at the Smithsonian Institute in Washington, DC (www.aaa.si.edu). Many major national (and smaller regional and local) libraries, museums, historical societies, art associations and art institutes maintain their own files and archives, as do some art dealers. Consult experts and check specific institutions according to who or what you are researching to see whether relevant archives exist and, if so, where they are located.

Auction Price References, Databases and Guides (see Appendix II). These references will be discussed at length in

Part IV. Briefly, price references tell you whether works by particular artists have sold or been offered at public sales (primarily auctions, but sometimes through dealers) and either specifically or approximately what prices they sold for or were offered at.

When you first start researching artists, have art librarians, art dealers and other professionals walk you through the basics, step by step. This is the best way to learn what you're doing, to identify the specific references best suited to your needs and, eventually, to learn how to streamline the process. Experts can teach you how to use any reference book or online database within a matter of minutes. Artist research is really that easy!

Even on your own, learning how to use books and online databases to research artists is not difficult. All you do is check those references listed in the appendices mentioned above that appear relevant to your situation, one by one, preferably in the order they have been summarised here (indexes first, encyclopaedias next and so on). This way, you maximise your chances of locating the information you need on whatever artist you are researching. The next few paragraphs provide several additional research pointers.

Whenever you research, check as many relevant references as possible. This is especially necessary when you're starting out. Since you do not know which books or databases to go to immediately and what their respective strengths and weaknesses are, you have to look up artists' names in every one that could possibly help you. This exercise also gives you practise researching and helps familiarise you with what specific references are all about.

If you find an artist listed in one book or database, don't stop looking and assume you have all the information you need. Different references often contain different information about the same artist, and combining what you find yields the best results. If you don't find an artist listed in the first two or three references you check, do not give up and decide that the artist is a total unknown. Continue checking; then decide.

Random online artist research is another story. So much information is available, some of it accurate, some of it not so accurate, that you really have to verify any source before taking it seriously. You can't believe everything you read just because you found it on the internet. Standard art references are best, but often the far corners of the internet can yield fascinating results as well. Time, practice and experience are the best teachers here. The more artists you research and the more research you do, the better you get at being able to parse and interpret the information you locate.

No matter who, what or where you're researching, approach the task of gathering information as though you are writing an essay entitled 'The Life of an Artist'. Write down, print out, copy or save the links of every listing or entry you find. Do this whether or not you think what you read has any significance or relation to the artist's art. The truth is that *everything* you find is relevant in one way or another.

Here's an extreme example of information that may seem irrelevant at first, but actually isn't. Suppose you have selected a work of art for possible purchase and discover that the artist was once implicated in some type of illegal activity or made the news in a less than positive way. These facts have nothing to do with art, but they may have something to do with whether you still want to own the piece you've selected. Maybe you do, but chances are you want to own it less than you did before finding out that information. Regardless of your preferences, collectors sometimes avoid art by artists with certain backgrounds or histories, which in turn may decrease those artists' prices and collectability in the market-place. While your artist's history has no direct bearing on the quality of the art, it may affect its overall marketability.

You won't have to go much further than the basic references listed in the appendices with the great majority of artists you research. The reason is that most artists are not that widely written about and are listed in few places other than in basic standard references, archives and files. The better known artists are, however, the more they have been written about, the more information exists and the more extensively you'll need to research in order to make informed decisions.

Information about better-known artists can be located in numerous books, exhibition catalogues and other publications in addition to online databases and the standard references discussed above. The most famous artists are included in dozens of references; many even have entire books written about them (a book about a single artist is known as a monograph and a book that lists every work of art an artist produced during his or her career is known as a *catalogue raisonné*). If you intend to collect art by important artists, have experts teach you how to research and assemble data from multiple sources. Such advanced research techniques are beyond the scope of this book.

INTERPRETING THE RESULTS
OF ARTIST RESEARCH

Finding an artist listed or included in standard references is a good sign, but that fact alone does not bestow instant collectability or justify the price that is being asked for a work of art. You must know how to interpret those entries in order to get an accurate idea of how accomplished the artist really is. Some of the general ways that information you find in books affects an artist's market and price structure are discussed here. Know that none of these is an absolute and you should not base your final conclusions on just one of them being true.

The more references that include an artist and the more sources of information you can find online, the more collectible his or her art is. An artist you find included in twenty books, all online databases and on numerous websites is better known than one who has only a few brief mentions or entries in only a couple of references.

The more significant the references and websites that include an artist, the more significant the artist is. For example, an artist listed only in a dictionary of Ohio artists and nowhere else is less important than one included in all major international art encyclopaedias or one that has significant coverage on multiple websites.

The more mentions an artist has in any given reference or website and the longer those mentions are, the more collectible his or her art is. A detailed multi-page entry is more significant than a brief two-line entry.

The longer an artist has been included in books, the more collectible his or her art is. For example, a contemporary artist who has been included in basic references ever since she started painting in the 1970s is more well known and well recognised than one who is approximately the same age and has been included only since 1995.

The more detailed the entries are in terms of art-related accomplishments, awards or distinctions, the more collectible the artist is. An artist who has participated in numerous national and international shows and exhibits, has won awards in prestigious competitions, has work in museums and has been represented by widely respected galleries is more important than one who has been involved in only small local or regional events, been represented only by one local gallery and so on.

The more respected the authors or the websites and the more widely accepted the references, the more seriously you may consider the artists they write about. For example, museum curators, art scholars and art historians who write scholarly texts are involved in the most non-biased sorts of writing. On the other hand, dealers or galleries who write and publish their own books or catalogues or websites about artists they represent or promote in order to increase sales have personal interest and financial gain in mind. As a result, such presentations are almost always prejudiced in favour of the artists and don't necessarily detail the facts accurately. Check with experts whenever you have questions about whether a reference is respected and accepted as standard by the art community or is not much more than a vanity publication designed to make money for those representing the artist.

The more respected the institution or business publishing the book or maintaining the website, the more seriously you may consider the information you locate. For example, inclusion in an important museum exhibition catalogue, on a respected online reference site, in a book published by a major university press or in a standard artist encyclopaedia is more significant than a mention in a catalogue published by a small regional or local art association.

With respect to price records, artists who sell for more money are generally more important and collectible than those who sell for less. That's not much to go on, but it's enough for now. You'll read plenty more about art prices and how to evaluate them in Part IV.

ASSESSING THE FACTS

Once you have a general idea of what resources include an artist, who wrote them, and how frequently and extensively that artist is mentioned, you have to focus on the individual facts you find. These facts fall into specific categories and mean certain things. Here are the categories of facts you normally encounter, a brief summary of what they mean, how to interpret them and how they tend to affect an artist's market.

Birth and death dates. An artist's age is always good to know. From it you can determine how long he has been an artist, how old he was when he started, how old he is now and so on. For example, if you like to buy conservatively, as you should in the early stages of your collecting, buying established artists who have been active for significant periods of time is less risky than buying art by young artists who are just starting out.

Where and with whom an artist studied. These facts are interesting to know, but they have little bearing on an artist's collectability or reputation. Studying under famous artists or graduating from the finest art academies is a step in the right direction, but what really counts is what the artist accomplishes after completing that education. Self-taught artists with little or no formal schooling can be just as accomplished and collectible as those with years of training. Watch out for dealers who try to get you to buy the work of particular artists just because they had great teachers or graduated from the best schools.

Organisational memberships. The organisations to which an artist belongs are not necessarily an indication of how collectible that artist is. Many groups or associations allow anyone to join. Certain memberships, however, do indicate a level of accomplishment on the artist's part, especially organisations that only admit new members by vote. For example, being elected to the National Academy of Design in New York City is a high honour and major accomplishment for any American artist and has been so for nearly two hundred years. Whatever art you collect, it's always good to know the names of the most important and prestigious organisations to which the artists who produce that type of art can belong.

Where an artist has exhibited. The more established, recognised and respected the galleries and institutions where an artist has exhibited, the better. For example, showing a painting at the Museum of Modern Art, New York, is a more prestigious accomplishment than showing one at the Tinytown Zucchini Bazaar.

Group exhibitions versus solo shows. In terms of accomplishments, having a solo show is generally more significant than participating in a group show. For example, having a solo show at the Museum of Modern Art is a far greater accomplishment than showing one work of art at that same museum in a group show with three hundred other artists.

Awards received. Awards always speak well of an artist, but you have to differentiate between important awards and not-so-important ones. Winning a gold medal or first prize at a major international art exhibition is more significant than winning the Minnie Ginchflower Award for Sunday Painting at the Acorn Valley Bake Sale.

Public or corporate collections that own works by an artist. The fact that museums or corporations own works by an artist is an indication that art-world experts and authorities have recognised the art as significant. You have to be a little careful here because although most collection listings are legitimate, some artists claim to be in certain collections when, in fact, they are not. If you have any questions about whether an artist's art is in a particular collection, contact that institution and ask whether work by the artist is actually in their *permanent* collection. One additional point: make sure corporations and other non-art-related institutions included on an artist's résumé are known and recognised for the quality of their art collections.

Private collections that own works by an artist. This is a sticky area. Basically, major private collections known for having quality art are good for an artist to be in and good for you to know about. Other collections, even though they sound impressive, may mean nothing. For example, suppose you read that an artist has an etching in the collection of the Countess Matilda of Lower Stregonia. This sounds significant, but for all you know the Countess may have no taste in art, the artist may have given her the etching for free or her entire 'collection' may consist only of that one etching.

Auction sales results and other price records. Briefly, finding any price results whatsoever for an artist is good and the higher those prices are, the better. Interpreting price records will be discussed at length in Part IV.

When you're just starting out, always double-check your final evaluations with professionals or other individuals knowledgeable about the artists you're researching. Get the consensus opinion from 'those in the know'. Make sure you're reading and interpreting the facts and data correctly and are not jumping to any erroneous conclusions.

WHAT TO DO WHEN YOU COME UP EMPTY-HANDED

Suppose, after all your research, you come up empty-handed. You find absolutely no data or information on the artist you are researching, and all you have to go on is what the seller has told you. This is never good, and whenever you find yourself in this type of situation, you've got a problem – and several possible solutions.

The most common reason why people come up empty-handed is that they either shortcut their research by not checking enough references, spend too little time searching online, use the wrong keywords in their searches, or research only at places with inadequate art reference resources.

The solution: check at least one or two major art libraries in major cities – both in their art reference sections as well as comprehensive online databases to which they subscribe. Also, explain your situation to specialist librarians or curators, and ask them for advice in case you've overlooked something.

If you still find no information, the problem could be that you are researching a very minor artist who is not accomplished enough to be included in references. This doesn't necessarily mean you should forget about buying the art. You can, of course, buy whatever you want, regardless of how little known the artist is. What a lack of data does mean, though, is that you probably shouldn't be paying too much for that art.

You have three possible options in any circumstance where research yields nothing:

- If the art is inexpensive and you like it, go ahead and buy it. You're not risking anything.
- If the piece of art is expensive, if you enjoy taking risks and if you don't care how you spend your money, go ahead and buy it. (This is not a particularly popular option.)
- If possible, show the art to qualified or experienced collectors or professionals you know and trust, and see whether

they think the quality of the art warrants purchase. Over time and with training, you'll learn how to make these decisions yourself.

• Forget about buying the art, no matter what the price, but especially if it's expensive. Look for another artist whose work you like just as much and who has a documented and researchable track record.

Example 1

Imagine you are considering buying a painting by John James Burton and find this entry on a respected art website:

Burton, John James, Painter
Born: Roundtree, Virginia; 22 May 1967. Studied: University of Texas, BA; Oregon Art Institute, MFA. Works Held: Smithville Art Museum, Municipal Museum, International Farm Equipment Company collection. Exhibited: Modern Art Museum, St Louis, 1995; National Art Association, Wash. D.C., 1998; Municipal Museum (one-man), San Francisco, 2002; Boston Art Museum Spring Show, 2008. Awards: Second Prize, Boston Art Museum, 2008. Member: American Art Association. Mailing address: 2345 Main St, Wildflower, AZ 11111.

You see from reading this that Burton is an artist who has achieved some recognition. In art-business lingo, he would be described as a *mid-career* artist. So far, he has a respectable and established track record. He has exhibited nationally and has work in several significant collections. He has had a one-man museum show and won an award. Assuming you want to know more, here's how you can follow up on this data:

- Contact the two museums and one corporation that own his art. Find out the circumstances of the purchases or acquisitions, whether the art hangs on a permanent basis, whether they can supply you with additional biographical information and so on.
- Contact the Municipal Museum for further information on Burton and details on the one-man show. Maybe they published a catalogue of that show and they can send one to you.
- Find out how important the 'Boston Art Museum Spring Show' is and how important the award is that Burton received at that show.
- Find out how important the American Art Association is and what its membership requirements are.
- Contact Burton himself and see whether he can supply you with a complete résumé of his career.

Example 2

Not all art galleries rely on standard references and traditional measures of artistic accomplishment to sell their artists to the public. Some try to distract you from the facts. I can think of several instances where galleries use well-known public figures to promote artists in much the same way that advertisers usc athletes or entertainers to endorse their products. Rather than provide the facts and résumés of their artists' careers, these galleries show you pictures of the artists in the company of well-known personalities, give you the names of famous people (again of the non-art expert or non-collector variety) who own their art or use other celebrity-related tactics to convince you to buy.

Know that celebrity endorsements mean nothing unless those celebrities also happen to be accomplished art experts or collectors, or have some kind of standing in the art world. No matter how glamorous or important a gallery makes an artist look, only standard art references and career résumés give you the straight story on fame and accomplishments.

Example 3

Researching and finding out nothing about an artist can be just as telling as finding pages of information. Over the years, I have seen art for sale online and visited occasional galleries that exhibit works by artists whom the sellers claim are nationally known or even world famous – and who also happen to be artists of whom I have never heard. Impressive-looking certificates or documents may accompany the art and make claims about how famous the artists are. I sometimes research these artists out of curiosity, mainly because I'm surprised I've never heard of them and suspect they may not be as well known as the sellers say they are.

Some turn out to be included in a few standard references, websites or other publications where 'famous' artists are normally written about. Others are virtually unknown. The truth is that some artists are misrepresented by sellers as being far more important than they actually are. Always corroborate any claims made with your own independent research no matter how official any materials with which you are presented look.

Example 4

Some 'art references', especially those published by special interests, have a tendency to bend the truth or misstate facts. I recall an occasion where I met with an artist who gave me a catalogue of her work to impress me with her accomplishments. She had written it herself, paid for it herself, and designed it to promote her art and her art only. On top of that, she was great at promoting herself in person. She regularly sold her sculptures at what I considered to be impressively high prices.

Her catalogue contained colour illustrations of her art, laudatory information about her career, and names of private and public collectors who owned her work. It also listed several museums as owning sculptures. I did not bother to check whether any of these claims were true because I did not plan on doing any business with this artist. I filed the brochure away and forgot about it.

Several months later, while speaking with another dealer, this artist's name came up. I told him about her catalogue and mentioned that her work was apparently in several important museum collections. He laughed, told me that no museums owned her work and went on to explain what the truth really was.

According to him, she had mailed sculptures free of charge to these museums as donations. The museums had accepted them, but not for their collections. They were probably sold at white-elephant sales or other fundraising events, the proceeds of which are generally used to finance museum operations. Works by this artist were not recorded as being in any of their permanent collections.

Example 5

Sometimes sellers are the ones who neglect to research artists and other dealers or collectors are the ones who profit. I have made more than a few such bargain buys from experienced sellers who normally sell art at top retail prices. For example, one gallery owner had hung and priced a small painting by an important but somewhat obscure artist who was outside his area of speciality, apparently without researching it. It wasn't a very impressive-looking piece of art but, nevertheless, I recognised it to be worth about $5,000. He had it priced at just under $1,000, and I bought it on the spot.

While I was paying for the picture, I asked what he knew about the artist. He said he had found small bits of information here and there, but nothing substantial. I asked what references he had checked and he told me. Apparently, he had only researched briefly and did not check the best references for that artist. If he had researched more thoroughly, he would have discovered that an entire book had been written about this artist and several other books contained complete chapters on the painter's illustrious career.

A LOOK AHEAD

Assembling biographical data about an artist is your first step in research. Assuming the artist remains under consideration after you evaluate your findings, you must now turn your attention to the particular work of art you have selected. The next chapter explains the procedures for researching and evaluating a specific work of art.

CHAPTER 14

RESEARCH THE ART

Imagine two different works of art by the same artist. One is priced at $500 and the other weighs in at a hefty $50,000. This may sound absurd – that the same artist could have produced both – but it's a relatively common occurrence. The difference in price between an artist's least and most expensive art is often substantial.

How can this be? The answer is simple. The same artist can produce great art, good art, average art, awful art, big art, little art, one-of-a-kind art, limited edition art and so on. The range and variety of art that the average artist produces during his or her lifetime can be astonishing. For example, Picasso is said to have produced approximately fifty thousand works of art during his lifetime. He's the exception, but many artists produce hundreds or thousands of artworks during their careers.

Unfortunately, you cannot automatically tell what art by an artist deserves to sell for a lot of money and what should be selling for just a little. No standard grading or rating system exists for labelling significance, excellence, quality or inferiority in art. There are no quality-control labels or stamps, no classification categories like Class A, Four Star, Extra Fine, Grade A, seconds or irregulars, but you can make these kinds of distinctions if you know how. *Methods exist for determining the relative importance of any art piece in terms of the total output of the artist who created it.*

Many novice art buyers never even think about the relative importance or significance of one work of art compared to another. They make the mistake of viewing a work of art as an isolated entity and neglect to relate it to anything else the artist ever produced. As long as it's by the artist, they reason, that's good enough for them. A Picasso is a Picasso is a Picasso. In art-dealer jargon, they buy the name and not the art. A common result of this oversight is that these buyers often end up overpaying for inferior art.

For example, I once met a man who was interested in buying a painting by a collectible American artist. He had seen the artist's work at several galleries, liked it and was aware that it usually sold in the $4,000 to $8,000 range. He decided to shop around until he found just the right picture.

One day at a gallery, he saw a painting by this artist for only $900. It looked similar to some of the more expensive ones he'd seen at other galleries, and it was about the same size. He decided he'd discovered a major bargain and bought it instantly. He now owned the painting he had always wanted.

Unfortunately, this story does not end happily. He brought the painting to me and proudly showed me what a great buy he had made. I took one look at it and had to inform him that his treasure was indeed by the artist, but that was the only good thing I could say about it. I told him that not only was it an inferior example of the artist's work, but it was one of the worst examples I'd ever seen. His 'bargain' was overpriced even at $900 and was worth only $300–$500 at best.

This collector made two common errors. First, he assumed that as long as the artist had painted it, it had to be good. Second, he believed that all paintings by the artist were worth about the same amount of money – $4,000 to $8,000 each. If he had known how to compare his $900 special to other paintings by the artist instead of briefly looking at name, size, composition, subject matter and price, chances are he never would have bought it.

The important point to remember is that when you purchase a work of art, you do not buy an isolated item; you buy a portion of an artist's total output and you have to evaluate it in terms of that output. You want that portion, as small as it is, to be a good representative example of the artist's work, not a poor one.

Let's assume you are in the process of researching one of your selections for possible purchase. You assemble biographical data according to the guidelines laid out in the previous chapter and decide that art by this artist is worth buying. Now, you have to evaluate the art.

1 *Begin by reviewing the results of your biographical research and look for clues about what the artist does best.* Note any statements relating specifically to the artist's art. Perhaps she won an award for an oil painting of a New York City street scene. Maybe you'll see a sentence describing her as a well-known abstract bronze sculptor. Note any information regarding what this artist creates that is most recognised by those in the art community.

2 *Familiarise yourself with the artist's total output.* Find out what she has produced so far in her career, when she did it, what it looks like, how her style has changed over the years and so on. You have to know and understand the whole in order to evaluate the individual parts properly.

3 *Study as many examples of the artist's art as you can.* See them at galleries; in exhibits; in books, magazines or catalogues; online; and wherever else you can locate them. Note characteristics of the most expensive examples you can find; note characteristics of the least expensive ones.

    See how large the price differences are between the high-priced and low-priced art.

4 *Most importantly, ask dealers, collectors and other experts familiar with the artist's work to tell you what the artist is best (and least) known for.* Have them describe the qualities, subject matters, time periods and other specifics related to those works. Whenever possible, view and discuss actual examples in the company of these experts.

Combine the results of research, repeated viewings and conversations with experts with your answers to the questions detailed below. Keep in mind when researching the relative importance of a work of art that you will occasionally find exceptions to these general rules and tendencies. They do, however, hold true in the great majority of cases.

Is the work an original piece of art executed by the artist whose signature it bears or is it a type of reproduction? Many art galleries, for example, sell limited edition copy-prints or reproductions of works of art that are signed and sometimes numbered by the artists who created the originals (as you read about in Chapter 2); some galleries sell them without even the pencil signatures. *No matter how beautiful they look, these prints are created by publishers and not by the artists who signed them.* They are produced by companies that first scan either the original themselves or photographs of the originals and reproduce them as digital prints or giclées. Other companies employ similar scanning techniques, but then reproduce the images as serigraphs, lithographs, screen prints and so on. All the artists do in these cases is spend several seconds pencil-signing (and sometimes numbering) the finished copy-prints.

    Reproductions (whether they are prints, photographs, sculptures or copies of originals made in any other mediums) are *not* original works of art and, as such, are not significant in terms of an artist's total output. In fact, it is debatable whether they should even be classified or evaluated as part of an artist's total output. If you have any doubts about art you are looking at, ask one simple question: 'Is this an original work of art produced by the artist or a reproduction or copy of an original work of art produced by a printing or publishing company?' If you buy, get the answer or precise description on your receipt in writing. Also review Chapter 2, which discusses the differences between originals and copies.

Assuming your selection is an original work of art created by the artist who signed it, continue with the questions listed here.

Is the art major or minor? The terms *major* and *minor* refer to the scope and complexity of individual works of art. A major work is often better composed, more original, more detailed, better executed, more complex and larger in size than a minor work. Important major pieces display an artist's total range of skills and talents. A major work takes more time and effort to conceive and create than a minor one and, consequently, major works cost more than minor ones.

Many collectors make common and often costly mistakes of oversimplifying the differences between major and minor, so before going any further, two warnings. First, don't confuse major with 'good' and minor with 'bad'. Minor works can be just as well executed as major ones. They're simply not as substantial in scope or complexity on certain levels.

Second, don't confuse major with 'bigger' and minor with 'smaller'. Bigger is not necessarily better, more important or worth more money. Legend has it that an art professor active during the Abstract Expressionist era (the time when large abstract paintings were coming into fashion) used to put in his two cents on the size issue by telling his students, 'If you can't paint good, paint big.' Never judge works of art based on size alone.

Enough warnings – now for a quiz. Consider two paintings by an artist known for his urban scenes. Let's say they are equal in size and painted equally well. One shows a city street with buildings. The other shows the same street and buildings, but it also shows children playing, people talking, pedestrians walking, midday traffic, parked cars, movers carrying a large piece of furniture up a stairway, a sky filled with billowing clouds and what looks like an approaching thunderstorm. Which one has more characteristics of a major piece?

Now imagine that the first painting measures 8 by 10 inches and the second measures 30 by 50 inches. Assuming again that they are equally well painted, which one is worthier of being called major?

Lastly, imagine that the first painting measures 30 by 40 inches and the second measures 20 by 30 inches. Once again, assuming equal quality, which one would be considered more major?

In all three cases, if you answered the second, you're absolutely right. The second is far more detailed, and the composition much more complex. In terms of labour alone, the artist would have had to spend many more hours conceiving and executing the second than the first.

The best examples of any artist's work are referred to as 'major' and no matter what artist you are interested in, you should tend towards major examples in your collecting whenever possible and avoid very minor ones. This does not mean you zero in on the most monumental works an artist has produced, but that you at least look for art that has some characteristics of what major pieces look like. If all you can afford is a minor work, you may wish to move on to a more affordable artist. Owning a minor example by a big-name artist is not necessarily better than owning a major example by a lesser-known artist.

You don't always have to buy major, though, or even close to it. If you love the art and it happens to be minor, at least make sure it's competently executed and fairly priced. Then go ahead and buy.

As an aside, you'll find minor works overpriced much more often than you'll find major works overpriced. Too many people – dealers and collectors alike – either promote or subscribe to the myth that the signature is more important than the art and that anything with the right name on it has to be expensive. To repeat, the truth is that even the greatest artists produce minor, inferior and just plain bad works of art that should be priced far below what their best efforts sell for.

Is the art typical or atypical of the artist's work? All artists are known for producing certain types of art. To begin with, most artists are best known for specialising in a particular medium. One may be a sculptor in bronze, the next a painter in oils and another a lithographer. Getting more specific, each artist is known for producing certain subject matters or compositions in their typical mediums. Our bronze sculptor may be known for his depictions of wild animals, the painter in oils for her abstracts and the lithographer for his Los Angeles city scenes. These works of art would be considered 'typical' of these artists.

If you're a beginner buyer, play conservative and lean towards purchasing typical works, that is, the art that artists are best known for producing. In the above three cases, these would be a bronze wild animal sculpture, an abstract oil painting or a lithographed Los Angeles city scene. In general, focus on typical works and avoid atypical, experimental, offbeat or unusual works of art that artists do not have reputations for producing. For example, avoid a floral still-life painting done by our animal sculptor, a landscape etching by the abstract painter or a watercolour coastal scene by the lithographer. Even though the quality of these items may be good or their prices substantially less than those of the typical works (as is often the case), they do not ordinarily make good buys. At worst, you could get stuck with a one-of-a-kind experiment that an artist tried, failed at and decided never to attempt again.

When knowledgeable dealers and experienced collectors think of a particular artist, they tend to think of that artist in terms of what he or she is best known for producing. When they buy work by that artist, they buy in those terms also. Take the animal sculptor who works in bronze, for example. Because the art community identifies him as a bronze sculptor who depicts animals, that floral still-life painting he did will be considered an oddity and have little appeal for collectors of his work.

Atypical works are not always to be ignored, however. Experienced collectors, for example, sometimes recognise atypical works as being outstanding and worth owning no matter who created them. Advanced collectors who are in the process of forming definitive collections of particular artists' works may also buy atypical pieces from time to time in order to complete their collections.

A final note is in order here. Some artists work in more than one medium or are competent in more than one subject matter. In these cases, find out what they are the most proficient in as well as what they're not so good at. For example, an artist who paints, sculpts and etches may be best known for her sculptures of famous people, reasonably well respected for her paintings of New England hills and not particularly well-thought-of for her etchings, no matter what their subjects are.

When does the art date from? *Art from certain periods in artists' careers is often more collectible than the art from other periods.* For instance, Paul Gauguin's Tahitian period is known to be his most brilliant creatively. Career high points can happen at any time – some early, some in the middle, some late – but works of art produced earlier in artists' careers are generally more collectible than later pieces, particularly early examples of the types of art artists go on to become best known for producing. Grandma Moses, of course, is an obvious exception to this rule.

When researching an artist, determine these peaks from biographical data and by speaking with experts. Get to know when the best periods are and what art from those periods looks like. Art from the best periods is often the most important, the most collectible and commands the highest prices.

Artists also experience career low points – difficult times, times of change, times when whatever they produce just doesn't quite work. Work from less productive periods is worth substantially less than work from peak periods. Sometimes, for instance, you find art that at first seems relatively inexpensive, but once you start researching it, you discover that it doesn't cost much because it has that 'low-point look' that few if any collectors are interested in owning.

How original is the art? *Original compositions, techniques and subject matters in art are more significant and collectible than repeats of things that have already been done.* Here we're talking about art that the art community recognises as a step forward in an artist's career or, even more so, works that advance the evolution of art as a whole. The example below helps to clarify what the term *original* means.

Suppose an artist devotes all his creative energies to producing twenty sculptures for a gallery show. They're like nothing he's ever made before. He agonises over them for months, experimenting and trying dozens of different compositional options before settling on just the right look.

He shows them at an art gallery and they receive instant acclaim from prominent members of the art community. Collectors also love what they see and the show sells out within a few weeks. The artist decides that since this work sold so well, he's going to produce the same sculptures over again. This time, he makes forty pieces and within several months they sell out, too. By now, the artist feels he has found a formula for producing art that he can sell regularly and decides to make nothing but similar sculptures for the rest of his life.

When dealers, collectors and other experts look back on this artist's career, they will regard the sculptures from that very first show and those produced shortly after as being the most original – and thus the most significant, collectible and valuable. Ones produced five or ten or twenty years later, even though they look the same as the earlier ones, will not be as desirable because they are basically re-enactments or repeats of creative moments that the artist experienced years before. They lack the originality, risk-taking, energy and vibrancy of the formative earliest pieces.

The ultimate repeats are works of art that have nothing original about them, but are instead little more than copies of what other artists have already done. Continuing with our sculpture example, suppose another sculptor sees how successful the first sculptor is and decides to produce similar sculptures. He rides the first artist's coattails and attempts to cash in on the buying frenzy. His sculptures completely lack originality, are purely decorative and are little more than knock-offs, commonly referred to in the art world as 'derivative'.

With respect to price, the most original art should cost the most; repeats by the artist who first conceived those originals should cost less; repeats by other artists who copy the original artist should cost the least.

Watch out for galleries that price any types of repeats close to what originals sell for. These galleries are aware that inexperienced collectors who don't know enough about art and art history to tell the difference will be more susceptible to paying higher prices. When you're just starting out, rely on the advice of experts and consult biographical information and an artist's résumé whenever you have questions about the degree of originality.

How well done is the art? Determining quality in art is important. It's also difficult to do when you've been buying for only a short while. *The only way you learn to recognise quality is through experience – by looking at all the art you possibly can, learning about the artists, discussing the strengths and weaknesses of particular works of art with experts, and learning what makes any given piece good, better or best.* A work of art may be typical, original, from the right period and so on, but if the quality isn't there, it's not worth buying. When you're starting out, protect yourself on the quality issue by consulting experts and dealing with respected galleries that have experience selling the types of art you want.

Example 1

Early in my career, an art dealer offered me a darkish, misty sunset scene by a well-known American artist. He wanted $2,000 for the painting and told me that it was a great bargain at that price. He backed up his claim by telling me that two paintings by the artist, approximately the same size as mine, had recently sold at auction for over $10,000 each. He intimated that I would have no trouble doubling or even tripling my money. I believed him and bought the picture.

Several days later, I learned that the seller had misrepresented the painting by not giving me the full auction story and, unfortunately, my 'bargain' was worth nowhere near what he had told me it was. Yes, the impressive sales had taken place, but both auction prices were for snow scenes, the scenes the artist was most famous for painting. My painting was atypical, nothing like what collectors wanted, difficult to sell and worth only about $2,000 at the most, making it an ill-advised buy since my purpose in buying it was to sell at a profit.

If I had known more about typical versus atypical subject matters at that time, I could have saved myself a couple of thousand dollars as well as the headache of trying to resell that painting. I took time to learn how to make this distinction, however, immediately after realising what a very poor buy I had made. I also decided never to do business with that dealer again.

Example 2

Suppose you are thinking about buying a watercolour of the Rocky Mountains by an artist named Marla Mathews, and you discover certain facts about her career. Here are those facts followed by explanations of how you should respond to that information:

- *She is best known for her abstract watercolours of Rocky Mountain scenes.* This is a point in favour of your buying the watercolour you are considering. Now you have to educate yourself about these mountain watercolours, look at as many as you can, find out what the best and worst ones look like, and compare them to the one you are interested in.

- *She did some of her finest work between 1980 and 1990 and worst work between 1960 and 1965.* Find out when the watercolour was painted and act accordingly. If she didn't date her watercolours, find out what characteristics identify pieces from those particular time periods.

- *She tried oil painting for several years but gave it up because she never quite mastered the medium.* You're lucky you aren't considering an oil painting. If someone offers you one by this artist, you should probably pass on it.

- *She had success selling her views of Mt Ardmore in the mid-1980s, and started mass producing them in the mid-1990s.* If the work you're considering is of Mt Ardmore and dates from the mid-1990s, either pass on it or pay less for it than you would for an earlier example – one that was done before 1990.

- *Mathews paints best in the 20-by-24 inch size range. Her watercolours that measure larger than 25 by 30 inches are not as well done.* Measure the watercolour you like, compare it to others of that size range and to others of different sizes, and act accordingly. If the watercolour you are evaluating is very large, think about shopping for a smaller one.

A LOOK AHEAD

Many works of art are accompanied by either certificates of authenticity (abbreviated COA), appraisals or both. In the art business, specific requirements must be met in order for these documents to be considered accurate, valid and appropriate to the circumstances in which they're presented. In Chapter 15, you will learn to tell the difference between valid COAs and appraisals and problematic or meaningless ones.

CERTIFICATES OF AUTHENTICITY AND APPRAISALS

Two of the most important, least understood and most abused documents in the art business are the certificate of authenticity (or COA) and the appraisal. By definition, a valid COA conclusively proves and/or confirms that a work of art is by the stated artist, and a qualified appraisal states how much a work of art is worth according to a predefined set of conditions. Unfortunately for those new to buying art, telling the difference between a credible COA or appraisal and a problematic or meaningless one is not necessarily easy. So, in order to avoid tricky situations, let's take a quick crash course on the basics of each. That way, the next time you're presented with either, you'll have a basic understanding of what you're looking at.

THE CERTIFICATE OF AUTHENTICITY

No formal standards currently exist for either authorising or providing certificates of authenticity. COA procedures are not regulated and are subject to no oversight or examination by any official agency or organisation (assuming no national, federal, state or local laws have been broken). Pretty much anyone can print up or write a COA and word it however they please, whether they're qualified to do so or not. As if that's not bad enough, unscrupulous individuals can forge official-looking COAs and use them to either sell outright fakes or misrepresent existing works of art as being more important than they actually are. To make matters worse, bogus COAs have been issued for decades; one that's dated 1975, for example, can be just as worthless as one written today. The good news is that within the established art community, the form and content of an acceptable COA are well defined by convention, follow set guidelines and satisfy specific requirements.

The most important requirement for a COA to be valid is that the individual who authors and signs it is qualified to do so. He must be a recognised and respected authority on the art and artist he certifies as being authentic, and he must have the credentials and acceptance throughout the art community and among his peers for his conclusions to be considered valid and definitive. Qualified authorities include academics, curators or scholars who have extensively studied the artists, authored books, catalogues, magazine articles or scholarly papers, or who have organised museum or major gallery shows about the artists in question. Qualified authorities may also be artists (in the case of authenticating their own art); publishers (in the case of authenticating limited editions they publish); respected and established dealers or agents of an artist who receive art either directly from the artists or from their estates (not third-party dealers or resellers); direct descendants, informed relatives, spouses, long-standing employees or heirs of artists; or individuals who have legal, formal or estate-granted entitlements or sanctions to pass judgement on works of art by specific artists.

A valid COA must be an original document, NOT A COPY, and must be hand-signed or otherwise certified by the authority responsible for composing it. That individual must be identifiable, and the document must also include or make reference to that individual's qualifications to authenticate the art, and her FULL CURRENT CONTACT INFORMATION. A COA cannot be considered valid if the signer is unidentifiable, the contact information is untraceable or the qualifications are unverifiable.

A valid COA must specifically describe the work of art in question. This prevents the same COA from being misused to 'authenticate' more than one work of art. A valid description must include:

- the full name of the artist;
- birth and death dates (when available);
- nationality or location (when relevant or available);
- the medium of the art (painting, print, lithograph, giclée, etc.);
- its exact dimensions;
- its title (when known);
- the edition size (when applicable);
- and other distinguishing features or relevant specifics.

Additional details, when known, must also be included such as:

- the date of the art;
- its condition;
- its publisher or creator (if other than the artist);
- names of dealers who sold it (when relevant to substantiating the authenticity of the art);
- names of previous owners of the art (when relevant to substantiating the authenticity of the art);

- and the names of any reference books, websites, publications or related resources that specifically mention the art.

For example, ALL limited edition prints by Pablo Picasso, Marc Chagall and Joan Miró are documented in books called *catalogue raisonnés* (a *catalogue raisonné* lists ALL KNOWN WORKS OF ART in a particular medium or mediums by a particular artist). In fact, many well-known artists have *catalogue raisonnés*, and whenever a *catalogue raisonné* exists for an artist, the corresponding catalogue number or entry for the work of art in question must be included in the COA. (If a work of art is supposed to be in a *catalogue raisonné* but isn't, and it has a COA anyway, this is cause for concern, and the possibility exists that the COA may be fraudulent.)

COAs authored by anyone other than recognised authorities on artists are WORTHLESS, no matter how important or official they look. These documents have no credibility in the art community; no opinions, assertions or conclusions made in those COAs can be taken seriously without support or confirmation by acknowledged experts on the artists in question. Here are some examples of meaningless statements commonly found in worthless COAs authored by unqualified individuals or galleries:

- The art is by the artist because either all or part of it looks like the work of that artist.
- The art is by the artist because it looks like illustrations in books about the artist.
- The art is by the artist based on independent research performed by an individual who is NOT a recognised authority on the artist. (The findings of such research are often accompanied by long convoluted hypothetical

explanations that are supposed to support the 'researcher's' conclusions.)

- The art is by the artist because it bears the signature of that artist. The more important an artist, the more outside proof is required to substantiate the genuineness of a signature on any work of art supposedly by that artist. As difficult as this may be to believe, a signature alone is NEVER enough to conclusively prove authenticity.
- The art is by the artist because 'that's what the last person who owned it said'.
- The art is by the artist because it was bought in Paris (or some other major art centre).
- The art is by the artist because it was bought at a gallery with a fancy-sounding name.
- The art is by the artist because a collector with a fancy-sounding name once owned it.
- The art is by the artist because a rich collector formerly owned it and/or it came from a great big house on top of a hill and/or everything in the estate it came from was valuable, and so on and so forth.
- The art is by the artist because the last owner bought it a long time ago.
- The art is by the artist because it says so in an appraisal. *FYI, art appraisals only state monetary values according to the conditions defined in those appraisals. Art appraisals are not COAs; they do not authenticate art* (unless the appraiser is also a recognised authority on the art being appraised). Appraisals and COAs are two entirely different entities; *NEVER CONFUSE THEM*.

A formal COA is not necessarily required to prove that a work of art is genuine. Any valid receipt, bill of sale or proof of purchase from either the artist herself or from a confirmed and established dealer, publisher or agent of the artist will do. An appraisal from a recognised authority on the artist is also acceptable. Always remember, though, that only documents from QUALIFIED individuals are acceptable. Here are some additional pointers to keep in mind whenever a work of art you are considering buying comes with a COA:

- Read and review the full text of that COA and the qualifications of the individual who authored it BEFORE you buy the art to make sure that it meets adequate requirements to be considered valid.
- Never buy art based on a promise that a COA will be provided at some point in the future. Never buy art based on a promise that the COA exists but will be provided to the buyer only after the sale is completed.
- If the art is for sale online, request a copy, either by fax or digital image, of the complete COA and not just portions of it. Most importantly, verify in writing from the seller that the COA in his possession is an original document personally hand-signed by the signer and not a reproduction or photocopy.
- Any conditional statements found in a COA such as 'in our considered opinion . . .' or 'we believe that . . .' are warning signs that the art may not be genuine or is problematic in some way. A valid COA conclusively states that the art is by the artist in question.
- A valid COA must present documented proof or evidence in one form or another that the art is genuine. (This proof may be as simple as a signed statement from a respected authority on the artist.)
- If you have any questions about the content of a COA, contact the authority who is responsible for it BEFORE you buy the art.

- When the contact information on a COA is no longer valid or is otherwise out of date, confirm that the information corresponds to where the authority actually lived or worked on the date of completion of the COA.
- A COA with only a signature, legible or not, is NEVER valid. Full contact information for the signer must be provided.
- Names of previous owners, names of dealers or galleries that once sold the art, or information about auctions where the art once sold are only relevant if they speak directly to the authenticity of the art. All names and contact information for such individuals or businesses must be verified in order to confirm that the sales transactions actually took place. All other statements or claims made in the COA must also be verifiable.

A WORD ABOUT 'ATTRIBUTED' ART

Works of art are sometimes presented as 'attributed' to certain artists in order to justify higher selling prices. In many cases, these so-called attributions are meaningless. By definition, an attribution means that in the best opinion of A QUALIFIED AUTHORITY on a particular artist, the art in question MAY BE by the artist in question. In other words, not even the authority is sure (the exception being when he clearly states that the art is very likely by the hand of the artist, and provides a detailed and comprehensive explanation to go with it). And if an authority isn't sure, how can anyone else be sure? So, basically, an attribution has minimal value. Either it is or it isn't – what good is 'may be?'

To make matters worse, all kinds of unqualified individuals claim to attribute all kinds of art to all kinds of artists all the time, especially on online auction websites, and 100 per cent of those attributions carry no weight whatsoever. In the art world, the only qualified attributions are those made by recognised authorities on the artists in question. And to repeat, all those authorities are saying in the great majority of cases is that maybe the art is by the artist in question, and then again, maybe it isn't. In other words, unless the authority is pretty darned close to saying the art is by the artist in question and makes that clear in the attribution, who cares? If you ever have questions about attributed art, ask three simple questions: 'Who did the attributing?' 'What are their qualifications to make that attribution?' 'What facts about the art are their attributions based on?'

ART APPRAISALS AND HOW TO EVALUATE THEM

An art appraisal states, in the opinion of a qualified professional appraiser, how much a work of art is worth according to a predefined set of conditions. As with COAs, the only appraisals worth the paper they're printed on are those performed by qualified appraisers or, in other words, professionals who know how to value art and have the experience and credentials to prove it. People who are not qualified to appraise art conjecture about what art may or may not be worth all the time. But when real money is at stake, relying on casual or informal opinions is never a good idea. Not only can an appraiser tell you how much the art is worth, but he can also explain why, put it in writing and sign it.

The tricky part about appraisals is that the same work of art can be 'worth' different amounts depending on specific conditions normally stated in the appraisal. There are several types of appraisals, so whenever you're handed one, you have to make sure it's appropriate to your situation. Sound confusing? Well, it is – but not so confusing that we can't sort things out right here and now.

The most common and widely accepted type of appraisal is called a 'fair market value' or FMV appraisal. In the United States, this is the appraisal required by the Internal Revenue Service (IRS) in any taxable instance where art must be valued for inheritance, donation, barter or gift purposes. A FMV appraisal is also the most relevant and realistic appraisal for people who buy or collect art – and that includes you if you are in the United States. Fair market value is defined in IRS Publication 561 as 'the price at which the property would change hands between a willing buyer and a willing seller, neither being under any compulsion to buy or to sell and both having reasonable knowledge of relevant facts'. In other words, you're familiar with the market for the art you're buying, the seller knows what he's selling, and neither of you are under any pressure to either buy or sell.

In the art world, FMV generally refers to what a work of art would sell for at auction (see Chapter 21 to learn about approximating a work of art's auction value), not at a retail gallery. However, depending on the artist and the conditions of the appraisal, retail gallery prices may also be considered. Auction selling prices are significant because, at auction, potential buyers bid against each other with the art selling to the highest bidder. The art is not offered at a fixed price, no one is compelled to bid, the auction company typically knows what they're selling, competing bidders typically know what they're bidding on, and the highest bid or selling price is essentially considered to represent an agreement of sorts among bidders as to what the art is fairly worth. This pretty much matches the FMV definition as stated in IRS Publication 561.

Retail gallery prices are not typically used to determine FMV in tax appraisals because, in the closed, controlled environments of galleries, prices may reflect gallery policies and costs of doing business more so than they do open-market forces (including the fair market value of the art). The asking price for a particular work of art may vary considerably from gallery to gallery and may depend more on factors such as a gallery's typical mark-up over cost, overhead expenses, commissions, location, the owner's beliefs about what art is 'worth', buying habits of the gallery's client base and the ability of the gallery staff to sell art effectively than it does on the art's FMV. In extreme instances, art priced at gallery retail can be many times the amount it would sell for at auction or at what would be considered its fair market value.

The IRS additionally prohibits an appraiser from being 'a party to the transaction in which the donor acquired the property', or in other words, an individual who either sells or is involved in the sale of a work of art is disqualified from appraising it for IRS purposes (for obvious possible conflict-of-interest reasons). This point is important for you to keep in mind when evaluating any appraisal. An essential question to ask whenever you're unclear about who appraised the art is: does the 'appraiser' have any personal or business interest in the artist, in galleries or dealers that sell the art, or any other interest or investment in appraising the art at a certain value? If yes, then you cannot assume the appraisal represents a fair assessment of what the art is worth. The most obvious example of this is when galleries provide their own 'appraisals' to go with the art they sell. I can assure you that a gallery will never 'appraise' its art for less than the sale price; however, it frequently 'appraises' it at higher than the sale price. When is an appraisal not an appraisal? When the seller and the appraiser are the same person (or people or gallery).

Ready to get practical and learn about the other kinds of appraisals? Good. Suppose you see a work of art you like, the seller says it's been appraised for a certain amount and that's what he's selling it for. If you're like most people, you're inclined to believe that since the art's been appraised, it's worth that amount and it's OK to buy. But as you may have already guessed, this is not necessarily the case. Art appraisals may or may not have any relation to the art's FMV (the most relevant value for you).

If a seller says a work of art has been appraised or that he knows its appraised value, the first thing you do is ask to see the appraisal. If the seller says he doesn't have an actual appraisal, but rather that an appraiser looked at the art and gave a value, THIS IS NOT AN APPRAISAL. If the seller tells you he hasn't actually had the art appraised, but that's what he's seen the art sell for elsewhere, THIS IS NOT AN APPRAISAL. If there is not a document that you can hold in your hands and examine, this means only one thing – the seller does not have an appraisal.

Let's say the seller does have an appraisal, and he hands it to you. Pay attention to two things – the qualifications of the appraiser and the conditions of the appraisal. Regarding qualifications, the person appraising the art must be a professional appraiser with experience appraising this type of art and have no conflict of interest regarding the art, the artist or any dealer or gallery that sells the art. The appraisal should contain contact information for the appraiser, a conflict-of-interest disclaimer and a statement of how the appraised value was determined.

Regarding the conditions of the appraisal, if it simply states what the art sells for at a particular gallery, this is generally referred to as a retail value appraisal. A retail value appraisal is almost always higher than an FMV appraisal; it represents what a work of art sells for at a particular gallery, not on the open market. A FMV appraisal must reflect what the art sells for on the open market, not only at one specific gallery. Often, a retail value appraisal is simply a statement from the gallery that it sold the art for the price that was paid (this means there is an obvious conflict of interest and, as mentioned above, it's not technically an appraisal at all). Remember, the appraisal that is most relevant to you is one that states the FMV – what the art sells for in general across the marketplace as a whole – not at one specific gallery.

A similarly irrelevant appraisal (and potentially the most deleterious to your wallet) is a replacement value appraisal for insurance purposes. This is the amount of money an insurance company is generally asked to pay when a work of art is either damaged beyond repair, stolen or destroyed. It represents the full retail price of the art and may also include whatever additional expenses may be incurred to either repair the art or replace it with an exact or approximate duplicate. Unfortunately, there is considerable abuse with respect to replacement or insurance value appraisals, particularly when galleries do them in-house for their own art (a conflict of interest) and then represent them to buyers as being what the art is realistically worth. Another problem with replacement or insurance appraisals is that, at worst, the monetary amounts they state can be entirely arbitrary and have little or no basis in fact. Anytime you see the words 'replacement value', 'insurance value' or 'insurance purposes' in an appraisal for art you're thinking about buying, watch out. This is about as far from an FMV appraisal as you can get. The best procedure when buying art is to disregard any replacement value appraisal and to instead request an FMV appraisal from a qualified appraiser with no conflict of interest.

ADDITIONAL POINTERS FOR EVALUATING APPRAISALS

- The amount of money someone paid for a work of art IS NOT AN APPRAISAL. What art sold for yesterday is not necessarily what it sells for today. What someone pays for a work of art is not automatically what that art is worth. People overpay for art all the time and you, as a buyer, are not required to compensate them for any overpayments they made if they try to sell that art to you for whatever they may have paid.

- A work of art that's 'been appraised' for $5,000, but is priced for sale at $2,500, is not automatically a bargain. As discussed above, if the $5,000 appraisal is a retail, replacement or insurance appraisal, that figure may well exceed the art's FMV.

- Make sure any appraisal you are presented with is current, certainly no older than a couple of years. Art prices fluctuate over time. An appraisal dating from the art boom of the late 1980s, for instance, may still state a monetary amount greater than what the art currently sells for. Likewise, an appraisal done at the peak of an artist's market may not reflect what that artist's work currently sells for today.

- Beware of free appraisals (especially if you are thinking about selling your art). People who offer free appraisals often have ulterior motives including trying to buy your art for much less than it's worth, giving your contact information to third parties who will try to buy your art for much less than it's worth (and then pay the 'free appraiser' a finder's fee if they succeed in buying it) or talking you into paying for 'better' appraisals than the 'free' ones you're getting. Also, keep in mind that auction houses offering 'free appraisals' do not really appraise your art. They give you estimates of what they think your art will sell for at their sales.

CAN ANYBODY APPRAISE ART?

A surprising number of people believe they can appraise art just as well as qualified appraisers, especially now that art prices are often accessible online. They take whatever advice they can get for free (we all know what that's worth), go online to see who's offering art for sale and for how much, post in discussion groups, maybe look in a couple of art-price databases, perhaps find a few lists of art prices and think that's all they need to price art accurately. But you know what? They have no idea whether the values they end up with are anywhere near the fair market values of that art. No matter how much information they find, if they can't interpret the prices they locate and apply them specifically to the art in question, they're no better off than when they started.

More often than not, they end up with casual ballpark figures, which may or may not have any relation to what the art is realistically worth, and that's fine for casual situations. But when actual money is at stake and you still have questions, whether you're on the buy end or the sell end, whether you've been shown an appraisal or not, consult a qualified appraiser or other knowledgeable, non-conflicted source before you act, not after. Qualified art appraisers are neutral professionals with no conflicts of interest who value art for a living and who work on your behalf to make sure you have the facts you need to make informed, intelligent decisions about art.

A LOOK AHEAD

An additional question to help you evaluate a work of art is, 'What other interesting facts can you find out about the art?' The answer to this question deserves its own chapter – the next one. When evaluating your selections, you need to know as many facts as possible about them, some of which may not be evident from simply researching the artist or viewing and evaluating the artwork itself. Particular works of art often stand out above others because of interesting incidental information and are more sought after by collectors than pieces that lack such information. In Chapter 16 you will learn what kind of information this is and how to go about acquiring it.

PROVENANCE IS PROFIT

WHAT PROVENANCE MEANS

You're standing in Triple-A Fine Arts Gallery considering a Vincent Picasso landscape painting for possible purchase. You have researched the artist, know the milestones in his career and what his most popular subject matters are, and have decided his art is worth collecting. You've studied a number of his paintings and have concluded that Triple-A's painting is a significant example of his work. You're done with your research. Right?

Not quite.

Additional facts about a work of art – facts not obvious from simply viewing the art, viewing other examples of that artist's work or researching the artist – can significantly impact on its value and collectability. This information is called *provenance* and includes printed, verbal or other forms of data relating specifically to that work of art's ownership history. Particularly with important art pieces, provenance can be a major factor in determining monetary value, historical significance and marketability. Though not always obtainable or necessary to possess, when you do have it, you must understand what it means, how to interpret it and how it influences value.

Provenance can be many things:

- A signed certificate or statement of authenticity from an art gallery.
- An exhibition or gallery sticker attached to the art.
- A sales receipt.
- A film or recording of the artist talking about the art.
- An appraisal from a recognised authority on the artist.
- Names of previous owners.
- Letters or papers discussing the art.
- Images of the art online.
- Newspaper or magazine articles mentioning or illustrating the art.
- A mention or illustration of the art in a book or exhibition catalogue.
- Verbal information related by someone familiar with the art or who knows the artist.
- Any data, in any form, relating directly to the art.

Provenance almost always increases the value and desirability of an art piece because, with it, more exists than the art itself. Let's say you own a painting that was originally commissioned by famous art patrons and hung in their personal collection. You own not just another artwork, but rather the one commissioned by the renowned Mr and Mrs So-and-so that hung on the living-room wall of their mansion on Main Street. The fact that your painting was commissioned, owned and maintained in an exclusive setting makes it, in a sense, a blue blood among paintings.

Proof that your art was executed by the artist who signed it is the most basic function of provenance. Even though the art is signed and looks authentic, additional documentation provides conclusive evidence that all is right. With the proliferation of forgeries these days, the fact that the art is signed and looks like a recognisable example of an artist's work does not always place it above suspicion. But having good provenance does. For example, you can't dispute a painting's authenticity when you have an exhibition catalogue illustrating the work or a newspaper article showing the artist standing next to that very painting.

Artists often generate provenance on their own and, as a result, influence the futures of individual works of art. Suppose a painter writes in his memoirs, or in a letter to a friend, that his *View of Slattersby Park* is one of his finest compositions. Even though some art critics may disagree, the Slattersby Park painting becomes exceptional among that artist's output because of the artist's documented opinion.

More unusual examples of provenance include documented incidents of controversy or intrigue. A work of art may have been stolen and recovered fifty years later, or have travelled across country in a stagecoach in 1856, been prominently displayed in a scene of a famous film or music video, or had other adventures befall it. Any facts or revelations that distinguish an art piece from all others created by the artist and make it more than just another painting or sculpture or etching or watercolour are what good provenance is all about.

Art galleries are well aware of the value of provenance. Given two comparable works by the same artist, one with good solid provenance and one without, the one with provenance will invariably cost more than the one without. Your task is figuring out what good provenance is and how much additional value you should ascribe to the amount and kind of provenance. You can overpay for inferior provenance the same way you can overpay for inferior art.

Let's examine and then analyse four hypothetical provenances that Triple-A Fine Arts could give you for their Vincent Picasso landscape.

Provenance 1: 'We bought the painting privately from a local collector who wishes to remain anonymous.'

Provenance 2: 'This painting hung in an American Art League show at the Boston Museum in 1989, where it won the Hubert D. Thorp prize for excellence in abstraction. It was purchased in 1990 by Peter J. Richard, an important New York art collector, and remained in his family until now. Accompanying the painting is a letter to Peter Richard from Vincent Picasso, dated 18 July 1990, stating that the picture is "the best abstract I have painted to date".'

Provenance 3: 'The woman who sold us this painting said the elderly man she bought it from told her the painting originally belonged to one of Laurence Olivier's best friends, a well-known art collector. According to the elderly man, the woman went on to say, it was supposedly one of Olivier's favourite paintings, and he always remarked on it when he visited that friend's home.'

Provenance 4: 'This painting once hung in the Presidential Suite of the Mayflower Arms Hotel, Detroit's finest accommodation from the 1940s to the early 1980s. From 14 to 16 June 1968, during their notorious *Rock the Solar System Tour*, the Purple Oranges, Britain's premier rock band at the time, stayed in the Presidential Suite. On the night of 15 June 1968, a wild all-night party convened two hours after the concert resulted in damage to the suite that exceeded $20,000. The Vincent Picasso did not escape unharmed. It received a minor tear when Bottomly Scrimpton, lead singer for the Oranges, threw a reproduction Ming table lamp at a cute but obnoxious groupie, and missed. The tear has long since been expertly repaired. Accompanying the painting is a signed statement from the hotel security guard who was stationed outside the door during the party, as well as photocopies of Scrimpton's letter of apology to the hotel manager for destroying the room and of the Purple Oranges' cheque for the painting's repair.'

How do you as a collector evaluate these four provenances in relation to what you are being asked to pay for the painting? Let's say that a good-quality Vincent Picasso, similar in size, subject matter and condition to this one, is worth $10,000 with no provenance. Now for the analysis.

Provenance 1: this is essentially no provenance at all, and as long as the painting is average-to-good quality and in good condition, the asking price should be $10,000. What you should get with your purchase is a signed statement or receipt from Triple-A Fine Arts affirming that the painting is an authentic Vincent Picasso. You should also receive a full money-back guarantee should the authenticity of the painting ever come into question, in the opinion of a qualified expert on the artist. These documents will become the painting's provenance.

Provenance 2: you've got an impressive history here. Vincent Picasso considered this painting to be one of his best, a jury of his peers concurred by awarding him a prestigious award at a significant national show, and a major private collector agreed by purchasing the piece. That sort of provenance should add at least several thousand dollars to the base price of $10,000 and possibly as much as $8,000 to $10,000 or even more, depending on how many other Vincent Picassos share those types of distinctions. On the high end, if critics, curators and experts concur that this picture is one of Vincent Picasso's greatest, an asking price somewhat in excess of $20,000 wouldn't be at all out of the question.

Provenance 3: what you're dealing with here is verbal hearsay. This provenance is valid only if the allegations can be investigated and confirmed. Otherwise, assume no provenance – and no increase in price above $10,000 – at all. Unless

Triple-A Fine Arts can provide specific names, dates, places or any other concrete information to support the woman's contentions, all you have is third-party gossip that may or may not be true. At the very least, you need the name of the woman, the name of the elderly man who gave her the information, and the name of Olivier's best friend and supposed well-known collector. As for Olivier's liking the painting, his preferences in art are basically irrelevant because he was an actor, not an art expert.

Be especially careful when presented with gossip or hearsay provenance. Sellers sometimes state it as though it's true and then charge more for the art because of it. No matter how good it sounds or how much of it there is, it's not valid provenance unless you can prove it.

Provenance 4: this is a good story. If you buy the Vincent Picasso and hang it in your living room, being able to relate that bizarre incident while showing it off to your friends does have a monetary value attached to it. Your friends would certainly be more entertained hearing about this moment in rock history than hearing the statement, 'Look at this wonderful Vincent Picasso landscape I just bought.'

Be careful how much you pay for this story, though, because it does not relate to the painting as a work of art, but only to the event, albeit a notable one. Assuming the object of Bottomly's indiscretion is average-to-good quality, in good condition and that the inflicted damage was minor as stated, the asking price could reasonably be increased by a modest amount, perhaps $500 to $1,500 at the very most, above the $10,000 base (unless, of course, your mission is to form the definitive collection of paintings damaged by famous rock stars, you're the major expert on the subject and you couldn't care less who Vincent Picasso is).

ACQUIRING AND MAINTAINING PROVENANCE

Make every effort to acquire and maintain provenance on all art you own. At the very least, be sure sellers give you signed statements attesting to authenticity, and whatever other relevant facts or information they have in their records, whenever you buy works of art. Keep individual files on each work of art you own, and save all pertinent receipts, guarantees, statements by the artists, exhibition catalogues and anything else relating directly to that art (for additional information about documenting your art, see Chapter 23). Each file becomes a part of the art it represents and should remain with that art for all time.

Take what the galleries give you but, at the same time, be aware that they have not necessarily had the time to uncover every single fact about every work of art that they sell. Depending on how fascinated you are with certain artists or art pieces and how industrious you feel, you may want to continue the job of acquiring provenance on your own. The more you find out, the better you understand the history or significance of what you buy, the more sophisticated and experienced you become as an art buyer, and the more your art may ultimately be worth.

Those of you who truly enjoy ferreting out facts should think of yourselves as detectives out to acquire the complete history of your art from the day it was created right up to the present moment. Trace its existence as far back as you can.

If you are buying contemporary art, the detective work is simple. Get a statement from the gallery and, whenever possible, a statement from the artist specifically relating to the piece in question, and you're done. Add to your file as new developments take place.

You have to work a little harder on older pieces of art with vague histories. For art by artists who are still living, contact the artists directly when possible. Email them images of what you own, and ask them to comment on it. If they're willing to communicate, ask them for general biographical information about themselves and their careers and, most importantly, any facts relating specifically to your art. Also ask any additional questions you have about the art and its origins.

When an artist is no longer living, contact anyone you know to have been associated with them or their art and specifically with the art you own. Locating these people is not always easy. Some collectors use techniques as sophisticated as researching family genealogies – online databases, death certificates, property records, probate files and so on. If you've got the inclination to check these sorts of resources, do so. It's a fascinating process, and you never know where you'll end up or what you might find.

Previous owners are another great source of provenance. Some galleries will give you the names of these people and allow you to contact them. When dealers won't name names (which is often the case), request that they contact those owners on your behalf, get whatever statements they can and relate them to you.

A sad commentary on the business of acquiring and documenting provenance on older art is that, in many cases, dealers would rather protect their sources than name names of previous owners or tell you what they know about the histories of the art. This dealer reticence comes about, in part, because of less scrupulous collectors who learn sellers' names and sometimes attempt to contact those sources themselves. They then try to buy directly, thereby cutting the original galleries out of the profit picture. Sadly, keeping provenance a secret is sometimes just good business sense for the galleries.

Families who sell their art may also wish to remain anonymous. The dealers with whom they work are not at liberty to reveal names because that was part of the selling arrangement. In any event, you still may be able to locate these people and acquire provenance. Your job is just going to be tougher.

When you are fortunate enough to make contact with a previous owner, an individual who knew the artist well, a retired gallery owner who used to represent the artist or anyone else who may have information you need, be aware that they sometimes overlook significant details about the art or never mention them simply because no one ever asked – so ask. By the way, these are also questions you should ask any gallery selling you art. Sample provenance-gathering questions include the following:

- *Where did you purchase this art?*
- *How long have you owned it?*
- *Do you know the names of any previous owners?*
- *Can you identify the specific subject, event, location or what it represents, or relate any other information about the piece?*
- *Do you know anything about when, where, why or how it was created?*
- *Do you have or know of any online information or printed materials relating directly to this piece?*
- *Was it ever in a public exhibition?*
- *Has anyone ever told you anything interesting about it?*
- *Do you or did you know the artist personally and, if so, what was his or her opinion of the art? What are they like?*
- *Do you know anyone else who can tell me more?* (You take these names and repeat the procedure.)

Additional, more specific or follow-up questions often arise as you pursue your investigations, but these will get you started.

Researching and acquiring provenance is rewarding in the long run because most discoveries you make influence a work of art's value upwards. On the flip side, lacking crucial information may result in art being undervalued. Many art dealers have sad tales to tell about selling artwork and then later discovering important, relevant information about it. Consider yourself fortunate indeed when you uncover something about an art piece that the person who sold it to you unwittingly overlooked; and the better you get at researching and locating provenance, the greater the probability will be of that happening.

Example 1

Provenance can be conveyed verbally, as well as in writing, which is how I acquired information about a painting by Frederick Judd Waugh, the famous American painter of coastal scenes. The painting's subject, a camouflaged merchant ship on the high seas *circa* the First World War, is not exactly a composition Waugh is famous for and, being atypical, not exactly desirable among collectors. The artist's fans prefer dramatic coastal scenes with waves crashing over rocks.

The written provenance consisted of the original owner's name and various lifetime addresses on the painting's back. Since I purchased the painting directly from this owner's estate, I had the opportunity to receive its complete verbal history first-hand from the executor who had been a long-time friend of the family.

According to her, Waugh and the original owner, also an artist, both worked for the US government during the First

World War. Together they researched and developed camouflage configurations for military and merchant ships. While working with Waugh, this artist invented the colour, 'Battleship Grey'. The painting had been a gift from Waugh commemorating their relationship.

The unusual subject matter was now understandable within the context of the artist's life and no longer a maverick, unexplainable composition. It fitted perfectly into Waugh's career as a historically significant work of art.

I subsequently sent a photograph of the painting to a curator of a maritime museum for further information. In his reply, he stated that it was one of the few extant full-colour examples of ship camouflage surviving from that time period. This meant the painting had historic naval significance also. The curator was so impressed by it that he requested it be donated to the museum and stated that, if donated, it would be prominently displayed in their First World War collection.

What initially appeared to be an atypical and, therefore, relatively unpopular picture with collectors, took on a whole new meaning with complete provenance. Because of the painting's significance with respect to Waugh's artistic career, as well as to First World War naval history, the tale accompanying the painting made the piece much more attractive to collectors than it would have otherwise been. Without this information, I would have been hard-pressed to place it in any collection.

Example 2

I own a painting by a well-known American artist who was active from the late 1920s to the 1950s. I liked it the moment I saw it, and I decided to buy it for my own collection. The only provenance the painting had was in the form of two pieces of paper glued to the painting's back: a museum accession sticker and the remains of another art exhibition label.

The complete sticker was from a local museum. The museum had apparently purchased the painting for its collection in the early 1930s, but had de-accessed the painting some decades later when it decided to go in a different direction with its collecting. The fact that a museum once owned a work of art is always a plus point, but what I discovered several years after buying the painting was an even bigger plus point.

One day, I was looking through an old handbook of this particular museum's collection, one that had been published in the early 1940s, and found, to my delight, that my painting was one of only several American pictures illustrated. I could conclude from this that the museum held my painting in special regard while they owned it. Not only had they considered it good enough to purchase, but they had also felt that it was one of only a few paintings good enough to be illustrated in the museum's handbook.

I continued to puzzle over the remains of the second label for several more years, trying to figure out what specific exhibition it was from. I eventually identified the show from the few words remaining on the sticker and, again to my delight, it turned out to be from a major international art exhibition that had been held in the late 1930s. My painting turned out to have a much more distinguished history than I was aware of, and in terms of monetary value, was actually worth substantially more than I had initially thought when I bought it.

A LOOK AHEAD

Suppose you have selected a work of art that, on the surface, appears to qualify for inclusion in your collection and that, according to the research guidelines you have been reading about so far, looks pretty good. Suppose, however, that it has either been damaged in the past, is prone to damage in the future or, worse yet, is an outright fake. In either of the first two instances, there's a distinct possibility you won't want to purchase the piece. That possibility becomes a certainty if the art happens to be a forgery.

The next two research chapters concern the topics of damage and forgeries. They are not topics that members of the art community – especially galleries – enjoy talking about, but they cannot be ignored. Inspecting any selection you make for damage and/or the possibility that it could be a forgery are the last two steps in your research before you address money issues and, ultimately, decide whether to buy.

CHAPTER 17

ART AND DAMAGE

Just about all art you see on display in galleries looks to be in perfect condition and looks as though it will last forever. Galleries make every effort to present their art to the public in top viewing condition. But what condition is it really in, and will you have problems with it after you buy it? These are important questions that must be answered before you spend your money.

Think of how long you expect the art you buy to last. A work of art is not like a car, a television or other disposable consumer product that, after a few years, you throw away or trade in and replace with the latest model. You keep art much longer than you keep other possessions. You may decide to sell it twenty or thirty years down the road. You may own it for fifty years and then pass it down to your children. They may pass it down to their children and so on. Whatever you do with it, you always want it to look its best.

Art dealers and galleries, unfortunately, don't do nearly enough to inform and educate their customers about condition, damage and the consequences of damage. Neither do they discuss the materials art is composed of, particularly contemporary art made with unusual or atypical materials. Only at the highest levels of collecting do dealers regularly discuss these topics with their clients. The average art gallery is in business to sell art. Since conversations relating to damage, condition problems and longevity issues are not usually conducive to making sales, such conversations don't usually happen unless they have to. Consequently, you have to arm yourself with appropriate knowledge in order to avoid problem art.

A substantial percentage of older works of art, for instance, have been subjected to various degrees of wear and tear over the years and been conserved, repaired or altered at various points during their lifetimes. Even though they appear to be in original perfect condition, underneath the gloss there may be histories of damage, condition problems and repairs.

Contemporary art can have problems, too. Just because you buy it brand new does not mean you'll never have to worry about it. Some pieces are not very well constructed and are predisposed to wearing poorly over time. Experimental materials might change or degrade or otherwise alter in appearance over the years. Dealers in contemporary art can often point out instances where art substantially deteriorated or otherwise changed in appearance after as little as only a few years in existence.

For example, several decades ago, artists were attracted to certain brands of water-based markers or 'water crayons' when they first came onto the market and used them in their art. Within five to ten years, the water-crayon portions of that art began to fade and, after ten years or so, they had faded so seriously that they had either totally changed colour or had almost completely disappeared. Early dye-based inks used in digital printmaking had similar issues. Artists now know to avoid these ingredients.

Contemporary art can also have damage repair, even though the art has only been in existence a short while. A gallery employee may have dropped the art on its corner while transporting it from the artist's studio to the gallery, it may have had coffee spilled on it, it may have repaired tears or abrasions, and so on. Artists can even damage their art in the process of creating it and, rather than start all over, repair or camouflage the problems themselves.

Whatever the situation and whatever the art, if what you are considering buying has either had problems in the past or has vulnerabilities in the present that will lead to problems in the future, you have to know about them. The reason is that damage decreases value. Art that has damage, is prone to damage or has suffered damage that has been repaired is worth less than art in perfect condition. It's that simple.

Damage reduces value in another way, also: you must pay to have it fixed. Art that develops problems over time or is damaged while you own it must be repaired, and those repairs cost money. Not only do they cost money, they often cost a lot of money. Art restoration and conservation is a highly specialised profession, and spending several thousand dollars to repair or restore an art piece is not at all unusual.

You should not automatically refuse to buy a work of art because it has damage, however. Damaged art is not necessarily worthless, as many people believe. For example, I once bought an old, torn, rolled-up canvas at a Texas junk shop for $7.50. The piece looked totally worthless to the shop's owner, but I had no trouble selling it several days later in 'as-is' condition for $2,500. The buyer invested several thousand more dollars in getting it restored.

The good news is this: *anyone can learn the fundamentals of how to inspect and evaluate the condition of any work of art on his or her own.* Whether damage has already happened or is yet to come, whether the art looks beyond hope or is in pristine condition, the better you are at assessing the art's condition history and, when necessary, its prognosis for successful restoration, the fewer problems and added expenses you will have to contend with in the course of your buying.

LEARNING ABOUT TYPES OF DAMAGE

No matter what kind of art you buy – oil paintings, etchings, bronze sculptures, watercolours, wood carvings, whatever – you need to learn what specific problems are associated with that type of art. You'll find that for every art form, an entire terminology exists for identifying and evaluating damage. For example, oil paintings can rip, tear, lose paint or accumulate dirt. Repair procedures include repainting areas of missing paint, closing rips and tears, and removing surface dirt. (The respective technical terms for these repairs are *inpainting*, *lining* and *cleaning*.)

If you're getting a little nervous and thinking that the subject of damage might be too difficult to understand, relax. You can get a good sense of the basics after only several hours of instruction. Then, after learning the basics, all you need to do is practise, practise and practise by looking at art and learning to spot problems.

The best teachers you can find are repair specialists called 'fine-art conservators' or 'fine-art restorers'. No matter what you collect, when it breaks, fades, dents, rips, yellows with age, cracks or anything else, an art conservator exists who knows exactly how to fix it. These people are trained experts in their particular fields of restoration. You can find out much of what you need to know by visiting and speaking with a conservator or two.

Locate fine-art conservators in your area by searching keyword combinations 'Art Restoring', 'Art Restorers', 'Art Conservators' and 'Art Conservation'. You can also get names by asking art dealers or contacting art museums. Museum references are especially good and, in fact, many larger museums operate their own full-time conservation facilities. Some of these institutions even provide formal instruction on the subject through occasional seminars or lectures. If you are in the United States, you can also visit the American Institute for Conservation of Historic and Artistic Works website (www. conservation-us.org) to access the group's membership roster, find out who specialises in the types of services you need and see whether any of their members are active in your area. Internationally, you can visit the website for the International Institute for Conservation of Historic and Artistic Works (www.iiconservation.org).

Assemble names from these various sources, and speak with the conservators over the phone. Tell them what you collect, and make sure they are experts at restoring it. Anyone with whom you decide to work should have years of experience and be able to provide you with adequate references. Assuming they are qualified, tell them you are interested in learning about damage and its treatment, and ask whether you can visit them at their studios. Most are happy to spend at least some time with you and show you first-hand how they work, especially if you're interested in hiring them.

While at conservation studios, make sure you do the following:

- See photographs of art in its 'before' and 'after' condition (you'll quickly realise that expert conservators can truly work miracles).
- See restorations in progress.
- Have conservators show you how to identify and diagnose existing damage as well as damage that has already been repaired.

- Have them show you or discuss specific problems that you could encounter with your art and what to watch out for.
- Find out how much each of those problems costs to repair (being able to approximate repair costs comes in very handy if you are ever offered a work of art that is not in perfect condition or may need periodic treatment).
- Learn what types of damage are easy to repair, which are difficult, and which are impossible.
- Pay special attention to learning how to recognise permanent irreparable damage. For example, paintings or bronzes that have been cleaned with excessively harsh solvents can have irreplaceable amounts of paint or patinas stripped off their surfaces. The better conservators can hide these sorts of problems, but they can never bring the art back to the original look that the artist intended it to have. Irreversible damage seriously reduces monetary value and collectability; avoid it at all costs.

Another way to learn about damage and condition problems, especially if you want to buy contemporary art, is from artists themselves. Have art galleries, art associations or museum sale and rental galleries recommend the names of artists who can teach you. As with conservators, speak on the phone first, make appointments and then visit these artists at their studios. Have them show what characteristics to look for in well-made art and how to avoid inferior pieces. Learn the difference between poorly constructed art and art that has been put together with quality materials by artists who know how to use them.

One important warning: never confuse artists with art conservators. Never ask artists to assess or repair damaged art, even if it is their own (artists who 'repair' their own art tend to rework it the way they think it should look now rather than reconstruct the way it originally looked). Unless they've had special training, most are totally uninformed about proper conservation techniques and procedures. Artists and art conservators are two entirely different professions. Artists create art; art conservators restore, preserve and maintain it.

HOW MUCH DAMAGE IS CONSIDERED ACCEPTABLE?

Experienced art dealers and collectors generally avoid art that has been damaged beyond a certain point. They also tend to avoid contemporary art that is not well made or that may be prone to developing problems over time. The most serious, investment-oriented collectors avoid damage at all costs, and prefer to buy art that is in its original, unaltered condition only and made of quality materials. The logic is clear: the more damage repair a work of art has or may need in the future, the less it is (or will be) as the original artist intended it to be, and the more it is (or will be) as the conservator has reconstructed it. In the extreme instance, some art you find for sale has had such severe damage that it is now primarily the work of the repair person and no longer that of the original artist.

Depending on the type of art, certain amounts of damage are considered minor and acceptable by most collectors; larger amounts become increasingly unacceptable and either significantly reduce or totally destroy the value of the art. What those precise amounts are vary according to factors such as the age of the art, rarity, importance of the artist and so on. For example, collectors of fifteenth-century Gothic panel paintings are more liberal in the amount of damage or restoration they consider acceptable than are collectors of contemporary oil paintings or watercolours.

Have art dealers – not conservators – teach you what amounts and types of damage are acceptable and not acceptable, how they affect collectability, and how they affect monetary value. Conservators want to restore art no matter how bad the damage is and are especially eager to get going when damage is severe. Repairing major damage is not only challenging to conservators, but also financially well worth their while. As a result, conservators tend to downplay the effects of moderate to severe damage on collectability or the monetary value of the art. Dealers, on the other hand, have substantially less conflict of interest here and give you more realistic assessments.

Two general rules can help you determine how the extent of damage affects the value of any given art piece:

1 *The greater the percentage of damage, the more value is reduced.* With most art, no damage is best; 5 per cent is usually considered minor, but beyond that point, things begin to get a little touchy (unless you happen to be collecting great rarities). Ordinarily, 10 per cent is about the maximum acceptable amount.
2 *The location of the damage is equally as important as the percentage.* A small amount of damage in the wrong place can substantially reduce or even destroy a work of art's value.

Consider, for example, a portrait painting of a figure against a black background. Let's say it's in perfect condition except for severe damage to one eye. Eyes are usually the most important details in a portrait and are crucial to understanding and appreciating the composition as a whole. When one eye is completely destroyed and has to be entirely repainted by a conservator, the essence of the painting is substantially altered and possibly even lost. That new eye will never look the same as the original and, thus, the painting's value is markedly decreased. If, however, that same percentage of damage is to the plain black background behind the figure and the rest of the painting is perfect, overall value is reduced only slightly.

INSPECTING CONDITION BEFORE YOU BUY

For every type of art that exists, a system also exists for inspecting and determining the condition of that art. You inspect oil paintings a certain way, watercolours a certain way, sculptures a certain way and so on. And you inspect everything, not just the front or the 'art part'. This includes the back, the sides, the bottom or any other details that are ordinarily hidden from view when the art is on display. Whether you buy period or contemporary art, learn proper inspection procedures for that art and always follow them before you buy. No matter what you collect, the general pointers given below will be of help.

Begin any condition inspection by asking the seller for a full condition report. When repairs have been made in the past, have the seller show you exactly where they are located and how extensive they are. Sometimes – not nearly often enough, but the practice is becoming more common – conservators provide full descriptions of their completed work on the art. This information includes what repairs have been made, how they were made, what chemicals or other materials were used in the process and photographs of the art in its 'before' condition.

Inspect the art using the techniques you learn from art conservators, artists and dealers. Always do this yourself, no matter how much information the seller gives you. You are the buyer; you deserve to examine all prospective purchases fully before buying.

How do you inspect for damage? Very carefully and closely. If you need a magnifying glass or small flashlight, buy one. Don't be embarrassed to study the most intricate details of an art piece. That scratch, chip or dent may be small, and that repaired tear may not be visible from more than two feet away, but they are there just the same, and they affect the value of the art.

Buy any specialised tools you may need to help check for damage. For example, a hand-held ultraviolet light is often used to inspect for damage repairs on old oil paintings, textiles, works on paper, glass and ceramics. Make sure you know how to use whatever equipment you buy before you try to use it to examine art you are considering buying. As always, it is best to have fine-art conservators, art dealers or other experts train you in proper use and inspection techniques.

Whenever you see any aspect of an artwork that you don't fully understand or that looks suspicious, ask about it. Whether it turns out to be damage repair or structural weakness or the way the artist intended the art to be, satisfy yourself fully before buying. If you have any doubts whatsoever about a piece, have a conservator independently examine it *before you buy*.

Be wary of sellers who give vague answers to your questions regarding materials or condition or, worse yet, discourage condition-related questions or examinations altogether. Your best option is not to patronise galleries where you experience such treatment. Unless you are skilled at inspecting the condition yourself and are willing to take the necessary risks, do your buying elsewhere. Whenever possible, get a written condition report and an accompanying guarantee that if the condition is not as it has been represented, you are entitled to receive a complete refund of the purchase price. This guarantee protects you from sellers who might deliberately misrepresent the condition of their art. Misrepresentation doesn't happen often, but it does happen.

MAINTAINING YOUR ART

Few people ever think of asking how to care for their art once they own it. They hang it on the wall or place it on its pedestal and forget about it. Years later, they discover problems and end up having to pay costly repair or cleaning bills.

Art has care and maintenance instructions just like anything else. Have dealers and conservators show you the best way to maintain yours. For additional instruction, read *Collecting and Care of Fine Art* by Carl David (New York: Crown Publishers, 1981). Also contact the American Institute for Conservation of Historic and Artistic Works or similar national bodies for advice and ask if they can recommend any publications you might read.

General rules for proper care and maintenance of fine art are as follows:

- Avoid excess dryness or humidity.
- Avoid exposure to direct sunlight.
- Avoid temperature extremes. An average room temperature of 70 to 75 °F is best.
- Avoid exposure to smoke from fireplaces, stoves or tobacco. If you have a problem with smoke, protect your art under glass or Plexiglas to save costly cleaning bills later.
- Protect art that has many intricate exposed edges or surfaces under glass or Plexiglas. Years of dirt and dust

accumulation on highly detailed surfaces can be costly, time consuming and sometimes even impossible to remove. Regular dusting does not necessarily keep dirt from accumulating on this type of art.

- Frame art using only top-quality archival materials, and have professional framers perform the work. Inferior frames, mats and other mountings can damage art over time.
- Never alter your art in any way for either protection or display purposes. For example, never cut down a painting in order to fit it into a smaller frame, never drill holes in a sculpture in order to mount a nameplate and so on. Alterations such as these substantially reduce collectability and monetary value.
- Inspect your art closely from time to time to make sure no problems are developing. Catch things early, before they get too serious, in order to avoid expensive repair bills.
- Never clean art using any chemicals (bleach, ammonia, window cleaner, paint thinner, furniture polish and so on). Use nothing more than a feather duster or a light-dry cloth (unless you are instructed otherwise by a dealer or conservator). Clean on a regular basis to prevent dust and dirt build-up.
- Never attempt to repair art yourself. Art dealers and art conservators can tell you horror stories of amateur repair attempts that reduced valuable art to worthless junk.
- Employ only qualified fine art conservators to treat your art – not artists, not your next-door neighbour who happens to be handy at repairing things, not any other amateurs who think they know how to fix it. If you damage your art or it becomes dirty with age, take it to at least two conservators, compare opinions on what needs to be done, on how treatment will be performed and how much it will cost; then get

the work done. Cutting corners by employing inexperienced or unqualified professionals or amateurs may save you a little cash in the short term, but such an approach could jeopardise the value of your art in the long run.

Example 1

I once attended an art opening for an artist who, at that time, had been painting for about ten years. He was showing a series of large paintings, priced between $3,000 and $5,000 each, done using a new technique he had recently developed. What was on the canvases was not really paint, but rather a heavily textured malleable substance that felt more like soft putty. The art looked great, but I had several strong reactions to it, all negative.

First, the paintings were unprotected. The slightest touch made an impression in the surface texture. Second, keeping the art clean would be extremely difficult. Even a light dusting would likely alter the putty-like surface. These problems could at least be avoided by protecting the paintings under glass or Plexiglas, but what if these paintings ever got damaged? Would conservators have the technology to repair them? Could they even be repaired or would conservators never be able to reconstruct damaged areas?

As if those worries weren't enough, I looked into the future and tried to imagine what would become of these pictures. Would gravity take its toll and eventually pull this substance down and off the canvases? Would the substance dry in five or ten or one hundred years and shrink or leave great cracks or exposed areas?

The artist had apparently not considered any of these potential outcomes. To me, spending thousands of dollars on one of these pictures seemed like something between an incredible risk and a complete waste of money. Sure, the art looked great at the moment of the opening, but more goes into creating art than producing temporary good looks. It must be made to permanently survive intact and retain the characteristics it was originally meant to have.

Example 2

Even standard household cleaners and polishes can destroy works of art. A collector I know completely removed the finish from a $3,500 metal sculpture simply by dusting it several times a month with a nationally advertised spray furniture polish and dust remover. The dustings gradually removed the finish along with the dust in a process that occurred so slowly that he did not realise what he had done until it was too late. The sculpture is now worth only several hundred dollars.

Example 3

Early in my career, I bought a landscape painting that I thought was in perfect condition. It was a little dirty, so I decided to have my conservator do a light surface cleaning. He took one look at it and immediately told me that something about it was not quite right.

At first, he wasn't sure what the problem was, but after studying the painting for a few minutes, he said he thought the sky looked a little funny. To him, it was painted in a style different to the rest of the painting. He proceeded to chemically remove a small area of the sky and, sure enough, the painting's original sky was underneath. Someone other than the original artist had completely painted it over.

My painting now needed to have the entire added sky removed in addition to the light surface cleaning. The surface cleaning would have cost $200 at most. Just to remove the sky would cost an additional $1,500, and once it was off, any damage to the original sky, if it was not in perfect condition, would cost hundreds of dollars to repair. My painting was not worth restoring, and I ended up selling it for less than what I had paid. I now know how to recognise when portions of paintings have been painted over by people other than the original artists, believe me.

A LOOK AHEAD

Related to condition inspection is forgery detection. Both involve close physical examination of art and both are often performed simultaneously. Now, more than ever, it is necessary for collectors to be fluent about the nature and detection of forgeries – the darkest side of art research. Chapter 18 will introduce you to the forger's art.

FORGERS, FAKES AND SCAMS

Ask any art dealer whether he or she has ever been taken advantage of by art forgers, and you will find that the answer is almost always yes . . . including me. Art is faked on a constant basis; anyone can be victimised at any time. The best forgers are skilled enough to fool even experienced professionals.

Forgers provide whatever collectors are looking for. They know which artists sell well in the marketplace, what their art looks like and how they sign. After carefully selecting works of art that have just the right look, forgers give those pieces fake signatures or documentation and the deception begins. Sometimes they even create them entirely from scratch.

Art collecting is more popular than ever and the internet provides more opportunities than ever for the unscrupulous to sell fake art. As a result, forgers and those who sell fake art are enjoying a good deal of success. These criminals have risen to the occasion and are hard at work keeping up with the increased demand. Now, more than ever, you take your chances when you assume that just because a piece of art is signed or otherwise stated to be by a given artist, all is in order. You've got to 'look under the hood', so to speak, and confirm for yourself that the art is being truthfully represented.

This does not mean you have to run around paranoid, never believing a single word sellers tell you. The great majority of art is authentic; the great majority of sellers are honest. Fakes, however, are a fact of the art business, and the less you know about them, the more likely you are to end up with one.

No matter where you buy art, you should be concerned about forgeries. Whether you shop exclusively at established galleries and are protected by money-back arrangements or you decide to explore alternative avenues for acquiring art like online auctions or classified ads, you could end up purchasing a forgery. However, adventurers who get the urge to wander outside established gallery settings, as many art buyers do once they get their feet wet, are particularly vulnerable. Flea markets, estate sales, traditional auctions, online auctions, online classifieds, antique shops, online fixed-price websites, travelling or transient art auctions or shows, and less established galleries are great places to look for art bargains, but they are also places where you're likely to come into contact with art forgeries.

No matter what your budget, you should be concerned about forgeries. You've probably heard occasional news stories about collectors being taken for a fortune by sophisticated forgers or about a valuable original being removed from the wall of a museum and a worthless copy hung in its place. Tales like these make great entertainment, but they're not characteristic of the techniques and methods of the average forger – the forger whose work you could well encounter as you shop for art. Art forgery is widespread and routine; forgers fake art in all price ranges, not only at the top of the market or expensive art by famous artists. Don't think you're safe just because you're not buying artwork by Picasso or van Gogh.

Be aware of the following three truths about forgers and forgeries:

- Forgeries are everywhere.
- Forgers fake all kinds of art.
- Forgers forge and sell art in all price ranges.

You or anyone else can take certain precautions to help identify and avoid questionable works of art, but a strong word of warning is in order here. *As long as you're unsure of your ability to spot fakes, stick with established dealers or venues that provide money-back guarantees of authenticity.* Buying art on your own without expert advice is always a risky proposition. Regardless of those risks, however, some of you are going to take chances anyway, so the balance of this chapter offers some tips and hints that might keep you from getting had.

KNOW YOUR ARTISTS

No matter where you buy or what you are buying, the number-one rule is to know your artists. An artist's style, subject matters, colours, favourite media, signature and other qualities of his or her art are as unique and individual as fingerprints or handwriting. Knowing what an artist's work looks like, how it is constructed, and how and where that artist customarily signs can protect you from buying a fake that happens to have his or her name on it.

The great majority of transactions involving forgeries could be instantly eliminated if only buyers took time to learn more than artists' names before heading out into the open market. Whenever you are offered art by an artist whose work you're not familiar with, locate known examples by that artist and compare them to yours. Also seek the advice of experts or authorities. Always do this *before* you buy.

HOW FORGERS SELL

Forgers have to sell what they produce, and they do so in a variety of ways. They victimise art dealers, private collectors, antique shop owners, flea marketers, gallery owners, estate liquidators and more. But nowhere can you come across more problem art than online, particularly at online auction sites, online classifieds and other platforms where private sellers sell art. To make matters worse, the most innocent-looking sale can have forgeries in it. Don't think you're safe just because you are buying from a little old lady who lives out in the country, far from big-city evils.

You, or anyone else, can come face to face with someone intentionally selling fakes (or unintentionally, but either way, the outcome is the same if you buy). The more skilled among them know all kinds of tricks including how to back you into a corner and limit your options in terms of deciding whether to buy. Here are several ways they work:

- They limit you from doing research by claiming that they don't have time to wait.
- They insist the art has been handed down in their families or that it was purchased directly from the artists, but have no tangible proof and offer no means of verification.
- They fabricate various forms of provenance, documents or certificates of authenticity.
- They distract you from normal research procedures by making you think you're getting great bargains.
- They tell you they have other buyers just waiting to buy if you don't.
- They claim to be either experienced collectors or reputable established dealers (usually private or online only) who have been in business for many years.

Forgers say whatever is necessary to fool you. Watch out when any aspect of a selling situation seems out of the ordinary or you feel pressure to act.

These days, forgers sell plenty at online auctions. They may also consign to smaller local or regional houses that don't employ full-time art experts, but even major houses get fooled from time to time. Online auctions, though, have become the main place where forgers ply their trade. At sites where sales regularly take place between private parties without supervision or oversight by specialists, for example, the forgers – not the online auctions – have total control over how their fakes are represented.

As with art dealers and antique shops that inadvertently buy and then sell occasional forgeries, auctions also innocently pass them on to private collectors. Auctions protect themselves with disclaimers, though – everything is sold 'as is', buyer beware. This situation makes auction buying, especially at small, transient, less established firms or at online venues, a risky venture for novice collectors. Unsupervised online auctions are particularly treacherous places for inexperienced buyers to shop. If you make a mistake buying art at any type of auction, *you* are generally the one responsible and not the auction house or website. (You can read more about auction buying in Chapter 24, 'Buying Art at Traditional Auctions', and Chapter 25, 'Buying Art at Online Auctions'.)

LEARNING TO DETECT FORGERIES

Learning to inspect art for signs of tampering is similar to learning how to evaluate it for damage, condition and durability problems. You should contact the appropriate experts – namely dealers, curators, experienced collectors and conservators – and ask them to teach you what to look for. Each specific type of art has a specific system of checking for authenticity, and you learn that system from experienced professionals or experts in those fields.

In order to distinguish a work of art that is totally original from one that has been manipulated in some way, you have to become familiar with every aspect of the art, not just the subject matter and the signature. You have to know it from top to bottom; inside and out; back, front and sides. With a painting, for example, you not only look at the composition and signature, but also at the framing, the back of the picture, the sides, the gallery stickers, the labels, writings or markings on any other parts of the painting or the frame, and so on. Every detail about a work of art is a clue to whether it is right. For example, if a painting by a particular artist looks good from the front, but the back looks different than backs of paintings by that artist normally look, this may be cause for concern.

Finding authentic originals to study and learn from is relatively easy. The hard part (and the important part) is finding forgeries to compare with those originals. Dealers are sometimes reluctant to show either images or actual examples of forged works, but you might be surprised at how many have one or two put away in the back rooms of their galleries or can tell you where to go to see them. Examine forgeries first-hand whenever possible and see exactly how and where the tampering has taken place. Encourage dealers, experienced collectors or other art professionals to show you examples and explain them to you at every opportunity.

Other ways to learn about forgeries include attending seminars sponsored by art galleries or museums, and reading about famous forgers and how they operate. For example, several major American museums have exhibited various

234

types of forgeries next to originals so that patrons and collectors were able to compare and contrast the different qualities of each. The BBC's *Antiques Roadshow* television series is another great resource for watching experts speak about forgeries. For you forgery fans who are intrigued by the topic, there is also the BBC series *Fake or Fortune* about trying to validate works of art. If you would like to do some further reading yet, two good books on the subject are *The Art of the Con* by Anthony Amore (New York: St Martin's Press, 2015) and *The Art of Forgery* by Noah Charney (London: Phaidon, 2015), and there are a number of other worthwhile titles as well.

Also contact the International Foundation for Art Research (IFAR). This non-profit organisation is dedicated to integrity in the visual arts and deals extensively with art theft, fraud, fakes and ownership issues. If you want up-to-the-minute news on the state of the art world's underbelly, visit their website at www.ifar.org. Their educational resources include information on art law, cultural property, provenance, collector information, programmes, events and more. They also publish the *IFAR Journal*.

SPOTTING THE ART AND CRAFT OF FORGERY

The great majority of forgeries involve manipulation of a signature. An old signature is altered or removed and a new signature is added. Or, if the art is unsigned to begin with, a new signature is simply added. Sometimes the art is actually by the artist whose signature has been added – it was originally unsigned and was then signed by a third party to increase its value – but this makes no difference. It's still a faked signature, and whenever someone other than the original artist signs a work of art without revealing that they have done so, you are dealing with a misrepresentation at best, and a forgery at worst.

Correct signatures should look natural and unforced, be located where the artist customarily signs, be in the colour or manner the artist customarily signs in, and match in other particulars such as how T's are crossed and I's are dotted. Checking a signature against an example online or in a reference book or signature dictionary sometimes helps, but just because the two look identical doesn't mean you should automatically assume the one you're checking is right. The forger could have copied the exact same example you're checking. You've got to go further and study multiple examples firsthand from a variety of sources, including book, magazine and online illustrations. Simply comparing examples online or in books is not enough. The best procedure is to study actual artworks themselves.

Beware of pencil or pen signatures on paintings, works on paper or sculptures (unless this is how the artists ordinarily signed). Forgers who are not very good at using brushes and paints sometimes sign signatures this way. With sculptures, for instance, writing fake signatures is much easier than carving or casting them. Even when such signatures are authentic, serious dealers and collectors may still tend to avoid them if they're not typically how the artists signed. They prefer signatures in the medium of the composition: oil on oil, watercolour on watercolour, gouache on gouache, wood carved into wood, metal sculpture signatures cast into the metal, and so on.

Make sure pencil or ink drawings are signed in the identical pencil or ink used to make the drawings. Sometimes a discrepancy between inks or leads is obvious; other times it is only visible under a magnifying glass or jeweller's loupe. The slightest difference between the ink or lead used on the signature and that used on the drawing often means trouble. Settle for nothing less than a perfect match.

Suspect signatures scratched into dried paint or sculpted surfaces. In these cases, you notice small chips or other irregularities around the lines forming the names. Usually, these are visible with the naked eye, but once again, magnifying names is a good idea. Scratched names are frequently added well after the art has been completed, not immediately after as is the normal procedure for any artist.

Check to see that names blend naturally with the rest of the art. Signatures that look out of place may have been added recently. For example, a name on an older painting or sculpture may look fresh and new, a name may be in a colour that seems out of place with the rest of the colours in the art and so on.

Sometimes original signatures are erased or painted out and replaced with different ones. Examine places where artists sign (usually the lower corners of pictures, bases of sculptures, margins of graphic works and so on) and see whether attempts have been made to alter or remove old names. Small areas differing in brush stroke, colour or texture often give this away.

Make sure names are spelled correctly. Surprisingly, this does happen! Artists themselves have been known to misspell, but you will most likely be dealing with a forger's error.

Watch out for paintings, watercolours and prints that are unsigned on the front, but signed elsewhere – perhaps on the back of the canvas, artist board, paper or stretcher bars. These pictures may be genuine but, once again, unless an artist is known for signing in locations other than on the front, watch out.

Art that is only initialled, as opposed to signed with a complete signature, can present problems. For one thing, forging initials is easier than forging entire names. For another, genuine examples of art produced and initialled by minor artists can be misrepresented as being by more famous artists who just happen to have the same initials. Here, the forger leaves the art exactly as it is. All he does is find a good, collectible name to match with the initials on the art and then claim that the work was done by the more collectible artist. Unless an artist is known for signing with initials only, exercise caution. (Similarly, forgers also misrepresent art that is signed only with common surnames like 'Smith' or 'Jones' and claim that it is by well-known artists who happen to have those same last names.)

Certain artists have names that are easily copied and often faked. Find out who those artists are from dealers and fellow collectors. Be especially careful when you are presented with art signed by those artists.

Some sellers have reputations for handling forgeries or forging art themselves. You'll learn who to watch out for the more involved you get with collecting. Art dealers and other art-business insiders are highly unlikely to name names or discuss the nefarious activities of others until after they get to know and trust you.

Some forgers do not sign names, but instead photocopy artist listings from reference books or take old newspaper or magazine articles and attach them to the backs of unsigned pictures, to the bases of unsigned sculptures and so on. The presentation may look official and indisputable, but no signature means no signature, and that's that. Additional proof of authenticity is required.

A variation on the photocopy or old-news-article ruse is the fabrication of official-looking documents or certificates that appear to authenticate unsigned works of art. Once again, the art is still unsigned, and unless these authentications are from respected experts or authorities, be very careful (of course, this information can be forged, too). If you have any doubts, get the art (as well as the documentation) re-evaluated by experts or professionals you know and trust before you decide to buy.

Don't assume that provenance automatically makes a work of art genuine. Some forgers list names of auction houses or galleries as previous owners with the insinuation being that because these establishments owned or handled the art, it is genuine. This is not necessarily the case, especially when these previous owners or sellers are not authorities on the art or artists in question, or the histories of the art previous to them owning it is not known. A fake is a fake no matter how many previous owners or sellers it's had.

Beware of unsigned works of art that identify the artists only by nameplates on the frames of paintings, the bases of sculptures and so on. Anyone can purchase beautiful, custom-brass, antiqued nameplates and have them engraved in any manner and with any artist's name. No matter how impressive the nameplate, the art is still unsigned and you need more proof.

Framing, backing, glass or special mountings and display cases are sometimes used to disguise forgeries and make close inspection difficult. Sealing the back of a picture, for example, may hide a new canvas that has been painted to look old. Enclosing a bronze in a Plexiglas case may make it difficult to tell whether it is an original or a recast. If you have questions, request permission to remove the art from its frame or case and examine it up close.

Pay attention to the asking price. Forgers often entice victims by offering big-name art at extremely cheap prices.

When the price seems to be a bargain and the seller is well aware of this, the reason could be that the art is a forgery. Sellers are rarely inclined to give valuable (or even potentially valuable) art away at bargain prices unless something is amiss.

Watch out for 'verbal' forgeries. This is the easiest way of all to fake authenticity. All a seller has to do is show you an unsigned work of art and insist that a particular artist did it or that it looks remarkably like the work of that artist. Unless that seller is a recognised and accepted authority on the artist and is willing to put all statements into writing along with an unconditional money-back guarantee, avoid the art.

Watch out when unsigned art is 'attributed' to well-known artists. Phrases such as 'attributed to', 'school of', 'manner of' and 'style of' are sometimes used to describe works of art, particularly at auctions. No matter which of these phrases a seller uses, the art is *not* by the artist in question. The seller is only stating that it looks like it could possibly be by the artist in question. Always pay substantially less for an attributed work of art than you would for a genuine one (unless you know something the seller doesn't). Also make sure the person doing the attributing is a recognised authority on the artist because, otherwise, the attribution is meaningless. Many dealers and experienced collectors avoid attributed works of art altogether. Three good questions to ask anytime you are considering buying attributed art (which you generally shouldn't), are these: 'Who made the attribution?' 'What are their qualifications for making that attribution?' 'What specific facts about the art are the basis for that attribution?'

In extreme cases, everything is faked. A nameplate is added, a special pedestal or frame is constructed, a signature forged, fake gallery or exhibition stickers are added, and a date, title or inscription is written or glued to the back or base. Do not assume that just because so many details point to the authorship of a particular artist that the art is automatically genuine.

Watch out for forgeries that were faked decades ago and have been on and off the market ever since. Forgers have faked art by a surprising number of artists for many, many decades. In certain cases, particularly with more famous artists, forgers began faking their art even while they those artists were still living (as they now do with some of today's most recognisable and collectible names). Be aware that older forgeries are among the most difficult to detect. Learn from galleries and dealers who specialise in the art you buy which artists' works you should be the most cautious about buying. As always, if you have any doubts about any work of art you are thinking about buying, consult a recognised professional who is knowledgeable about the life and work of the artist.

As you can see, forgers manipulate in many ways, so thoroughly inspect all details of any art you're not 100 per cent sure about. Never shortcut the inspection procedure; get outside expert opinions whenever you have questions. And don't try to be too clever, especially when you're buying out there in the wilds. That bargain you think you are sneaking past some unsuspecting dealer may well be bogus.

SOME METHODS FOR INSPECTING PAINTINGS

Inspecting signatures on paintings in darkened surroundings under ultraviolet light is a relatively common practice. Forged signatures sometimes 'fluoresce' or appear to float above the rest of the composition. Art dealers, conservators and other experts can teach you how to examine art under ultraviolet light.

Infrared rays are also used to inspect paintings. This technique, known as 'infrared reflectometry', involves the use of a special video camera that transmits pictures of an infrared exposed painting onto a television screen. Infrared reflectometry can detect previous restorations, paint inconsistencies and sometimes act like an X-ray to identify paintings under paintings.

Pocket microscopes (those that enlarge details in the range of anywhere from thirty-two to a hundred times) sometimes come in handy when examining paintings. As paintings age, the paint tends to shrink and surface cracks eventually appear. Many cracks are so small that they are not visible to the naked eye. These 'hairline cracks' are visible under microscopes, however, and studying the cracks around a signature helps to determine whether that name is as old as the painting itself or has been recently added (forged). Old, original signatures hairline-crack right along with the rest of the paint. Newly added names, on the other hand, do not show cracks and appear to rest over the original hairline cracks. The paint of a faked signature can also 'bleed' into adjacent hairline cracks. Have professionals show you how to use a hand-held microscope to recognise these and other signature problems or inconsistencies before you go out diagnosing paintings on your own.

Chemical detection and examination techniques also exist for identifying forged or tampered-with paintings. Solubility tests, for example, have to do with how quickly paint dissolves in certain chemical solutions. Basically, paint that dissolves quickly in mild solvents tends to be newer. Paint that dissolves slowly is older. For example, if a paint sample from a signature that is supposed to be a hundred years old dissolves easily, that signature could be forged. *Never* do any sort of solubility testing or chemical analysis on your own – only expert conservators and similarly qualified technicians and investigators know how to do it properly.

Pigment identification is another test conservators and investigators use to identify problem art. Usually, this is done using a technique called 'polarising microscopy', which involves studying the way paint samples look under a microscope when exposed to polarised light. If a painting is signed and dated 1889, for example, but polarising microscopy reveals that the signature contains a pigment that wasn't invented until 1930, something's obviously not right. Another situation where authenticity could be questioned is when signature pigments don't match those of the rest of the painting. Once again, only qualified professionals should perform these types of tests.

FORGED LIMITED EDITION PRINTS

Prints are easier to doctor than most other works of art because only pencil signatures need to be added. Forged signatures on prints are also more difficult to detect than those on other types of art because just about anyone with writing skills and larcenous intent can practise signing a particular artist's name five hundred or a thousand times and get reasonably good at it. Forgers who forge print signatures do not have to worry about mixing special paint colours, camouflaging existing signatures, matching special pencil leads and so on. A few seconds with an ordinary everyday pencil is often all that's necessary.

Forgers manipulate prints in several ways, the main one being that they add signatures to unsigned prints. Unlike paintings and other works of art, prints with fake signatures are usually the work of the artists whose names they bear; the print may be an authentic image by the artist, but the signature is not. So, don't automatically believe, for example, that just because an authentic Picasso, Warhol or Dalí lithograph happens to have what appears to be Picasso's, Warhol's or Dalí's signature on it that these artists actually signed them. You may need to consult an expert.

One of the more common techniques of print forgery is for forgers to remove or cut out unsigned original lithographs or high-quality reproductions of original art by famous artists from deluxe books, magazines or portfolios and then fraudulently sign them. Some forgers even cut worthless illustrations out of ordinary books, magazines or portfolios, forge signatures on them, and offer them for sale as original hand-signed limited edition prints or lithographs. Sometimes these prints are even accompanied by bogus certificates of authenticity. Book, magazine and portfolio prints are usually smaller in size (about the size of book or magazine pages) and usually have no margins. If you are offered such a print that is signed by a famous artist, ask the seller whether the print was originally published as a stand-alone, signed limited edition or was instead part of a book, magazine or portfolio. If he answers the latter or is otherwise unclear or evasive about where the print came from, watch out.

Copy-print reproductions (see Chapter 2) of original prints by famous artists are sometimes marketed as hand-printed originals. Here, the prints are either signed with fake signatures and sold as originals or are left unsigned, 'verbally' doctored and sold as originals. Copy-print reproductions of prints have decorative value only, no matter how famous the artists are and whether or not they're hand-signed. For example, a signed original Picasso lithograph might be worth $30,000. That same lithograph unsigned might be worth anywhere from $200 to $2,000. A copy-print reproduction or illustration of that lithograph cut out of a book or issued as an unlimited mass-market print would be worth under $100, often significantly under.

Have print experts show you how to recognise the difference between reproductions or copy-prints and originals. One way to tell an original is to look for the 'plate impression' around the image of the print. When the plate containing the original image is pressed onto the paper by a printing press, the pressure is so great that the paper under the plate is compressed, thereby leaving a border, visible to the naked eye, in the shape of the plate. Copy-prints and book illustrations are rarely pressure-printed with plates and, therefore, lack plate impressions and have a uniformly flat appearance.

Most reproduction prints are composed of dot-matrix or inkjet printer patterns – much like newspaper or magazine illustrations – while originals are not. When you magnify reproductions, you see series of tiny dots or dot patterns. When you magnify originals, you don't. Certain digitally reproduced prints, however, do not show dot-matrix patterns and can be more difficult to detect (but they won't show plate impressions either). Whenever you have any doubts, check with experienced print dealers or related professionals, in addition to the sellers themselves, *before buying*. An excellent resource for locating reputable print dealers is the International Fine Print Dealers Association (IFPDA). For information about the organisation and a list of their members, visit their website (www.ifpda.org).

Problem prints are especially pervasive online, particularly on eBay. The most faked signatures are those of Modern Masters like Picasso, Chagall, Miró, Dalí and Matisse, but signature problems extend well beyond them. eBay is an exceptionally risky place to shop for art by famous artists if you're not an experienced buyer, but for those of you who insist on doing so or who like to beat the bushes at other risky venues like flea markets, offbeat auctions or estate sales, here are some additional problem print pointers to keep in mind:

- The most common sources of excised prints are *Derrière le Miroir* (portfolios), *Verve* (periodicals), *XXe siècle* (periodicals) and books called *catalogues raisonnés* that list and show the complete prints of famous artists, like those of Warhol, Chagall, Picasso and Miró. If these publications are mentioned in descriptions of prints, this very likely means they have been removed from books or portfolios and signed with fake signatures. Most knowledgeable dealers will tell you that famous artists like those mentioned above rarely signed prints that were originally published in books, periodicals or portfolios.

- Beware of vague explanations like the print came 'from a major estate', or 'from a well-known collector', or 'was purchased in a bulk lot from the publisher', or came from 'a Beverly Hills [or other impressive location] gallery'. Claims such as these are not adequate proof that a signature is genuine unless accompanied by solid documentation.

- Sometimes prints are removed from art gallery exhibition catalogues and signed. These may be even smaller in size than prints cut from books.

- Prints that are described as being heliogravures or photogravures are not original prints but rather reproductions of originals. The two names may sound impressive, but they are nothing more than photo-reproduction techniques. Furthermore, artists rarely hand-signed them.

- Double-page prints, particularly those removed from *Derrière le Miroir* portfolios, often have visible creases or folds down their centres, although sometimes these creases have been pressed out and are difficult to detect unless you look closely. Other multiple-page prints may have as many as three or four creases. Always check prints for creases because this is generally a good indication they have been removed from books or portfolios and signed with fake signatures.

- Signatures on prints and lithographs removed from publications are often in the compositions themselves (since the images were usually published without margins). Be wary of any hand signatures in the compositions themselves as this is atypical; the overwhelming majority of genuine limited edition prints are published with margins and then signed (and often numbered) in those margins.
- Sometimes a seller represents a print as being 'signed in the plate'. This does not mean that the print is hand-signed, but only that it was printed with a signature already on it. Do not confuse hand-signed with 'signed in the plate'. Prints that are sold only as being 'signed in the plate' are nowhere near as valuable as those that have been signed by hand.
- Some prints are posthumous impressions – printed after the artist is dead. These are also commonly referred to as 'restrikes'. For example, a recent impression of a Rembrandt etching made from an original plate has nothing to do with Rembrandt. Rembrandt died in 1669 – well over three hundred years ago – and has had no involvement whatsoever with this restrike. And, of course, a posthumous impression hand-signed by the artist (not all forgers check artist death dates before they fake the signatures) would be proof of life after death.
- Some prints are created by other artists or publishers 'after' the original images by the original artists. In other words, another artist makes a copy of a print, drawing or painting by a famous artist. Copies or reproductions of art by famous artists typically have only decorative value and are almost never signed by those original artists.
- Prints removed from books, magazines or portfolios may be painted, coloured or otherwise embellished by hand as well as signed with fake signatures. This is not a common occurrence, but it does happen.

- Exhibition posters from museum or gallery shows of art by famous artists may have signatures that are not authentic. Beware of any poster that was originally published unsigned and is now signed.

FORGED SCULPTURES

The most common problem encountered when buying sculptures is identifying whether you are being offered a reproduction or an original. Most art dealers tell you when they are offering reproductions, also known as 'restrikes' or 'later castings', but others simply say nothing. If you don't ask, they won't necessarily volunteer the information.

Another problem with sculptures is known as 'posthumous casting'. This means that a sculpture is cast from an artist's prototype after the artist has died. Or it is cast from a cast made from an original sculpture. Often these are produced without skilled supervision and without the knowledge of the artist's descendants or estate executors. As with reproductions, less scrupulous sellers may attempt to market these later or posthumous castings as originals.

A relatively recent development in sculpture forgery is the replacing of minor names on sculptures with those of major artists during an actual casting process. In this type of forgery, bronzes by minor sculptors are recast from old castings. But before the recasting, original signatures are covered over or filled in and replaced with more important names. This used to happen only on rare occasions but has become somewhat more prevalent.

Learn how to evaluate sculptures from reputable established sculpture dealers, or even sculptors themselves. They can show you how to recognise differences between later castings or inferior reproduction castings and originals. The evaluation techniques that dealers can teach you include ways to tell the difference between new and old patinas, ways to compare variations in detail between originals and reproductions, and how to spot other tricks that forgers use to make new sculptures look like older originals.

Example 1

I've bought forgeries. In fact, I've bought them on several different occasions, each time under different circumstances. I'll recount three incidents of who took me, what I bought and how I got taken, or, as I prefer to think of it, how I took myself.

First incident

Who took me: The owner of a small-town antiques shop.

What I bought: Two paintings by well-known American artists.

How I got taken: The paintings were way under-priced, and I was more interested in getting bargains and maximising my profit than in examining the paintings and requesting provenance. I asked the seller no questions about the art because I didn't want him to suspect that he was selling so cheaply (clever me). I figured I was safe because he was way out in the country, appeared to know little about art and seemed like an innocent antiques dealer who just happened to have miscellaneous paintings hanging on his walls. He turned out to know a lot more than he let on. He was a forger well known among established dealers, and who had sold many fakes during his career. I did not discover that my paintings had forged signatures until well after this dealer had closed up his shop and moved on. He left no forwarding address.

Second incident

Who took me: A local art dealer.

What I bought: A small painting by a well-known American artist.

How I got taken: I was familiar with the style and signature of this artist. At a glance, all looked right. The painting matched perfectly in both respects, so I felt no need to examine it in depth, plus the fact that I trusted the seller. When I got home, I realised the artist's name was spelled wrong. I then took a look at the name under ultraviolet light, and it 'floated', as some fake signatures do. I returned the painting the next day, and the dealer gladly refunded my money. I later found out he too had a long-standing reputation for selling art with fake signatures. This was an excellent forgery, by the way; I still think about how good it was except for that spelling error.

Third incident

Who took me: A seller who found my name online and emailed me about a painting he had for sale.

What I bought: A painting signed by a well-known American pin-up artist.

How I got taken: I was quite familiar with the artist, but had never seen any examples of his work first-hand. I asked the seller how he knew the painting was authentic. He gave me a somewhat vague story about how he had purchased it at a small local auction, intimating that they had no idea what they were selling. I believed him and bought the painting. It looked good to me. The signature, the quality of the work and even the back looked like they came from the right time period. I offered it to a local collector and made the sale. A week or two later he called to tell me that he had contacted an expert on the artist and the expert told him it was a fake.

Sure enough, I followed up on his call, realised I had been taken and refunded the collector.

I subsequently contacted the seller and he as much as admitted he knew the painting wasn't right. But it was such a good fake that I offered to keep the painting if he agreed to refund a significant amount of the original purchase price . . . which he did. To this day, the painting hangs in my collection and serves as a constant reminder that I'm not always as smart and clever as I think I am. I also take it down off the wall on occasion to show people how talented and deceptive experienced forgers can be.

Example 2

Several years ago, word was out among dealers that a certain art restorer was faking signatures. His primary outlet was a small local auction house where he would put as many as five to ten forgeries through every sale. Dealers and experienced collectors knew which pictures to avoid, but no one had enough evidence to accuse the man directly and inform the auction-house owner about what was going on. In the meantime, plenty of unsuspecting 'bargain hunters' with no idea what they were bidding on were getting taken for hundreds, and sometimes thousands, of dollars per forgery.

I did occasional business with this restorer and, on one occasion, sold him a pleasant nineteenth-century landscape painting signed indistinctly in the lower right corner of the canvas. Some months later, the picture appeared for sale at the local auction house. The original signature had been removed and replaced with a new and more important one in the opposite corner. I saw the painting at the auction preview and had all the proof I needed to inform the auction house about what was going on.

The good news is that this restorer was permanently barred from consigning to that auction. The bad news is that he remained active as a forger for years afterwards. His work continued to show up at other locations, as he got better at covering his tracks.

Accusing, arresting and convicting forgers is almost impossible. In order to prosecute someone for producing forgeries, that person must literally be caught in the act of adding a fake signature to a work of art; that is, a third party must actually *witness* the signings first-hand. Keeping forged art off the market is harder yet. Works of art have been forged for hundreds of years; art forgery will never stop and, in fact, the proliferation of art fakes will most likely become even more of a problem with the passing of time. The responsibility for detecting and avoiding bogus art lies with you, the buyer. Make sure you protect yourself.

A LOOK AHEAD

This completes your basic course in art and artist research. At this point, assuming the initial selections you made during the course of your Part II art gallery and artist explorations are still under consideration after reading and applying what you've learned in Part III, you have only one additional detail to evaluate: the asking prices. If you're like the great majority of art buyers, you want to pay fair and reasonable prices for whatever art you buy. Part IV, the final part of this book, shows you how to determine what those fair prices are and explains how to go about buying the art once you have made those determinations.

PART IV: BUY

The relationship between art and money has become much more formalised in recent years than it's been in the past. An ever-increasing number of art prices are determined not arbitrarily, but rather according to documented pricing practices, asking prices and past sales results in the fine-art marketplace. An increasing number of people buy the art that they do for more than purely decorative purposes and, these days, whenever the word 'art' is mentioned, you can bet that the word 'investment' won't be far behind. Unfortunately, a good number of people take their art buying to extremes and buy thinking that they're buying assets or commodities similar to stocks, bonds or pork bellies. But this gold-rush-style hubbub does not mean you should blindly follow suit. You can still approach buying art with love, passion and common sense, *as well as* the wisdom to pay fair prices for the art that thrills you the most.

The final and, in many ways, most important step in buying art is understanding the selections that you are considering for purchase in terms of what you are being asked to pay for them and, in the end, buying them if they seem acceptable in price as well as according to all the other guidelines laid out in this book. Do not confuse this process with procuring art for 'investment' purposes. The goal of Part IV is merely to assure your fair treatment in the marketplace, nothing more, or, in other words, that you're getting good value and paying a reasonable price now. You accomplish this by acquiring a working knowledge of the general relationship of art to money, learning how to evaluate specific asking prices and learning how to consummate art-business transactions properly. As for the future, you'll just have to wait and see.

CHAPTER 19

THE ECONOMICS OF ART: AN INTRODUCTION

Art is a commodity, or as certain more investment-oriented sectors of the marketplace like to call it, an 'asset class'. This statement may sound crude, but it's the truth. Art is bought, sold and traded much like all other articles of commerce. The fact that money changes hands as art moves between artists and dealers and collectors requires that it be examined, at least in part, from a purely economic standpoint.

Fine art never starts out as just another thing to buy and sell. Its creation is one of the most inspired, personal and unique forms of expression known to humankind. It is the product of an artist's perspective, thoughts, feelings, experiences and the specific reality in which he or she lives. But the moment a work of art is completed and leaves the artist's studio, it becomes subject to many of the same laws of buy and sell, and supply and demand, as do other hard goods.

To begin, let's examine two fundamental truths about the art economy:

1 *Some art is worth more than other art.* Certain works of art provide us with more to look at and think about than other art. These works may be historically significant, unique in special ways, technically superior, the products

of pure genius, masterworks by great artists and so on. Collectors pay more for art with such distinctions or histories than they do for art that does not possess such levels of depth, significance or quality.

2 *Art prices can fluctuate over time.* The values of works of art do not necessarily remain constant over time, and they certainly don't only go up. Changes in value can be the result of general outside forces such as taste, fashion, hype or the overall economic climate. They can also be the consequence of progressions of events within particular artists' lives or careers or within the scholarly art community.

Dealers and collectors respond to these two phenomena by evaluating financial worth, as well as aesthetics, when they exhibit, represent or otherwise transact in art. Beauty, visual appeal and critical acceptance are considered in varying degrees right alongside price, demand in the marketplace and thoughts about projected financial performance over time. Dealers, of course, must seriously consider the financial implications of all art that they sell because they have to sell enough of it in order to stay in business.

Some collectors place a similar emphasis on the money aspects of art; others buy or collect primarily because they love art and don't care that much about the money. No buying pattern is right or wrong, better or worse. There are pure speculators and pure art lovers – and everything in between – buying, selling, trading and otherwise transacting in art according to their own personal feelings and beliefs about art and money.

The total of all of this activity results in what can be called the art economy or art market. Whether the art involved ends up in a museum, in a private collection, in an historical society, in a dusty attic or damp basement, or in the rubbish bin, anytime it transfers from owner to owner, monetary values are assessed according to certain criteria, and money in some form or other – cash, trade, tax-deductible donation, gift tax, etc. – frequently changes hands. But before learning what these criteria are and how to apply them to what you want to buy, you need to know some basic facts about the relationship of art to money.

THE LIQUIDITY OF ART

The first, foremost, and number-one truth about art and its relation to money is that art is not immediately liquid. Repeat: art is not immediately liquid. You cannot simply cash in the art you own like stocks, bonds or other investments whenever you feel like generating funds. Selling art takes time, sometimes months, sometimes years, and that's longer than many people who want quick cash are able to wait.

Art is more like real estate in terms of liquidity. If, for example, you put your house up for sale at a certain price, you have to wait until the right person comes along and buys it. You may get lucky and sell it quickly; it may remain on the market unsold for months.

Certain art galleries and dealers would like to make you think that art is instantly convertible to cash. But no matter what sort of profit-positive tales they tell, you take your financial life into your hands when you 'invest' non-discretionary capital in art with the idea that you can convert it back to cash at any given moment.

Many people are not aware of how *illiquid* art is. They don't realise that art galleries have to wait quite a while for customers to come in and buy what they have for sale. A small percentage of art does sell immediately, but the great majority takes weeks, months and sometimes even years to sell. Art galleries will tell you that, on average, a work of art takes between two and eight months to sell.

As for auctions, the art sales you read and hear about in the media may seem immediate – as if sellers are cashing in their art instantly – but that's not true at all. With auctions, you often have to wait six months or longer between the time you notify the auction house that you're interested in selling and the day you finally get your cheque in the mail. At worst, your art may not sell at all, in which case the auction house returns it to you and you have to try and sell it all over again somewhere else. Online platforms have considerably shortened the time period necessary to consummate auctions, but the prices you net when you auction art online tend to be unpredictable, uneven and frequently less than those you can net when selling through established galleries or auction houses.

Art is immediately liquid in one sense, though not a pleasant one. Most art is convertible to cash within a week or so but, unfortunately, you have to accept whatever buyers are willing to pay you at the moment you decide to sell. If you need money fast, you have no time to solicit or wait for acceptable offers. For example, if you have one week to sell a sculpture you paid $5,000 for and the best offer you get is $750, that's it. Either sell the sculpture or keep it.

The bottom line: *spend only discretionary capital on art.* Never tie up emergency funds or money you need for day-to-day expenses to buy art. That's an extremely high-risk proposition. And don't ever believe that art only goes up in value or will always be worth at least what you paid for it. Sometimes it does, sometimes it doesn't. Only time will tell.

UNIQUE ASPECTS OF THE ART ECONOMY

The art economy may resemble other economies in how sales are transacted and how works of art change hands, but it is very different in several important ways.

With art, no obvious relationship exists between price and product. Suppose you have three paintings that are identical in size, quality, subject matter, cost of materials, amount of time they took to paint and all other physical characteristics. The only difference is that each was created by a different artist. Even though all else is equal in physical terms, one painting may be priced at $200, one at $2,000 and the last at $200,000. Whereas the price differential between a Hyundai and a Rolls-Royce, for example, is based on concrete variables like manufacturing time, amount of labour involved in production, quality of materials and end-product performance, with art this is not necessarily the case.

No formal laws, standards or regulations exist for pricing art. People selling art can price it as high or low as they want, for whatever reasons they want, and change their asking prices whenever they feel like changing them. A seller can ask $100 for a work of art or $100,000 for it. Any price structure or reasoning is legal as long as the seller makes no intentionally false claims about that art and does not misrepresent it in any way.

Art is not subject to quality controls. No law requires artists to have produced art for a certain period of time, to be licensed or to reach a certain level of accomplishment before being allowed to sell their art (at whatever price they decide to sell it for). Anyone can claim to be an artist, anyone can create anything and call it art, and anyone can sell it.

What does all this mean? It means you've got to be aware of the unique aspects of the art market and take them into consideration every time you evaluate an asking price. Explaining price differences between Painting A and Painting B, for instance, may not be as straightforward as explaining price differences between a Rolls-Royce and a Hyundai, but the differences as well as how they are arrived at can, without question, be explained and understood by anyone – including you!

ART AS INVESTMENT

Buy art because you like it, not for investment purposes. *Again: never buy art purely for investment.* Artists do not sit in their studios deliberating about how to create commodities that will compete well with stocks, bonds, oil futures or other artists' art. Monet did not wonder, for example, about how his Giverny canvases would perform financially over time or how they would compete against works of the Munich School. Don't insult artists or art dealers and trivialise their art by viewing it as currency.

Unfortunately, many buyers are attracted to art because they have either heard, read or otherwise become aware that certain works of art have substantially increased in value over time. They don't know much about art, but they do know they would like to make some money by owning it. The most unfortunate of these speculators end up paying highly inflated prices to unscrupulous dealers who talk only money and speak of art as the path to riches.

We are all aware that some art does increase in value over time and that many art experts and advanced collectors consider the financial ramifications of their purchases. But if you ask these people what attracts them to art above all else, money is always far down the list. If you also ask these people what percentage of art increases in value over time, their unanimous answer will be, 'Not very much.' The great majority of art produced on this planet fades slowly into obscurity. You'll have a much easier time, for example, finding an $8,000 work of art that will be worth $1,500 in ten years than you will have finding a $1,500 work of art that will be worth $8,000 in ten years.

And don't forget those pesky commissions you almost always pay when you either buy or sell art through a third party other than the artist, like an auction house, a website or a gallery. When transacting in stocks or bonds, commissions rarely exceed 2 per cent. When buying or selling real estate, commissions in the United States are usually in the range of 3 to 6 per cent. With art, paying a commission under 10 per cent to either buy or sell is rare (this sort of commission structure applies only to extremely valuable works of art). Commissions to sell art at auction normally range from 15 to 35 per cent; commissions to buy art at auction generally range from 10 to 20 per cent; commissions to either buy or sell art through galleries usually range anywhere from 20 to 60 per cent. Buying online is no different; commissions are generally worked into asking prices unless you're buying directly from the artist.

OK, maths hounds – are you ready for a story problem? Mr Jones buys a painting at Susan's Art House for $1,000, 40 per cent of which is Susan's commission for selling the painting. ($400 is Susan's profit; the remainder, or $600, is what Susan has to pay for the painting.) Now if Mr Jones were to return to Susan's Art House several months after purchasing the painting and ask Susan to resell it for him because he needed the money, she would again likely price the painting at $1,000 and take her standard 40 per cent commission, meaning she would pay Mr Jones only $600 when it sold, or a 40 per cent loss over what he originally paid.

Or let's say several years later, Mr Jones decides to sell the painting at Bill's Auction Company and to pay Bill a 20 per cent commission for making the sale. Buyers at Bill's Auction Company pay Bill a 20 per cent commission above and beyond the hammer price (what the painting sells for). So, here's the question: how much does Mr Jones's painting have to increase in value, beyond what he originally paid for it, in order for him to break even when Bill sells it?

OK, time's up. It has to increase in value by 45 per cent or, in other words, be hammered down at $1,250 (Mr Jones paying $250 of that to Bill), then add to that the buyer's premium of 20 per cent ($200 paid to Bill by the buyer) for a total selling price of $1,450.

Either way, not a great outcome for Mr Jones, but the good news is that any reputable gallery or dealer will tell you that if the art you buy happens to go up in value, that's great and you're fortunate. If it doesn't, that's fine too because it will continue to beautify and enrich your environment and provide you with pleasure for as long as you own it. In other words, buy art for art reasons, not money reasons.

WHY SOME ART INCREASES IN VALUE

Only the very best art is destined for fame, fortune and financial stardom. When you read in the major art publications and websites or hear on the news on mass media, for example, that 'art' has increased in value by a certain amount per year over the past so many years, know that they're referring to a very skewed sample, namely the best works of art by the world's best artists. They do not mean every piece of art by every artist that has ever been produced.

Art that increases in value does so based on a consensus of acknowledged art experts and professionals such as museum curators, critics, influential art dealers, major collectors and art scholars who regard it as significant in some way and agree that it should be recognised, honoured or distinguished above all other art. For example, when a major museum decides to put on a one-person exhibition of a particular artist's work, anything that artist has done in the past or will produce in the future tends to increase in value. The museum show focuses attention on the artist, legitimises the art in the eyes of the art-buying public, attracts new collectors and, in general, increases demand for the artist's work. Art that is 'worth more' in the opinion of the experts also tends to be worth more in terms of money.

A distinction must be made here between real and artificial increases in value. Real increases, as stated above, have to do with general agreement among experts in the art community that certain art has merit above and beyond most other art. Artificial increases have to do with art galleries or artists arbitrarily raising their asking prices or making claims regarding the collectability of their art, either for no apparent reason or for reasons they concoct on their own, independent of what the majority of the art community thinks.

For example, suppose you walk into Triple-A Fine Arts Gallery and see a limited edition print. The asking price is $3,500. The gallery owner tells you that only last year the print could be purchased for $1,750. When the edition sells out, she adds, the price will go even higher, and that art by the artist is on its way to becoming highly collectible in the future.

Assume the increase in value is artificial – not real – and that the claims of continued appreciation in the future are tenuous at best if the artist has not accomplished anything over the past year. Nor does the increase have much basis in fact if no significant career events are on the artist's near-term horizon, there has been no dramatic increase in demand for his art, if no one in a position of authority or influence has recently recognised the artist for outstanding achievements, and if no other outside evidence can be presented to substantiate the gallery owner's statements. Assume instead that she has simply decided to increase prices in an attempt to influence the artist's market on her own. She may totally believe every word she tells you about the artist's bright future, but unless the art community agrees, she's doing little more than hoping.

Sooner or later, art that has been artificially inflated in price or marketed as collectible when, in fact, it's not, deflates back down to realistic levels. Art that increases in value based on artists' tangible track records of accomplishments, on the other hand, tends to hold or even increase in value. Only the passage of time combined with continued progressions of accomplishments together with positive assessments by art experts, not hype or self-declarations, determine what is great in art, what increases in value and what is destined to be forever forgotten.

A LOOK AHEAD

Individual works of art can be categorised in terms of how well known the artists are, how significant they are in relation to all other art produced by the artists, how early or late they were produced in the artists' careers, how long the artists have been producing art, how much art the artists have yet to produce, and how much art the artists have already produced. All of these variables influence art values. The next chapter takes a more in-depth look at the relationship between art and money.

CHAPTER 20

MORE FACTS ABOUT ART AND MONEY

On the most fundamental level, a work of art can be categorised in terms of its age. Older art is generally referred to as antique or period art; newer art is referred to as contemporary art. Period art is generally associated with artists who are either no longer alive or with living artists who have completed the majority of their careers. Contemporary art is associated with living artists who have significant percentages of their careers still ahead of them. An artist who has either completed, or is close to completing, his or her career has basically produced all the art that he or she will ever produce. Contemporary artists, on the other hand, have yet to produce dozens, hundreds or even thousands of works of art, depending on the artist, the rate at which he or she produces art and the number of productive years remaining in his or her career.

Period art, because it exists more or less in fixed quantities and is older, is evaluated differently from a financial standpoint than is contemporary art, which is newer and steadily increases in quantity. Additional factors such as expert opinions, fame of the artists, fashions and trends, and tastes of collectors also affect the way art is evaluated from a financial standpoint, but a significant degree of art-market activity can be explained directly as a function of the age of the art and the passage of time. Suppose, for example, that two career artists, Bruce and Sharon, are equally respected in the art community, their art is equally in demand by collectors and art by both artists sells at the same rate. Let's say that Bruce and Sharon have each produced one thousand works of art, but Bruce is retired – one thousand works of art is all that he will ever produce – and Sharon is still in the prime of her career and will continue to produce art for several decades to come.

Each time a collector buys a work of art by Bruce, the total number of his artworks remaining in the marketplace decreases by one. This is not the case with Sharon, however. Assuming that she produces at least one work of art for each one that she sells, the total number of her works on the market during her active career either remains constant or increases. Bruce's art becomes scarcer with the passage of time; Sharon's art does not. As a result, collectors must become increasingly competitive to own Bruce's art whereas with Sharon's art, all they have to do is wait for newly produced pieces to come onto the market. In monetary terms, and assuming all else is equal, selling prices for Bruce's art tend to escalate more, due to the dwindling supply and resulting competition than do selling prices for Sharon's art, which are inclined to hold steadier because supply remains constant or may even increase somewhat – she replaces her sold art with new art.

As Sharon approaches the end of her career as an artist, however, the values of her art will begin to fluctuate in much the same way that the values of Bruce's art have fluctuated. Her earliest pieces, which are constant in number (that is, she can never produce her early pieces again, but only brand-new ones), will begin to increase in value with the passage of time. As collectors buy up her early works, those pieces become increasingly scarce in the marketplace and, as a result, competition to own them becomes greater. Once Sharon completes her career, all of her art becomes subject to increasing scarcity and resulting price rises in the same way that Bruce's art has, assuming of course that the artists continue to be recognised and revered for their accomplishments.

I'm now going to take a big leap and, for the benefit of all of you readers who understand the *Wall Street Journal* or *Financial Times* better than you understand art periodicals like those listed in Appendix III, further elaborate on relationships between art and money by making several general analogies to the stock market. Art and stocks are somewhat similar to one another in terms of how old or new they are and how they tend to fluctuate in value over time. Art and stocks are also very different, however, in terms of their liquidity and in the percentage commissions that people pay dealers to buy or sell them, as you saw in the last chapter. Hopefully, you will not misinterpret the following comparisons to mean that art is the same as stocks and that you can go out and buy art in much the same way as you buy stocks . . . because it's not, and you can't.

Established dealers, experienced collectors, curators, critics and other respected figures in the arts community, of course, frown on analysing art from a strictly financial standpoint (as do I), but doing so provides a fundamental insight into how the art business works for people who don't know much about art, but do know something about money. And money must certainly be addressed because, although no one knows the total monetary value and number of artworks sold worldwide on an annual basis, that monetary amount certainly ranges into the billions, and the number of pieces sold easily ranges into the low millions.

Before we get started with the art-to-stocks comparisons, let's lay out the ground rules. The only art that can fairly be compared to stocks is art produced by artists who are recognised within the art community as having talent and as showing potential to become recognised for their accomplishments at one stage or another during their careers. The better known and more significant an artist becomes, the more the following analogies apply to that artist's art. Art by artists who are not well known, amateurs or hobbyists, who are not serious about their art and their careers as artists and who do not get involved with the established arts community, is not particularly relevant to the following comparisons. Now, before we get going here, remember this: *never buy art for money reasons alone. You'll end up disappointed far more often than not.*

THE SPECULATIVE GROWTH STOCKS OF THE ART WORLD

A speculative growth stock is that of a company that exists based primarily on a concept, such as an internet start-up firm. From a time standpoint, that company is brand new and their ideas about how to make money remain unproven over the long term. A business model is in place and employees of the company work to turn the company's concept into reality, but the company is most likely operating on borrowed capital and has yet to turn a profit. From an investment standpoint, buying a speculative growth stock is a high-risk proposition. The company may go bankrupt, as happens to countless start-ups, in which case you lose your investment. Or it may one day become part of the Fortune 500 – a far less likely outcome, but possible – in which case you're in line for early retirement when you decide to sell your stock.

The 'speculative growth stocks' of the art world are works of art by artists who are either fresh out of art school or who are otherwise just starting out in their careers, but who manage to attract the attention of various segments of the art community very shortly after beginning to show their work. These artists have progressive ideas about art, their art is fresh or new or original, it engages viewers and people get interested in what they create. Whether they can consistently bring those ideas to fruition in ways that ultimately resonate with the established art community over extended periods of time remains to be seen.

At present, these artists are totally unproven, they're just starting out, they've likely made little money-producing art, they probably do not make their livings producing art, they have not produced extensive bodies of work, and nobody knows at these early stages whether they'll become career artists or disappear into the ether. Of those who continue, few will ever become well known; far fewer than that will ever become famous. Over time, the large majority will either stop creating art altogether or will approach it as more of a hobby or pastime, and go into other professions – some art-related, some not.

From a purely financial standpoint, art by these artists tends to be inexpensive (or at least it should be) and, from a financial perspective, a high-risk proposition in terms of whether it will even hold, let alone increase in value over time. If you buy art by a relatively unknown artist who eventually succeeds, you usually do very well financially; if the artist fades into obscurity, so probably does the monetary value of your art. From a purely entertainment standpoint, however, buying art from artists who are just starting out is often great fun and a wonderful adventure. It's also a great way to support them when they need it the most. And the perennial upside, of course, is that no matter how the art fares financially, you hopefully bought because you like it, it enriches your life and it gives you joy when you look at it.

THE AGGRESSIVE GROWTH STOCKS OF THE ART WORLD

The two most important characteristics of an aggressive growth stock are that the company is growing rapidly and, at the same time, showing a healthy profit. Such a company tends to be smaller, younger and growing at a rate in the area of 20–50 per cent annually. From a time standpoint, the company's business model has not yet been proven over the long run, and the company's ultimate survival is still somewhat in doubt. From an investment standpoint, buying an aggressive growth stock is a relatively risky proposition. Growth may suddenly go flat or even negative, in which case you either break even or lose money. On the flip side, the company may continue its high rate of expansion for years, in which case you get to buy a larger house and more art when you sell your stock. Overall, the chances that the company will survive and that you'll retain and eventually profit from your investment are better than with speculative growth stocks, but still by no means a sure thing.

The 'aggressive growth stocks' of the art world are works of art by emerging artists. These artists tend to be younger and relatively early in their careers, but have survived beyond just starting out and being total unknowns. Most are making respectable numbers of sales, have either garnered gallery representation, participated in significant group shows or been otherwise recognised within the art community as having the talent and potential to perhaps one day go on to bigger and better things. Selling prices of art by these artists tend to be reasonable, but can also be on the rise due to their increasing exposure in the art community. The price rises are based on excitement and anticipation in combination with frequency of sales and belief among collectors that the artists have talent. They tend to be more rational and predictable than those of artists who are just starting out, but are still relatively vulnerable to fluctuations.

From a purely financial standpoint, the jury will be out on these artists for some years to come, and the chances they'll become well known or famous and sell their art for big prices are still relatively small. The monetary values of their art will depend on how consistently they perform in their careers and how well their work is received by the art community. Unless they become famous, their selling prices will in many cases ultimately level off and then fluctuate modestly – sometimes up, sometimes down – with the passage of time. From enjoyment or entertainment standpoints, the emerging-artist sector of the art community is a vibrant and exciting one where things can happen fast. And, as always, the upside to owning any type of art is that no matter how it fares financially, you bought it because you like it, it enriches your life and it gives you joy when you look at it.

THE CLASSIC GROWTH STOCKS OF THE ART WORLD

Classic growth stocks are those of well-known companies with established track records. These stocks tend to steadily increase in value, but not as fast as speculative growth or aggressive growth stocks can potentially increase in value. Return on investment over time is generally good as these companies tend to have quasi-monopolies and, therefore, significant control over their markets. Classic growth stocks are not particularly dependent on product cycles and are not affected that much by overall economic conditions.

The 'classic growth stocks' of the art world are the best works of art by artists who are established, well known and even famous. They have either completed substantial portions of their careers or are no longer living, and have been recognised as significant, influential or important by the art community for anywhere from decades to centuries. Like classic growth stocks, art by these artists also has quasi-monopolies in the marketplace. The art of Picasso, Warhol or Koons, for example, will never lose its place in art history, be displaced from museums and replaced with different art by newly determined famous artists that the scholarly art community one day decides are more important.

The best, most significant artists may or may not be household names, but their reputations – whether regional, national or international in nature – are well established within their respective areas of the art community and will remain so for all time. Their art is the art you see at museums, in major collections and at other significant public institutions; their names are the names you see featured on major online art sites and read about in art books. Their art sells at the best galleries and at the major auction houses around the world.

From a purely financial standpoint, art by these artists tends to be the most expensive art of all and also tends to steadily increase in value over time. In most cases, the amount of this art available in the marketplace is either tightly controlled by those representing the artists (or sometimes by the artists themselves) or tends to be decreasing in availability because, as mentioned above, many of the artists who create it are either no longer alive or are approaching the ends of their artistic careers and are, therefore, producing either little or no art. When this type of art decreases in availability or gradually disappears into private, public or institutional collections, this segment of the art business is basically a sellers' market.

Resale values of the best art are well documented in art-price references like those that you'll learn about in the next chapter. When a collector decides to sell such a piece, he's generally able to locate a willing buyer, most likely through an art gallery, broker or an auction house, without too much trouble. That buyer, in turn, often pays more than the collector paid for the art. At the risk of sounding boring, remember, once again, that the overwhelming majority of collectors buy great art not because it tends to increase in value, but because it's beautiful to look at, superbly executed, is among humankind's greatest achievements and continually enriches the lives of all those who appreciate it.

THE CYCLICAL NATURE OF ART PRICES

Art in general is similar to cyclical growth stocks in that both are sensitive to the performance of the overall economy. Art prices tend to fall when the economy slumps, bottom out and start to rise when the economy begins to recover, and continue to rise steadily during healthy periods of growth. The simple explanation for the cyclical nature of art is that it's one of the last things people need in order to survive and, therefore, it's one of the first things to get cut out of the budget when money gets tight or the economic going gets tough. With few exceptions, fine art is the ultimate discretionary expenditure, which means most people buy art only after they feel very financially healthy.

When the economy turns down, virtually no art is immune from devaluation. However, different types of art lose value at different rates. As mentioned above, the great art by the most famous artists is the most resistant to bumps in the economy, tends to drop in value the least and recovers the fastest. This relative invulnerability is related to the size, strength and wealth of its collector base. The wealthiest collectors almost always have adequate funds available and are prepared to compete and buy when the right work of art comes up for sale. And when it does, this may be the one chance they ever have to compete for a work of such great quality or rarity – weak economy or not.

Art by artists who are just starting out or who are not that well established in their careers fares less well in a poor economy. The more unknown an artist is and the greater the uncertainty surrounding his or her future as an artist, the more that artist's prices tend to fall when times get tough. In general, less well-known artists have weaker collector bases, not only with respect to solvency, but also with respect to commitment.

Mediocre works of art, no matter who the artists are, hardly ever fare well in a poor economy. In general, mediocre works of art tend to be owned by less experienced collectors who buy more by name than by quality and are not particularly committed to collecting. These collectors also tend to be more speculative, impulsive and fickle than are experienced, dedicated collectors who know how to recognise quality art, are willing to wait for it and hold on to it once they have it.

THE MYTH ABOUT HOW AN ARTIST'S DEATH AFFECTS PRICES

Many people believe that when an artist passes on, his or her prices skyrocket. This is a myth often perpetrated by art sellers who are OK with sometimes bending the truth and saying whatever is necessary in order to make a sale. The worst way to buy or sell art is based on financial considerations alone, and for a dealer to infer that an art sale or purchase should be based on an artist's age or health status is not only misleading, but also disgusting.

The truth is, in the overwhelming majority of cases, an artist's death has little or no impact on the value of his or her art. Most artists die of old age; all changes in the markets for their art have taken place slowly, sensibly and in an orderly manner for decades. Death comes as not much of a surprise to anyone and consequently, supply, demand and prices of the artist's art remain relatively unchanged.

The rare instances when death significantly impacts on artist price structures occur when artists are relatively famous, their art is higher priced, they're in demand and collectible, and, most importantly, they die suddenly and unexpectedly. During the time periods immediately following the deaths of Andy Warhol and Jean-Michel Basquiat, for example, the markets for their art became unstable and inflationary. Dealers and collectors were caught off-guard, they scrambled to buy up art that they had perhaps been only thinking about purchasing when the artists were still alive, a temporary buying panic set in and prices spiked in the upward direction. As time passed, however, panic buying subsided, prices gradually settled at realistic levels and the markets for the artists stabilised.

In some instances, an artist's prices can actually drop on the occasion of his or her death. For example, an executor or family member may mismanage an artist's estate by dumping all of the art on the market at once and, in doing so, temporarily flood the market and depress prices. Prices can also decline when the market for an artist's art is based more on the artist's personality, charisma, media profile, flamboyance, social contacts or sales skills than on the quality of his or her art. With the artist's number-one promoter gone (namely the artist herself), art values fall flat.

SPECULATIVE ART MARKET 'BUBBLES'

Every once in a while, an uncontrolled, uninformed, speculative art-buying frenzy results in a 'bubble', or rapid and unjustified rise, in art prices. In the late 1980s, for example, credit was cheap, the economy was strong (particularly in Japan), record art sales were being reported almost daily in the news media and, consequently, a large number of speculators jumped into the market to make some 'easy money'. Similar spikes happened during the dotcom era of the late 1990s and the real-estate boom of the early 2000s. Unfortunately, many speculative buyers lacking the knowledge and perspective necessary to understand what was going on entered the market, paid high prices and, when the downturns hit, the art parties ended and they lost plenty of money.

As usually happens during these inflationary spirals, too many people who don't know what they're doing chase after too little art or whatever gets hyped as hot, and not only does the best-quality art spike upwards in price, but so does art of mediocre and even poor quality. Inexperienced speculators jump into the market and buy indiscriminately, thinking that just because an artist is getting press, or a piece of art has the 'right' signature on it, they'll have no problem selling it at some point down the road for more than they paid – similar to the progression of a chain letter. Sooner or later, though, the economy cools, the money supply dries up and, as mentioned above, art is one of the first extravagances to get cut out of the budget. The speculators attempt to cash out and suddenly realise that no new speculators are waiting in line to perpetuate the myth.

The art-price inflation of the mid-to-late 1980s, for example, was extremely intense, and the fall-back in prices in the early 1990s was equally drastic. Likewise in the dotcom-era debacle and the real-estate crash. In some cases, mediocre art by famous artists, as well as large percentages of art by many secondary artists, still sells for less than what it was selling for during the high times. The good news is that prices of the best-quality art almost always recover and even go on to exceed their boom-time prices in a number of instances. The really good news is that the speculators tend to disappear, prices stabilise, and the serious dealers and collectors are no longer being held hostage by fine-art Philistines who spike the markets with their indiscriminate buying. Regardless of how bad things get, though, people always seem to forget what happened, and we can look forward to repeat performances of speculative waves periodically impacting on the overall health of the art market.

Smaller speculative price run-ups also happen in the art market with some frequency. Individual artists get hot, dealers and collectors buy in advance of major museum shows hoping prices will surge upwards once the shows open, art of particular geographic regions suddenly becomes all the rage and so on. Unless you can buy, sell or collect on the level of the professionals, your best approach to any inflationary situation where everyone seems to be scrambling to get in on the action is to sit back and wait until the dust settles.

ALL ART PAYS DIVIDENDS

No matter what happens to art prices or what happens to the artists whose art you buy, if you buy art because you like it, you're already experiencing benefits that will continue to accrue for as long you own it. It's all yours, it beautifies your environment, you learn from it, it enriches your life and no one can ever take those positives away. No matter what a work of art is worth on the open market, it pays dividends in ways that no other material possessions can.

Example

Collectors often ask me whether they should buy particular works of art. I ask them whether they like the art and, of course, they all answer yes. But on further questioning, that 'yes' is sometimes based on beliefs unrelated to the art itself, such as how much they think it's going to appreciate in value, how much of a deal they think they're getting or how famous they think the artists are now or will become in the future. If you find yourself in the position of trying to decide whether to buy a work of art that you honestly believe you like, ask yourself a few questions like those below.

- *Would I like this art as much if the artist was virtually unknown and just starting out in her career?*
- *Would I like this art as much if the artist's prices haven't gone up in fifteen years and aren't expected to rise anytime soon?*
- *Would I like this art as much if I found out I was paying a top-of-the-market price?*
- *Did I start liking this art more when the seller began telling me how important it is and how famous the artist is?*

Be careful whenever considerations unrelated to how you experience a work of art when you first look at it begin to influence your decision whether to buy. What's important is how the art impacts on you and makes you feel, not so much all the chatter and noise that goes on around it.

A LOOK AHEAD

With these basic art and money facts in mind, let's move on to the specifics – namely, evaluating the asking prices of whatever works of art you have selected for possible purchase. Being able to understand a given work of art in terms of a set monetary value is the final goal of buying art intelligently. How much art are you getting for how much money? That's the question you will learn how to answer in Chapter 21.

EVALUATE THE ASKING PRICE

Any work of art you see for sale and are interested in owning has a price attached to it. If you're like most people who buy art, you're not looking to make a financial killing, but you do want to make sure the asking price is fair and reasonable before you pay it. You determine that by evaluating that price.

You may wonder how you can possibly determine whether art asking prices are fair, but it's really not that difficult once you know how. In fact, evaluating art prices is much like evaluating the price of any consumer product you are considering buying – you find out what you want to know from the firm representing the product, and then you check independently to make sure what they tell you is accurate.

Unfortunately, not all art galleries and dealers appreciate people who know how to evaluate art prices. Some may even resent buyers who ask too many questions and prefer selling to clients who believe that monetary values are set according to mystical procedures only art dealers can understand. Know right now that this is simply not the case!

The single most important truth about art prices is that they are purposefully set according to methods that you or anyone else can understand. Furthermore, they may be verified as reasonable or unreasonable just as purposefully. You need a certain amount of knowledge to evaluate prices and reach those conclusions, of course, but once you learn how price research works, you'll be capable of making them entirely on your own. Never let anyone tell you otherwise.

Before going any further, be advised that procedures for evaluating art prices are not meant to take the place of the art and artist research described in Part III of this book. Buying art based on financial considerations alone without any understanding of the artists, the art or the history behind the art falls into the category of pure speculation and is definitely a high-risk proposition. You cannot intelligently evaluate an asking price without first researching and evaluating the art, the artist and the provenance. Assuming all is in order and you know what you're being offered, then the time comes for the price research.

Many novice art buyers don't fully understand what price evaluation entails. They ask a few price questions at the galleries selling the art, instantly accept everything they are told and assume no further investigation is necessary. They believe whatever the seller tells them constitutes adequate insight into asking prices when, in fact, it's only one side of the story. Galleries are, of course, more than happy to answer money questions about their art, but in the great majority of cases, they have an obvious self-interest, and the less business you've done together, the more you need to corroborate what you're hearing.

What gallery do you know that believes their asking prices are anything but fair? What gallery do you know that will advise you not to buy their art because they think it's overpriced? The answer to both of those questions is none. Buyers don't necessarily get taken advantage of when their complete price research consists of asking sellers price questions, but at the very best, they get biased opinions.

Comprehensive price evaluation means more than having a quick chat with the seller. You've got to accumulate a variety of data from throughout the art community in order to get a balanced overview of the value of any art you are considering. You acquire this data from three primary sources:

- *The seller.* When evaluating asking prices, acquiring information from the seller is the only sensible way to begin. They are experts at what they sell and can provide extensive data and reasoning around their asking prices.
- *Art auctions.* By studying price results of art that has sold at auction – specifically, art that is comparable to what you are considering buying – you can get an idea of what your art would be worth outside of its gallery setting and of the overall strength of the market for that art.
- *Online.* For many artists, not only can you find information about art that has already sold, but you also can often find galleries, private individuals, secondary market websites, the artist's website or other venues offering their art for sale.
- *Resources that do not have conflicts of interest.* By consulting independent art professionals who have no vested interest in whatever art you are considering, you can get informed, unbiased opinions on the prices you are being asked to pay.

This check and balance system protects you from overpaying for art. Learn how to use it and profit.

ASKING THE SELLER

As mentioned above, art-price research always begins with the seller. The single most important and only absolutely necessary question to ask any seller, no matter what you are being offered, is this: *How did you arrive at your asking price?*

A satisfactory answer – that is, the type of answer you want – is one that explains and justifies the price you are being asked to pay in terms of specific, current market information about the art and its artist. Without exception, a satisfactory answer must include concrete data about other works of art by the artist that are for sale or have already been sold, the circumstances under which they are for sale or have sold and, if sold, how much they sold for.

You want facts here, actual sales results – names, places, dates, monetary amounts – and the more you get, the better. You want proof that work by the artist is changing hands on a regular basis at prices comparable to those you are being asked to pay. Or, if the artist is younger or just starting out and has few sales, you want to know from the seller how they determined their asking prices. You also want information about where the art is selling *in addition to* the gallery you are doing business with – auction houses, other art galleries and so on. When you get these sorts of detailed responses to that most important price question, you can be reasonably sure you're dealing with reputable dealers.

An unsatisfactory answer to the big question – one that may appear to justify an asking price but actually does not – is when you are told that other dealers' asking prices are comparable to what you are being asked to pay. Knowing that other galleries are offering art at similar prices is a start, but you need more. Asking price alone is never an indication of market strength or fair market value. Asking price is not relevant until someone actually pays it. To repeat: *the amount of money a work of art is being offered for by an art gallery is not how much that art is worth*. It's only how much the gallery hopes to sell it for.

Another unsatisfactory answer is one that only relates price information about sales that have been made at the gallery trying to sell you the art. Price records solely from the seller's gallery are never adequate proof that what you are being asked to pay is fair or that a market exists for the art outside of that gallery's doors. Even when a gallery has sold numerous works of art at prices comparable to what you are being asked to pay, this could mean nothing more than the gallery personnel are experts at talking people into buying that art or that they sell primarily to clients who tend not to evaluate the prices of what they buy before they buy it. You need additional information about what level of recognition (in financial terms) the artist is receiving in other sectors of the market.

Whatever answers you get to the big question, document every single detail. You are then ready to continue your price evaluation outside of the gallery selling the art and see what the rest of the art community has to say.

CHECKING ART AUCTION PRICES

The amount of money a work of art sells for at auction is an excellent indicator of how liquid that art is, how strong its market is and what it is worth when it has to sell immediately for cash. High auction prices often indicate that a healthy, no-hype market exists for an artist. Low auction prices, on the other hand, may indicate a weak or unstable market. It's that simple.

Assuming the artist sells at auction, a major goal of your price evaluation is to approximate how much whatever work of art you are interested in buying would sell for at auction and then to compare that value to the price you are being asked to pay. You need to make this comparison not because you intend to sell the art, but as a person who buys art intelligently, you want it to have some degree of financial strength on the open market, outside of its biased retail environment, and in a neutral auction or marketplace setting. In other words, you don't want your art to be worthless the moment you walk it out of the gallery door.

Art auctions continually take place around the world. Some hundreds of thousands of significant works of art are auctioned annually. Auction houses internationally sell everything from Old Masters to contemporary art, and an average specialised art sale consists of between one hundred and three hundred pieces, sometimes more. All major international auction houses and a number of regional ones publish catalogues, either hard copy or online, of every art sale they conduct.

Learning how to read auction catalogues or online descriptions is an essential part of art-price evaluation. These are the most important sources of art-price information in the art business. A single catalogue or auction can supply you with comprehensive sales data on several hundred works of art.

Many art galleries and dealers have at least a handful of auction catalogues in their libraries and will be happy to teach you how to read them, assuming you're doing at least a modest amount of business with them and are not simply asking for free information. A few minutes is all it takes. For our purposes now, what you need to know is explained below.

Auction catalogues individually list each work of art to be sold along with basic facts about it. An average catalogue entry for a work of art includes the lot number of the art in the sale; the name and nationality of the artist; the artist's birth and death dates (when applicable); the title, medium and dimensions of the art; the location and spelling of the signature as it appears on the art; relevant incidental information relating to provenance (a previous owner's name, where the art was exhibited, etc.); and the amount of money the auction house believes the piece will sell for, known as the pre-sale estimate. Entries also note whether the art is illustrated (most art is). The catalogues for significant sales at better, more established houses usually illustrate every work of art they sell.

Let's imagine you are studying an auction entry for a painting by an artist named Blake Stoneman that provides the following information:

Lot Number: 4027
Artist: Blake Stoneman; American (1961–)
Title: *Northern Coast on a Stormy Day*
Signature and location: B. Stoneman in the lower left
    corner
Medium: Oil painting on canvas
Dimensions: 27 by 36 inches (68.5 by 91.5 centimetres)
Estimated selling price: $3,000–$5,000.
Illustrated in the catalogue.

No matter what auction house is selling this picture, the actual entry in either the catalogue or online would probably look something like this:

*4027 BLAKE STONEMAN (1961–) NORTHERN
    COAST ON A STORMY DAY
Signed lower left: B. Stoneman Oil on canvas, 27 by 36
    inches, 68.5 by 91.5 cm
See illustration (Est: 3,000/5,000)

After an auction sale is held, all prices realised at that sale become a matter of public record. Anyone can contact the auction house to find out for how much any item in that particular sale sold. Let's say the Blake Stoneman painting sells for $4,500. You can call the auction house and ask them how much it sold for (this amount is known as the *auction record* for that painting). You may also be able to ask for auction records of other Stoneman paintings the auction house has handled in the past. The auction house will usually give you those results, within reason.

Supposing you are interested in finding out how much Blake Stoneman paintings have been selling for at auction houses around the world. This would involve contacting auction house after auction house to see whether they have ever sold his art and, if so, how much it has sold for. You can see that this would be a rather difficult, expensive and time-consuming task. To make matters worse, auction houses are not generally enthusiastic about taking the time to give out price information to people doing art-price research and who are not interested in buying.

Fortunately, you don't have to bother auction houses with continual price requests; most of the major houses now have searchable online databases of their past sales. You or anyone else can also locate all the relevant auction records you want from multiple houses simply and easily because a number of publishers keep track of international auction sales for you online, maintaining what are referred to as *auction price databases*. These databases are continually updated with results from the latest sales and contain anywhere from several hundred thousand to millions of auction records from several thousand significant auction houses around the world, documenting sales taking place during periods ranging from the most recent few years to several decades. See Appendix II for a list of online auction-price references and databases and brief comments on their respective strong points.

Online database services offer various subscription options ranging from affordable single-day or single-artist access to annual memberships that can run as high as several thousand dollars, but you don't need to pay to use them. Many major public library, museum, college and university art departments subscribe to at least some auction-price services and databases. Find out what libraries offer which, and when you need information, just call or visit these institutions and ask the art librarians to show you how to find whatever auction records you need.

Make sure you have access to multiple online databases because they sometimes differ in the quality and amount of information they provide. Not every library has them all, and some libraries carry only one or two. If you have to contact more than one library in order to cover most of the main ones, do so. Art dealers and serious collectors generally have auction-database access in their galleries too, but most are reluctant to share them with you unless they know you well or you do regular business together.

Auction records are easy to read and understand. Each database has instructions on how to read results and all list results in basically the same format. Artists are listed alphabetically and individual price results for any particular artist may be viewed in a number of ways including by medium (painting, sculpture, works on paper, etc.), by price (highest to lowest, lowest to highest, etc.) or by date of sale with the most recent sales first. Under Blake Stoneman, for example, you would find the $4,500 entry and entries for other Stoneman paintings that sold during whatever time period the particular database you're using covers.

The $4,500 Stoneman entry would look something like this in a database:

Stoneman, Blake   American (1961–)
$4,500; *Northern Coast on a Stormy Day*, signed lower
left, (05/12/07, Smith's-NY, #4027, illus.), 27 by 36 in.
(68.5 by 91.5 cm), oil painting on canvas.

This entry gives the same basic information about Stoneman
and his painting that you find in the auction house's sale catalogue. Inside the second set of parentheses are the date of the
sale (05/12/07), name of the auction house (Smith's), location
of the auction house (New York), the lot number of the painting (4027) and the notation that it is illustrated in Smith's
catalogue of that sale. Online databases include images of the
art when available. Some service plans or memberships
charge an additional fee for access to images. Another way to
find out what a particular work of art looks like is to either
search for it by artist, title and auction house online, or refer
to the original sale catalogue.

APPROXIMATING A WORK OF ART'S AUCTION VALUE

Suppose you have selected a work of art for possible purchase,
have reached the point in your research where you are seriously considering buying it and are ready to determine its
approximate auction value. The procedure is the same no
matter what type of art or artist you are evaluating but, for our
purposes here, let's say you are considering a Blake Stoneman
oil on canvas of a mountain scene that measures 24 by 30
inches and has an asking price of $4,500.

Your first step is to locate as many auction records as possible of Stoneman paintings that have sold at auction in recent
years. Here's how you do this for any artist:

- *Personally check or have art librarians check online art-price databases for sales results, especially ones with images.* Ask art librarians, experienced collectors or other experts to work with you until you know what you're doing. Also check as many different databases as possible, not just one or two, so you can not only access the most results, but also learn the relative strengths and weaknesses of each database. As you get more experienced, you'll learn which will be best to check depending on what you are researching.

- *Start with the most recent auction results and locate all entries under the artist's name.* Go back through at least three years' worth of records, and preferably five to ten. You want to get an idea of price trends over time.

- *Save the links to pages listing all pieces of the artist's work that sold during the time period you are checking.*

- *Whenever possible, look at images of sold works.* You need to visually compare as many artworks as possible to the one whose value you are in the process of approximating.

You are now ready to take the auction records you have located and approximate an auction value for your Stoneman painting or whatever art you are evaluating. Below are some general rules that will help you analyse, interpret and understand those records and apply them to your art.

The most significant auction records for your purposes are those that describe works of art most similar in size, subject matter, medium, date executed and other particulars to the one you are researching. The amounts of money these works sell for are the best approximations of your art's auction value. In our Blake Stoneman example, since you are researching an oil painting of a mountain scene measuring 24 by 30 inches, pay special attention to auction records of mountain-scene oil paintings with similar characteristics to yours. You would not pay much attention, for example, to records of very dissimilar works of art like a painting of ships on the ocean measuring 6 by 9 inches or a floral still-life watercolour. Comparing the selling prices for the ship scene or the still-life to your mountain scene would be like comparing apples to oranges.

Auction prices of art similar to the art you are evaluating should generally be at least 40 per cent to 50 per cent of what the gallery is asking you to pay. The higher the percentage, the greater the art's resale value on the open market. Unless the gallery selling the art has a very good reason, you do not, for example, want to pay $4,500 for the Stoneman painting you are considering when similar paintings sell at auction for only $300 to $500 each. Remember that auction prices are an excellent indicator of value on the open market and, in the great majority of cases, records that are consistently far below gallery retail indicate either a weak or unstable market for that art and artist, as well as overly ambitious pricing on the part of the gallery that's selling it.

The works of art that sell for the greatest amounts of money are usually the ones that collectors of that artist prize the most. If, for example, Stoneman mountain scenes fetch the highest prices at auction, assume they are more sought after by collectors than any of his other subject matters. The more characteristics a work of art you are researching has of the higher-priced works, the more you should think about buying it.

The works of art that sell for the least amounts of money are usually the least desirable in terms of collectability. If Stoneman mountain scenes sell for less than all other subject matters, assume they are not in demand by collectors. When art you are researching falls into the low end of the artist's auction-price continuum, think about perhaps looking for something a little more collectible, unless, of course, you really love it, in which case at least you're aware of where you stand market-wise.

Pay the most attention to those monetary amounts that the majority of the art in question auctions for, not the minority. For example, if you locate twenty different auction sales results for Stoneman paintings, nineteen of which are in the $2,000 to $4,000 price range and one for $15,000, assume that Stoneman's art generally auctions in the low thousands of dollars, not the tens of thousands. Isolated high (or low) price records are not accurate indicators of the overall market for the art; focus on averages, not extremes.

See how auction prices change over time. You want indications that an artist's art is at least holding steady and preferably increasing in value. Watch out when you see decreasing or erratic records.

You need at least half-a-dozen auction records to establish any meaningful pattern for an artist. One or two isolated records of pieces selling at auction cannot be relied upon to provide any concrete conclusions about a particular artist's market. What you can conclude from one or two auction records, though, is that the artist has at least been through auction and is viewed by auction galleries as saleable in a public arena. In other words, any auction records are better than no records at all.

Let's return now to our Blake Stoneman mountain scene and analyse it in terms of some hypothetical auction records. Suppose you locate ten auction records of Stoneman oil paintings that have sold over the past five years, with characteristics as follows:

• The selling prices range from a low of $300 to a high of $4,000.

- Four are mountain scenes, five are coastal scenes and three are landscapes.
- Two mountain scenes are about the same size as the painting you like; the others are much smaller. They sold for $2,500, $2,000, $400 and $350 respectively. The $2,500 painting sold two years ago and the $2,000 painting sold four years ago.
- The three highest records, $4,000, $3,500, and $3,000 are all coastal scenes and all about the same size as your mountain scene.
- The remaining records are for landscapes with no mountains, the smallest selling for $300 and the largest for $900.
- In general, Stoneman's prices have been slowly increasing over the past five years.

Based on this data, you can make certain assumptions about Stoneman's market, determine an approximate auction value for your mountain-scene painting and compare it to the gallery's $4,500 asking price. The following interpretations and conclusions would generally be considered reasonable by a majority of art professionals:

- Stoneman collectors prefer coastal scenes to mountain scenes and landscapes (his three highest auction records are all for coastal scenes).
- Mountain scenes are acceptable to collectors as evidenced by the fact that the larger ones sold for respectable prices.
- Stoneman's landscapes without mountains are not that collectible; they all sold low.
- Collectors prefer larger paintings to small ones; the small ones sell inexpensively.
- The auction value of the mountain scene you are thinking about buying would probably be between $2,000 and

$2,500 today. This price estimate is based on the similarity in size and composition of yours to the mountain scenes that sold for $2,500 and $2,000. The $2,500 high estimate is in line with the most recent sale, the $2,000 estimate is in line with the older sale, and the range takes into consideration the fact that the Stoneman market appears to be stable and gradually strengthening.

- Comparing that $2,000 to $2,500 auction approximation to the $4,500 asking price, you could conclude that $4,500 is, at worst, just slightly on the high side, but not overly so. You could call it fair retail because even the lower auction value of $2,000 falls within 40 per cent to 50 per cent of the gallery retail.

Suppose you are evaluating an asking price and find only a few low auction sales results for the artist or, worse yet, none at all? This is not usually a good sign in terms of the artist's resale value on the open market. In most cases, this means that the artist's market is weak, the artist is minor or younger, and that auctions are not interested in handling his or her work because it won't sell for very much money. Exceptions do exist, though. For instance, an artist might be so collectible or rare that collectors hold on to their art, rarely resell it and, when they do, rarely put it up for auction. Art research combined with conversations with the seller and no-conflict resources usually sheds light on what the auction situation might be and how seriously to take the lack of sales-price results. Regardless, you're still in the dark as to performance at auction.

No matter what the reason for a lack of auction data, you are by no means at a dead end. You can still approximate an auction value on the art. It's a little different from normal procedure, but not very difficult.

To obtain an approximate auction value in such a case, contact at least several auction houses, both regional and national, that conduct regular art sales and are familiar with the art or artist in question. (See Appendix VIII for a list of significant auction houses.) Ask every specialist with whom you speak the following two questions:

- *Are you familiar with this artist?*
- *Would you auction his or her work if given the opportunity?*

It's good when the auction experts answer yes to both parts of this enquiry, not so good when they say yes to the first and no to the second, and worse yet when they say no to both.

Whenever someone at an auction house gives you at least one yes answer, ask whether that person can give you ballpark estimates on what they think art similar to the art you are considering buying might sell for at one of the auction house's sales. Don't automatically assume that the values you get are the approximate amounts that the art would actually auction for. These figures do come from informed sources, though, and should be given a respectable degree of consideration. This is especially true when every firm you call gives you the same approximate values. Regardless of the responses you get, always combine them with seller and no-conflict resource enquiries.

As an aside, don't get into the habit of constantly calling auction houses for this sort of advice, especially when you can locate adequate price information elsewhere. Auction firms are in the business of selling art, not running price-information hotlines.

CONSULTING NO-CONFLICT-OF-INTEREST RESOURCES

The consulting of no-conflict-of-interest resources – sources of honest straightforward information – is equally as important as auction-price evaluation and as the other procedures you must employ in order to corroborate any price information sellers give you. Here, you solicit prices, thoughts, feedback and prognostications of informed outside sources and individuals regarding your selections. The best way to access this data is, of course, online, but also from art people you know and with whom you have established relationships. Relevant websites and artist pages often contain price or sales information as well as contact information for people who can help you; your friends or associates can provide the rest. This information, combined with auction-price evaluation and what the seller tells you, is, in the great majority of cases, all you need to determine the fairness of an asking price.

No-conflict research becomes all the more important when little or no auction records exist for an artist whose art you are considering. In these cases, no-conflict resources often provide the best conclusive primary and secondary price information you have to go on outside of what a seller tells you. For example, you might find websites offering or selling art by the artist or showing images of art they have for sale. If prices aren't posted, you can always call or email and ask.

No-conflict-of-interest resources are exactly what they sound like – they are websites, galleries, dealers, collectors and other informed individuals who are independent from and have no vested interest whatsoever in the art or artist you are researching or the gallery you are patronising. Ideally, they do not sell or collect that art on a regular basis, and profits from any related transactions in which they may be involved do not constitute a significant percentage of their incomes. Above all, these resources should be individuals you know and trust, not total strangers whom you email at random.

A no-conflict resource can be anyone you meet in the course of your art-buying activities, either in person or online. Over time, you get to know certain people who eventually become friends or acquaintances you can confide in about your buying. The better you know each other, the more they'll be willing to help you by giving you honest advice whenever you need it.

For example, an art dealer you have never done business with before is not likely to comment on a work of art you are considering buying that hangs in another dealer's gallery. To her, you are a stranger asking pointed questions that could involve her taking sides or incriminating the other dealer. But the better she gets to know you and understand your intentions, and, most importantly, the more business she does with you, the more likely she'll be to give you the valued opinions you want.

Be patient about acquiring no-conflict resources. These are people you'll meet in the course of your buying, particularly those with whom you'll be doing business. You'll eventually figure out who you work best with and are able to trust as honest, unbiased resources for consistent and accurate art-price information.

Here are the types of questions you should ask every no-conflict resource you have about a piece of art you are considering buying, assuming you have an established relationship:

- *Have you ever heard of this artist?* The more recognisable the artist's name, the better. If they don't recognise the name, on the other hand, that's not a good sign. Combined with poor or non-existent auction records, this could mean that unless you're completely in love with the art, you stop here, forget about the artist and look for something else to buy. Assuming you get at least some name recognition, proceed with your questions.

- *What do you think about the artist's art and his or her progress as an artist?* You want to hear that no-conflict resources respect the work of the artist and have good things to say about his or her future.

- *What do you think about the market for this artist's work?* In response to this question you want indications that the market is broadly based and increasing. The greater the number and variety of galleries, curators, critics, professionals and collectors supporting an artist's work, financially as well as critically, the better. Look for signs that prices the art sells for are at least holding steady and preferably increasing.

- *This question is for no-conflict dealers or galleries only: Would you handle this artist's work if someone offered it to you for sale or consignment and, if so, how much would you charge for it?* This is an important question. The more galleries who answer 'yes' and the closer their hypothetical selling prices are to what you are being asked to pay, the better. Also, the more enthusiastic no-conflict galleries are about handling the art, the better.

- *Again, for dealers only: If you are willing to sell this artist's art, how fast do you think it might sell?* This gives you an indication of how in-demand the artist is. A month or less selling time is a sign of an active market and a promising artist. A year is not. In fact, galleries who think a year or more is necessary to sell the art would most likely not be willing to sell it in the first place.

- *For no-conflict collectors and other informed individuals who do not buy and sell art for a living: Do you own work by this artist and, if you don't, would you consider buying a piece for your collection?* You want 'yes' answers; you want enthusiastic answers.

- *Here's what the art I'm thinking about buying looks like, and here's how much I'm being asked to pay for it. What do you think?* This is the most important question because the more no-conflict resources, online and otherwise, that view your situation as acceptable, the more you should consider buying the art. It's also the most difficult question because anyone who answers it is required to take a position on a gallery and their art. Since it is so direct, ask it only to those no-conflict resources you know well, with whom you have established relationships and confide in the most. Seriously consider all answers you get here in making your final decision.

Get to know as many no-conflict resources as possible, people qualified to answer your financial – as well as your aesthetic and informational – questions about art and artists. If you're at all serious about buying and get involved with the art community, these people will come into your life as your adventures progress, both in person and online. The greater the number of these people you know and speak with, the more data you can acquire and the better informed are the decisions you make regarding whatever art you select. Remember to cultivate these relationships gradually and diplomatically so you can ask sensitive questions like those listed above and get straightforward, honest and helpful answers.

By the way, you don't need 100 per cent enthusiasm, perfect agreement and purely positive answers to every question from every individual you consult. A variety of responses is fine – different people have different tastes and opinions.

What you should look for, though, is an overall positive response to the art and artist in question.

In summation, when no-conflict resources recognise the name of your artist, you're off to a good start. When they say positive things about the artist, that's better. When they express a willingness to actually tie up gallery space and sell the art or display it in their collections, that's best. When they comment favourably on the asking price of the particular piece you are thinking about buying, that's about all you need to go ahead and buy.

One final note: just because an asking price turns out to be too high or an artist turns out to be not that well known throughout the art community, do not automatically refuse to buy the art. If you really love it, go ahead and buy it no matter what it is. *You can buy any art at any time for any price and for whatever reason. Always remember that.* Price evaluation techniques provide you only with a knowledge of the financial aspects of that art and are never a verdict on what it means to you personally.

EVALUATING ART BY YOUNGER ARTISTS

For the most part, auctions sell art by established artists, that is, artists with healthy collector bases, good name recognition, strong markets and art that is in short enough supply or otherwise hard to find that bidders will compete to own it. Auctions are not typically interested in selling art by younger, unproven or less experienced artists. These artists tend to have limited name recognition as well as unclear or unstable collector bases, modest career accomplishments or art that is readily available from multiple sources in the marketplace. For most of these artists, years or even decades may have to pass before their work shows up at auction (assuming it ever does at all).

Evaluate the prices of art by a younger artist by assessing the artist's online profile, following, résumé, career accomplishments, exhibition experience and recent sales history. When the art is for sale at a gallery, ask to see the artist's résumé; when it's for sale online, look for the résumé. A healthy résumé should include solo shows, group shows the artist has participated in, interviews or articles or reviews about the artist, awards or distinctions the artist has won, collectors or institutions that own the artist's work and so on. The deeper the résumé in those regards, the better. In order to be taken seriously, a résumé must include names, dates and places of shows, events, reviews and so on. Watch out when instead of a résumé, you're given an essay about the artist, especially if it's peppered with generalities like 'the artist has exhibited internationally' or 'the artist is world famous'. Babble like this means absolutely nothing unless accompanied by names, dates and facts to back it up.

In addition to the résumé, speak with galleries or other venues that sell the art, your trusted no-conflict resources and, when possible, with the artist directly in order to best assess how their career is progressing and the overall market for their art. And don't be afraid to ask questions including ones about prices. As someone who is considering spending money on art, you are entitled to ask as many money questions as you want. Below are several factors that tend to indicate whether a younger artist's art is priced fairly.

- *At least half of the pieces in the artist's most recent shows have sold.* This means collectors see merit in the art and believe it is reasonably priced. The greater the percentage of art that sells and the more shows the artist has had with similar results, the better.

- *Multiple galleries or websites offer, sell or represent art by the artist.* This indicates not only a demand for the art, but also that the artist is productive and capable of satisfying the needs of more than one seller. Productivity is one of the best measures of how serious an artist is about succeeding. The more galleries and websites that represent an artist and the more widespread those venues are, the better.
- *The artist has been represented by the exhibiting gallery for a significant period of time and has had more than one show with them.* This means the dealer can consistently sell the art and believes in the artist's future potential. The longer an artist has been with a gallery, the better. If the artist is showing at a new gallery for the first time, he or she should be able to show evidence of past sales and extended relationships with other galleries, and talk about the show with the new gallery in terms of its being a logical career move.
- *The artist's prices have risen in recent years without a decrease in sales.* Increasing prices, even if as little as 10 to 20 per cent, and steady or increasing sales indicate a healthy market for the art. (Remember that arbitrary price increases are meaningless if not accompanied by increased sales; price increases based on increased demand, popularity of the artist, critical acclaim and recognition by the art community are what you're looking for.)
- *The artist's prices compare favourably with those of artists who produce similar art, live in the same geographical area and have similar career accomplishments.*
- *The artist has had at least one or two significant shows per year in recent years.* This is another indication that the artist is able to consistently produce art and that collectors are consistently buying it. Infrequent or sporadic shows are not generally a sign of a dedicated and committed artist.

- *The artist regularly shows in different parts of the country or, better yet, internationally – both online and at physical locations.*
- *The artist has received awards, grants or other distinctions for his or her art.*
- *The gallery is able to support and document the artist's current selling prices with records of consistent completed sales of comparable work at comparable prices.*
- *The gallery can show you at least one or two favourable reviews or comments about the artist from respected critics, academics or comparably accredited members of the art community.*
- *The artist has been featured in articles, interviews or reviews in art magazines, significant art websites or other respected publications.*
- *Books or exhibition catalogues, other than those that are self-published or printed by vanity presses, have already been or will soon be published about the artist.*
- *The artist has either been or will soon be included in museum or similarly notable shows.*
- *Established or well-known collectors, both private and institutional, own art by the artist.* Collectors are considered to be established or well known if they are recognised and respected for the quality of their art collections, not if they are famous or well known only for accomplishments unrelated to art collecting (such as business leaders, actors, sports figures, politicians, etc.).

GENERAL ONLINE ART-PRICE RESEARCH

A wealth of art-price information is available online from all kinds of websites and all kinds of sources. The sources we've been talking about so far are mainly standard, conventional, art auction-price databases and websites, established auction houses and qualified galleries or websites that represent or specialise in certain types of art and artists. The tricky part is that there are also plenty of prices posted by all kinds of people for all kinds of reasons, especially by private sellers and dealers who buy and sell secondary market art, but also people trying to find how much their art is worth, people who think they know how much art is worth and so on. Places where you can find all kinds of priced art for sale include online auction sites like eBay, fixed-price sites like 1stdibs.com, rubylane.com, etsy.com or artbrokerage.com, general question/answer sites and buy/sell sites like craigslist.com.

The problem with many of these prices, particularly prices on art that's up for sale, is that they're not necessarily accurate, at times can be completely arbitrary or random, and the people who post them are not necessarily knowledgeable. In many cases, overly optimistic sellers have mistaken ideas that their art is worth substantially more than it really is, and as a result post prices that are unrealistically high. Other sellers know their asking prices are high, but they're simply trying to sell for as much as possible, hoping they'll get lucky and find the perfect buyers (which they usually don't). In other words, you can't automatically accept every online price you find, no matter how good it might make you feel about whatever artist you're researching.

Here are some warnings to keep in mind when doing general online price research:

- Asking prices are not necessarily accurate indications of what art is worth. They're often better indications of what sellers hope their art might be worth than what it is realistically worth.

- Selling prices are better indications of what art is worth or at least what people are willing to pay for it under certain circumstances. While asking prices are good to know, selling prices are far more meaningful because they document what people are actually willing to pay.

- When possible, get a sense of the difference and range between asking prices and selling prices for whatever artist you are researching.

- Many online sellers accompany their art with elaborate descriptions, facts, claims or terms like 'rare' or 'museum quality' that may or may not be accurate. Do not automatically believe everything you read. Always consider the source and, if you have any questions regarding any statements sellers make, ask for corroborating facts, evidence or documentation. You need names, contacts, citations in standard references and so on – not unverifiable generalities.

- Additionally, if you have any questions about a price, ask the seller or whoever posted the information about how they either set or arrived at that price. Simply accepting a stated price or taking it at face value is not enough. You need to understand how people arrive at their conclusions, and whether those conclusions are based more on facts or fantasies.

The bottom line is this: Be cautious about general online price information and never make a decision about whether or not to buy a work of art based only on information from private sellers or sources you cannot verify. Diverse resources on the internet are always good to search for and check because you never know what you might find, but combine any such general research with more conventional research and information from standard accepted sources. Note whatever additional miscellaneous price information you find and where you find it, but always check with those in the know for the full story on exactly what has sold for how much or what reasonable values might be.

Appendix II lists some of the more popular secondary market websites where art is bought and sold on a regular basis.

A LOOK AHEAD

At this point, you should have no trouble deciding how fair or reasonable an asking price is. In other words, you're finally done with all your research and evaluations! Can you believe it? You're ready to buy art.

But wait one last minute. Suppose you could buy that art for less than the seller is asking for it? If you find this possibility appealing, then the next chapter is for you.

CHAPTER 22

NEGOTIATE THE BUY

You're ready to write your cheque or hand over your credit card and buy a piece of art except for one small detail: you'd like to pay less for it. Whether you think the price is too high, you have a policy never to pay full retail or you love to bargain, you're not quite ready to complete the transaction. So where do you stand and what are your options?

You happen to be in luck. Art dealers have been known to leave room in their asking prices for negotiation or, as it is more commonly called, bargaining. You may just get a break on your impending expenditure if you know how to conduct yourself.

Reasons for flexibility in asking prices vary. Both artists and dealers know that certain collectors or clients expect 'deals' or that they enjoy bargaining; some galleries leave room for employee commissions; outside market factors sometimes force dealers to pad asking prices; dealers themselves may accept or, in rare instances, encourage bargaining as part of the art-buying process; and so on. Whatever the situation, art buyers and sellers negotiate final selling prices all the time.

In its most primitive form, bargaining consists of two opposing parties battling against each other for no reason other than money. The seller wants to sell for as much as possible, and the buyer wants to pay as little as possible.

Anything goes, and the one who manages to outsmart the other with the cleverest tactics wins.

More mature bargaining or negotiating, on the other hand, is far from a simple battle over who can make who pay the most or sell for the least amount of money. Good bargaining in a fine-art setting is a cooperative venture in which both buyer and seller sit down together with the intention of reaching an agreement on how much a particular work of art is worth. Research results are studied, price data is evaluated, arguments from both sides are considered and fair value is determined to the satisfaction of both parties. When agreement is reached, the art sells.

Negotiating art prices is not a sport. It is a tool for addressing any situation in which you believe an asking price is too high. Rather than throw up your hands and walk out the gallery door, you speak with the seller about what you think a more reasonable price should be. And you follow that up with your offer. Consider bargaining for art as a petitioner's process where you request that the person in a position of power (the seller) reconsider his or her decision to price the art at the level that he or she has.

Intelligent bargaining or negotiating begins by your presenting a well-constructed and well-documented case about what you think a particular selling price should be and why. The seller, in turn, either accepts that offer, makes a counter offer or states that the asking price is firm and refuses to consider any offer. You then respond to the seller, and so the process continues until the two of you either agree or else agree to disagree.

The procedure may sound easy, but negotiating for art is an art in itself. You can do it right, and you can do it wrong. Learn the fine points and etiquette of bargaining in order to get what you want and get it without offending anyone the next time you think you should be paying less than what you are being asked to pay.

HOW A NEGOTIATING RELATIONSHIP EVOLVES

When you first consider the possibility of buying art from a gallery, you have no idea how the owner feels about bargaining, and the owner has no idea how you feel about his asking prices. The moment you begin to find these things out about each other is the moment you decide to negotiate an asking price. At that point, opinions about how high or low prices may happen to be begin to emerge from both sides.

This first negotiation over money is a challenging time in any dealer–client relationship. At the very least, you have to be diplomatic and sensitive to the seller's feelings. You can easily offend by making an offer that's too low, for example, because you are essentially saying that you think the art is worth significantly less than the dealer thinks it's worth. Make mistakes at the outset, and you can seriously damage or even destroy a relationship before it ever begins. Make an intelligent offer, though, and you'll find that the seller will listen to and respect whatever you have to say about the art.

The outcome of a first negotiation affects you in two ways. The obvious one is that a particular asking price is evaluated and agreed upon to the apparent satisfaction of both you and the seller. The not-so-obvious outcome – but much more far-reaching one – is that the two of you begin to discover each other's positions on how art transactions should progress to completion. You set the tone for all future dealings with that seller.

During the next few negotiations, you pretty much determine the course of your business relationship together.

Consistent positive outcomes mean that you each come closer and closer to understanding exactly what the other wants and, as a result, every successive negotiation becomes easier than the last. The seller develops a good idea of the most you are willing to pay, and you get a feel for the least he or she is willing to accept.

The twofold object of successful negotiating is, therefore, to buy art at prices you want to pay and, at the same time, to keep sellers working for you, keep them on your side. Poor bargaining technique may net you a good price on an art piece or two in the short run but, in the long run, your collecting suffers because dealers become put off by your bad buying etiquette. Knowing how to negotiate means knowing how the art of buying art works.

PROPER BARGAINING ETIQUETTE: DOS AND DON'TS

The first and most important step towards becoming a good negotiator is knowing when *not* to negotiate. *When you see art you like and determine through research that the asking price is fair, buy it without making an offer.* Intelligent collectors respect sellers' abilities to price art accurately and recognise when those prices are fair to begin with. Sellers, in return, treat those collectors with equivalent respect.

When you honestly believe an asking price is too high, go ahead and make an offer. Before you present that offer, though, research and organise evidence to back it up. Take time to build your case. Make sure you can give a solid presentation, and support everything you say with facts. Dealers do not appreciate frivolous offers and can quickly tell whether you have a legitimate concern or are just trying to pay less for the sake of paying less.

Do make your offers reasonable ones that dealers can conceivably accept. Extremely low offers lead to bad feelings much more often than they lead to completed sales. Dealers can only reduce prices so far before they are taking losses on their art, and no dealer is interested in doing that. When the offer you want to make is far below the asking price, think seriously about not making it and buying something else instead. Dealers never appreciate 'lowball' offers.

Do be tactful, and pay close attention to sellers' reactions as you go. Sellers should be receptive to what you say at all stages of the negotiations. They love having intelligent discussions about art, even when the end result might mean that they may have to lower their prices. Know when to stop, though, once they begin to lose interest in what you have to say. With experience, you'll be able to tell exactly when that is.

Do base offers on facts about the art, not facts about your personal financial situation. For example, you see a sculpture you like and determine that the $1,000 asking price is fair. If your budget is only $500 per work of art, don't arbitrarily offer the dealer $500 for the sculpture. Either wait until you can afford to buy it, or shop instead for sculptures more in your price range.

Do learn how individual dealers react to your offers. You will find that every dealer has his or her own peculiarities in bargaining situations. Knowing what those quirks are helps reduce friction during negotiations. There is no universally 'right' way to negotiate. Tailor your bargaining techniques appropriately for each of the sellers with whom you negotiate.

Do make an offer only after the seller has had the art for a while and has not been able to sell it. A month is a good minimum waiting time. If you're not sure how long the art has been for sale, ask. If you make an offer on a fresh new arrival before the dealer has a chance to show it to other potential buyers, that dealer will almost certainly take offence.

Do pay close attention to dealers' overall responses to your offers. The best dealers give you positive, constructive responses during negotiations that teach you about art and the art business. Whether or not they accept your offers, they supply you with important information about why they feel their asking prices are fair and how they set them, and thus they continue to educate you at all times. Avoid dealers who are not interested in having price-related discussions or who consistently refuse your offers without giving any reasons why.

Knowing what not to do in a negotiating situation is just as important as knowing what to do. You make offers in the hope that they will be accepted, so you certainly don't want to sabotage yourself during the bargaining process. Avoid certain behaviours and maximise the chances of getting what you want.

The most important don't is this: don't start talking price the moment you see something you like. This is not only rude, but it also alienates sellers. You give them the impression that all you care about is money, and are inclined to give as little of it away as possible. Even when you know precisely what you want to offer the moment you see a piece of art and can back that offer with facts, get to know the seller before diving right in and making your offer.

Don't make an offer without carefully thinking it through, because the seller just might surprise you and accept it. When a seller accepts your offer, you are obliged to buy the art. Dealers do not appreciate collectors who make offers, have them accepted and then decide that they are not interested in buying the art after all. This is bad etiquette and will seriously impair future negotiations.

When no price tag is visible on the art and you have to ask how much it costs, don't give the impression that you think it's too high the moment you hear it. Avoid rolling your eyes, groaning, making faces and that sort of thing. Dealers dislike collectors who have knee-jerk reactions to selling prices.

Don't negotiate for the sport of it or suggest that an asking price is too high on art that you're not really interested in buying. Make offers only when you're serious.

Don't badmouth art you're trying to buy or focus on negatives rather than positives. For one thing, this strategy makes no sense. If you have problems with it, why are you trying to buy it in the first place? Additionally, sellers are not big fans of complainers – especially when the complaint is about those sellers' selections of art. Talking about how much you like the art and how much you want to own it is a far better strategy.

Don't get a reputation as someone who always wants it for less, someone who thinks that the asking price is always too high, no matter what it is. Dealers will stop showing you good, saleable art, and show only second-rate or hard-to-sell pieces that they don't mind getting rid of at bargain prices – and that's assuming they'll want you around their galleries in the first place.

Don't bargain when you're shown special consideration. For example, when a dealer or artist calls you first to see a piece of art that has just arrived or is newly completed, either buy it or pass on it. Do not bargain. He is showing you special treatment, and you should return the favour. If you think the price is too high, wait until they've had the art for a while, had a chance to show it to other collectors and have not been able to sell it. Then make your offer.

Don't talk about all the great art bargains you've got in the past while in the process of negotiating a price. Not only is this irritating, but it also gives the seller the idea that you only buy art when it's cheap. Why should he bother showing you anything if all you talk about is how little you paid for something similar two years ago or how a dealer across town once sold you such-and-such for half what it was worth?

Don't beat a seller over the head with an offer. When a dealer tells you he would rather not sell at the price you want to pay, don't continue to give reasons why you should get it for less. Even if the seller does eventually give in, you'll pay for that saving in future negotiations.

ADVANCED NEGOTIATING

Gain experience negotiating with dealers by keeping your offers conservative at first and making them only when you feel absolutely justified in doing so. As with any learned and practised skill, the more offers you make, the better you get at making them. After a while, you acquire a feel for how far you can go in any given situation, even with dealers you've never met before. You'll not only know more about the art you collect and what it's worth on the open market, but you'll also know more about how to bargain for it.

Expert bargainers can closely approximate how much dealers they've never met before are willing to accept for their art even before negotiations begin. They recognise differences between sellers who are firm on their asking prices and those who are flexible. They know just the right moments to offer just the right amounts. Offers are still based on fact and reason but, in advanced negotiating, a little more strategy comes into play in terms of timing, the way the offer is proposed and so on.

The ideal situation for you or any buyer is to determine the least amount of money a dealer is willing to accept for an artwork without being offended or insulted. The fact is that in any negotiating situation, this 'least amount' does exist. The more money you can save without damaging a relationship, the more money you'll have to spend on future acquisitions and, oddly enough, the more respect you'll get from sellers for your negotiating skills. Being able to determine 'least amounts' is not really a skill you can learn through study, so don't start signing up for 'How to Get What You Want' seminars or run to the library and read all the books you can on negotiating technique. You learn only through real-life experience.

Another point that advanced negotiators are aware of and take into consideration is that art prices often fluctuate according to sellers' moods, financial situations, frequency of recent sales, feelings about particular works of art and so on. For example, a dealer who hasn't made a sale in several weeks and needs to pay bills is more willing to consider offers than one who is making regular sales.

Some dealers are more inclined to entertain offers at certain times of the year than at others. For example, the summer months are often slow months for art galleries and, therefore, good times for making offers. On the flip side, autumn and late winter/early spring are busy times of the year, times when your offers are less likely to be accepted.

In many instances, the longer a dealer has had a work of art in stock, the more he or she will be open to taking offers on it. Sooner or later, dealers get tired of looking at the same old art, decide to increase available storage space and so on.

With time, you'll be able to take greater risks when the moment of monetary truth is at hand. For now, play conservative and don't take too many chances too fast. You want negotiations to be cooperative ventures, not combative ones.

Surprisingly, the most advanced and mature form of negotiating is no negotiating at all. Here, you and a seller understand each other so well that selling prices are agreed upon instantly. This goal of complete understanding and total trust is one you should strive for. In the end, the less time you waste bargaining, the more time you can devote to learning about art and forming a meaningful collection.

A LOOK AHEAD

So let's say you make an offer on a work of art, and the seller accepts it. The big moment has arrived. You pull out your chequebook or credit card and proceed to pay. Time to buy!

Or is it?

Buying art is a little more complicated than simply completing the transaction and walking out the gallery door with your new acquisition. You've got to follow certain procedures and take a few precautions at the point of purchase in order to assure yourself a lifetime of happiness with your art. The next chapter considers these procedures and precautions.

CHAPTER 23

MAKE THE BUY

When you buy art, you can pay for it, take it home, display it and forget about it – as many people do – but that would be rather ill-advised. Your purchase is a long-term investment in more ways than one, and you should be concerned about its future. Your relationship with this art is just beginning, and you want it to be a successful one. What you do now could easily affect the art's value – historical value, scholarly value and monetary value – for generations to come (and for your descendants, in particular).

You must also be concerned about possible negative outcomes of your purchase. Two important points to consider are these. What if the art has been misrepresented to you in some way or, in a worst-case scenario, is not even by the artist it's supposed to be by? Obviously, you have to protect yourself. Attend to certain details now in order to maximise your enjoyment of the art, enhance its desirability and resale value, and save yourself potential complications later.

PAYING FOR YOUR ART

Before looking to the future, let's deal with the present – the moment at which you actually pay for your art. You have two options here. You can either pay for it all at once or you can pay for it over a period of time.

Many art galleries are amenable to allowing clients time to pay for their art, especially when the art is expensive. In these cases, collectors sometimes need to pay in several instalments or make other special purchase arrangements. Even with moderately priced art, collectors may be given the option of making several payments over time, whether they need to or not.

The best procedure, assuming you can afford it, is to pay the full price at the time of purchase. That way the transaction is complete and clean, you own the art outright, the seller has no further claim to it and you have an immediate sense of how much money you've just spent. Even when you are offered optional payment plans, if you can afford to pay the total amount at once – which should be almost always – pay it.

Then again, if you are the type who likes to take advantage of terms just because they are available, that's fine, too. Never use them as an excuse to overspend, though. A good procedure is not to ask for or insist on terms unless you need them. The best procedure is not to need them at all.

For you first-time buyers who are paying over time, know that art galleries do not charge interest. *Instalment payments should never total more than the agreed-upon purchase price of the art, assuming you pay within a reasonable period of time, usually three months or less.* If you need any longer than three months, you're probably spending too much and should consider tightening your budget and choosing another work of art that you can more easily afford.

When you buy art in instalments, always make your payments on time. Artists and galleries are quite flexible in sitting down with you and deciding how much you should pay by what dates. All you have to do is make those payments when you say you're going to.

Don't get a reputation for dragging things out. If you don't pay when you're supposed to, sellers will lose interest in extending you any financial considerations at all and, at worst, they may refuse to do business with you. They'll also tell other sellers to watch out for you, and that can seriously impair your ability to buy. The art world is small, word travels fast and no gallery or artist likes doing business with clients who don't pay on time.

DOCUMENTING YOUR PURCHASES

Formally document every work of art you buy. If problems ever arise with any art you own, proper written documentation leaves no question as to how the art was represented at the time of purchase. Never assume that verbal assurances are all that is necessary.

The first document you need whenever you buy art is a proof of purchase – a receipt. That receipt should accurately describe the art according to size, medium, artist, date executed and any other pertinent details. It should be fully signed and dated by the seller.

The second document you need is a guarantee that the art is by the artist who it has been represented as being by. This is often in the form of a certificate of authenticity (COA; see Chapter 15) signed and dated by either the seller, the artist or an independent authority qualified to make the determination of authenticity. It confirms that the art in question is by the artist the seller says it is by. Also stated should be any other facts relating to authenticity or authorship that have been told to you by the gallery.

The third document you need, especially when you are buying art that is not brand new, is a condition report; that is, a statement of the art's condition at the time you are buying it. This document should either state that the art is in perfect original condition or accurately describe any damage that the art has incurred over the years and specify whatever actions have been taken to conserve or repair it.

Along with this documentation, you need one more thing: an unconditional money-back guarantee. Included in or attached to your receipt, authentication and condition report must be a guarantee by the seller to return your purchase price in full at any point in the future should the art turn out to be other than how it has been represented in any of those three documents. Sellers must take full financial responsibility for all statements they make about the art they sell.

Your receipt, authentication, condition statement and money-back guarantee are the core of your documentation process (they can all be contained in a single document), but they are also just a portion of the records you should keep. Start and maintain a file, beginning with these documents, on every piece of art you buy. Inside that file goes anything relating to that art or artist. Along with the core documents go relevant gallery or artist correspondence, relevant articles or publications, exhibition catalogues, invitations to openings and so on (if you have questions about how to acquire additional data for your files, review Chapter 16, 'Provenance is Profit').

Never alter or destroy any of your file documents. Some collectors, for instance, throw away their original bills of sale because the art has increased in value since they bought it, and they don't want anyone to know how little they originally paid for it. They believe that the receipt will decrease the art's value or, if they ever decide to sell, buyers will offer less if they find out the original cost. Nothing is further from the truth! The art is worth what it's worth no matter how little it originally sold for.

For example, when you see a van Gogh painting, do you think about how little it sold for decades ago? Do you think it would be worth less to a collector today because he or she knows that it sold for a pittance over a hundred years ago? Would you be interested in seeing an original receipt for a van Gogh painting dating from that far back? Do you think that receipt would have historical significance and be worth money in and of itself? Of course it would. Case closed.

Summarising, always include the following in your art files:

- The original bill of sale.
- The authentication or statement of authorship.
- The condition report.
- A money-back guarantee protecting you if condition, authenticity or any other data the seller gives you ever turn out to be other than as they were stated.
- Any incidental material that the seller gives you.
- Any pertinent correspondences from the gallery, the artist, relatives of the artist and so on.
- At least two good, clear photographs or digital image files of the art in case the art ever gets stolen or significantly damaged.
- Any materials or information you acquire at any future date relating to that art or artist.
- A current appraisal of the art (less than three years old).
- Full instructions on what to do with the art should anything ever happen to you.

Each file becomes a record of the art piece that it represents. It protects your investment in case the art gets damaged, destroyed or stolen. It is a source of information and details that you otherwise might forget. It educates and informs all interested parties. And, at any point in the future, that art's history can be traced right back to the day you bought it – and to an earlier time if you did extra research or were provided with its previous ownership information from the seller.

Above all, such a file becomes part of the art itself and can be passed on to all subsequent owners of that art. The truth is that you won't be around forever to provide a verbal explanation of your art and the history behind it. Whoever owns it after you will have the information you accumulated on hand to help explain its value and significance. And should subsequent owners – your descendants in particular – happen to be people who don't care that much about the art and would rather sell or donate it than keep it, they'll have adequate data on hand for income-tax purposes or to protect themselves from being taken advantage of by unscrupulous buyers.

RETURN AND EXCHANGE ARRANGEMENTS

Before beginning any discussion on returning or exchanging art, remember that art is not currency. Artists and galleries are not banks where you exchange money for art and then, at some later date, return that art for any percentage of the initial purchase price. Return and exchange arrangements are not convenience services for transforming art into cash whenever you feel like it. You should, however, buy art only after you completely understand the return or exchange policy of the gallery selling it.

Many galleries offer what is called a *short-term return privilege* and provide it in writing. Here, for a limited period of time immediately following your purchase, you are allowed to return the art for a full cash refund. This period can range anywhere from one week to a month or so, depending on the gallery, during which time the art is returnable for whatever reason you have for deciding not to keep it, no questions asked. Of course, it is hoped by all involved that you will choose your art wisely and never have to take advantage of this option. Remember that if you have any doubts whatsoever about whether you really want to own a particular work of art, take it home on approval *before you buy it*.

Galleries (and sometimes artists) may offer *long-term return/exchange arrangements*. Such policies, which vary from seller to seller, have to do with how your art is to be handled if you decide to bring it back months, years or even decades after you buy it. The two main options offered under such arrangements are taking your art back on consignment and selling it for you or allowing you to exchange your art for credit equal to your original purchase price. When art has increased in value since you purchased it, terms will have to be worked out with sellers on a piece-by-piece basis.

Galleries are often willing to take your art back on consignment at any time and sell it for you, especially if it's in demand in the marketplace. This saves you the trouble of having to resell it yourself. The galleries display your art, offer it to their clients and assume the responsibility of completing the sales transactions for you.

Not all consignment arrangements are the same. Understand what fees or commissions a gallery charges for reselling your art in this manner. Some galleries attempt to net you your original purchase price, some give you a portion of the profit if they sell your art for more than you paid for it, and others take a set percentage of the selling price no matter what the art sells for. Whatever the arrangement, know what it is and get it in writing before you buy.

Consignment selling has one major drawback: there is no guarantee your art will sell within a reasonable time period, or even at all. Galleries typically have no problem offering consignment services because they involve no financial risks on their part. They only pay you if and when your art sells, not before.

Galleries (and sometimes artists) may offer options to exchange your art at any point in the future for a trade value equal to the full original purchase price. In this instance, you are credited that cash amount towards any new purchase you make from their current stock at the time of the return or after. This gives you the luxury of returning your art effortlessly and at no cash loss should your tastes change or should you decide to upgrade your collection.

Exchange policies vary from gallery to gallery. Some galleries allow exchanges for anything in their stock; others allow exchanges from only certain portions of their stock. The most common arrangement allows you to exchange your art for any art that a gallery owns outright, but not for art they have on consignment from other owners. If trade on consignments were allowed, a gallery would have to pay a consignor immediately upon receiving your art, which would be basically the same as giving out a cash refund without taking any cash in. With rare exceptions, immediate cash is not issued to any buyer who decides to exchange their art. Cash is paid out only after art sells.

Return or exchange policies at the same gallery can even vary from art piece to art piece, so understand what your options are on each individual work of art you buy. Never assume anything and, as always, get whatever you are told in writing.

As part of a sales presentation, some sellers may lead you to believe that if you ever decide to sell, all you have to do is bring your art back, they'll resell it within a short period of time and you'll have your payment, possibly with profit over your original purchase price. Don't believe this for a moment. Unless the art or artist is in high demand, selling on consignment takes time, and you may not recoup anywhere near the amount of money you originally paid. At worst, your art could sit for sale indefinitely without selling, in which case, you recoup nothing.

When galleries make consignment sound like a sure thing – like you can cash in your art at any time (usually with profit) – call them on it. Insist that they put their promises in writing and guarantee those returns. How many galleries do you think will be willing to go that far? You guessed it: none. The best approach is not to do business with these sorts of galleries in the first place.

One final note about consignment: honest and experienced art dealers will tell you that, looking back on their years in business, they have sold some art that they would love to resell and other art they would just as soon never see again. *No one can predict the financial future of any art or artist.* The passage of time is the ultimate determinant of how easy, difficult or impossible reselling your art under any circumstances might be.

Here's a scenario that puts consignment selling into its proper perspective. Suppose you buy a sculpture from a gallery that guarantees in writing to take it back on consignment at any point in the future. Ten years later, you ask the gallery to resell it for you. The gallery owner tells you he'll take the sculpture back on consignment, but he'll have an extremely difficult time selling it, if he can sell it at all, because the sculptor is no longer popular and has totally dropped from public view. He suggests that you'd be better off donating it to charity for a tax deduction.

Another circumstance where consignment arrangements become worthless is when the gallery where you bought the art goes out of business. Minimise the possibility of this outcome by making sure galleries you do business with have been in operation for years and have good reputations in the art community. In either of these situations, the final outcome is that you'll likely receive none of your original cash outlay with the gallery's help and will be pretty much on your own in terms of how or where to sell.

One final word: *never abuse a return or exchange privilege.* Becoming known among galleries or artists as someone who regularly returns art is bad for your reputation, and galleries will become reluctant to do any further business with you. When you buy art, be pretty sure you like it, pretty sure you can afford it and pretty sure you're going to keep it.

ART PURCHASES THAT ARE LESS THAN IDEAL

Not all sellers provide buyers with proof of authenticity, condition reports, data about the art they sell, consignment or trade-back arrangements and other amenities. They sell art pretty much 'as is' and have the attitude that once you buy it, you own it, and they want nothing more to do with it. This is their privilege and should not be taken as an indication that the art they sell is inferior in any way to 'guaranteed' art.

The fewer assurances you get at the point of purchase, though, the more informed you have to be about what you are buying. When you're just starting out, the best procedure is to avoid buying art that comes with few or no guarantees and protections. Buy only from sellers who stand behind what they sell and who take full responsibility for representing it properly. As you gain experience and learn more about what you're doing, however, you can become more adventurous in your buying habits.

Whenever you buy art under less than ideal circumstances, still record and file whatever information the seller gives you. With no authentication, condition report or money-back guarantee, at least try to get a receipt that accurately describes the art as to artist, size, subject matter and other particulars. Ask for a signed statement telling how the art was acquired and whatever additional facts the seller knows about it. If you are shown any documents relating to the art, ask that they be included in your purchase. When that's not possible, borrow them and make copies for your records.

Maintain a file even when you get no written information from a seller. Write a statement yourself recounting the circumstances of your purchase, the purchase price, what the seller told you about the art, where it supposedly came from and any other interesting details surrounding how the acquisition was made. This sort of documentation can eventually prove to be just as valuable and informative as the official material you get from established galleries.

Example 1

I once bought a painting from a dealer who gave me no guarantees on it. That was fine with me because I felt sure it was authentic and knew that for the size, subject matter and quality of work, the price was fair. Several months later, however, another dealer saw the painting and told me she thought it could possibly be a forgery.

I decided to show it to an expert and see whether he would authenticate it for me. He declined to do so. He didn't come right out and say the picture was a fake, but I got the idea that it (and I) obviously had problems. I contacted two other experts and they gave me the same response: no go on the authentication.

I returned to the seller and explained my situation. He told me that although my plight was unfortunate, he was not willing to take the painting back and return my money. He had sold the art 'as is'; I had bought it 'as is'. I was stuck with the painting. I, of course, stopped doing business with this dealer, but only after learning an expensive lesson – do everything possible to get guarantees, no matter how limited they might be. No matter how much you think you know, you can always be fooled.

Example 2

An art collector told me about a time she tried to return a limited edition print to the gallery she bought it from. When she purchased the print, the gallery verbally guaranteed that she could have an immediate full cash refund if she returned it within two weeks. However, nothing was put in writing.

About a week after purchase, the collector had second thoughts about the print and decided to return it. She brought it back to the gallery, explained her decision, and was told that the employee in charge of returns and exchanges was on vacation and would be back in several days. The person she was speaking with then attempted to convince her to keep the print. He said that the value was only going up, that the artist was on the verge of having a major museum show and so on. According to him, she was making a terribly wrong decision.

She insisted on returning it, however, and came back to the gallery several days later to complete the process. This time, she was introduced to the gallery owner, who talked to her about exchanging the print for one of equal value rather than taking the cash. She refused, demanded her money and was finally allowed to 'officially' return the print.

At that point, the owner took the print back, but the woman still received no cash as she had been led to believe she would. He told her that restocking forms had to be processed and she would have her money back within six to eight weeks.

The happy ending is that she did eventually get her money back, less 'restocking fees'. The lesson: *get it in writing and understand the terms*. No matter what you are told and how wonderfully you are treated in the moment you buy your art, know gallery policy and have it in writing.

A LOOK AHEAD

An art-buying and -selling situation in which sellers regularly provide little or no guarantees on what they sell happens to be, oddly enough, extremely popular with art buyers. In the great majority of cases, the sellers do their best to properly represent what they have for sale but, in the end, you – the buyer – are the one charged with researching and evaluating any art you are interested in buying. You must decide whether or not it is authentic, what condition it is in, how significant it is and what you think it's worth, because once you buy it, it's yours for keeps. The next two chapters address the highest-profile and risk-riddled art arena of them all – an arena that no book about collecting art is complete without discussing – *the auction*.

CHAPTER 24

Buying Art at Traditional Auctions

This chapter about buying art at conventional established auction houses and the following chapter about buying art at online auctions are placed at the end of this book, because that is exactly when novice art buyers should consider buying art at auction: after, and only after, they understand fully the differences between buying at galleries and buying at auctions. This is not to say auctions are bad places to buy art and you should avoid them. Quite the contrary. Auctions are great places to buy art, but only on the condition that you know what you're doing when you buy there.

More people than ever before are excited at the thought of buying art at auction. More people than ever before actually do buy art at auction. The great majority of auction-related publicity, most of it generated by the auction houses and art-industry interests themselves, is overwhelmingly pro-auction. In response to all this hype and hubbub, someone has to take the conservative, sober and sensible approach to action at the auction. We'll do that here.

Anyone can attend auctions for the purpose of buying art; no law prohibits them. Auction houses have no knowledge or skill requirements for people who participate in and buy art at their sales. As far as these establishments are concerned, the more bidders they attract, the better.

Auctions are places where art experts, art dealers and seasoned collectors go to buy art. Auctions are also places where beginners who aren't too sure about what they are doing go to buy art. In fact, even people who have no idea what they are doing buy art at auction. The less experience buyers have, the more substantial the risks they take when they buy at auction. Unfortunately, many amateur auction patrons don't realise this.

The auctions we are mainly concerned with here are less established, less well-known, secondary, and regional or local firms. These smaller houses are the ones that conduct the great majority of sales worldwide and are also the ones where you often have to take your chances when buying art. In the substantial majority of cases, staff and owners of smaller auction houses are not particularly qualified to oversee and accurately evaluate every piece of art that is placed for sale at their establishments. They do their best, of course, but don't always get it right.

This chapter is also applicable to some of the major houses, in spite of the fact that they are a great deal more selective in what they sell. Even though they employ qualified experts to carefully examine and screen all art before it is accepted for sale, you still take significant risks buying at these establishments if you don't know what you're doing. The very best auction houses (see Appendix VIII) do employ experts who can consult with you about what you're buying, but this is the exception rather than the rule. *No matter what calibre of auction house you patronise, though, the bulk of the responsibility to know what you are buying and how to go about buying it lies with you.*

AUCTIONS VERSUS ART GALLERIES

Buying art at auction is different from buying at galleries. Sure, the art you see at auctions looks basically the same as the art you see at galleries. It is often attractively presented, displayed and lit, and hangs on the walls and sits on the pedestals just as an art gallery would display it. But that's where the similarities end.

Auctions are less specialised than art galleries. For example, you can find galleries dealing in types of art as specific as Minnesota art and artists, American art from the 1930s and 1940s, contemporary French sculpture and so on. Specialised galleries are experts at what they sell; they spend all their working hours focusing exclusively on the art that they specialise in and, as a result, are able to provide their clients with the maximum amount of knowledge about that art.

Auctions, on the other hand, do not specialise and, thus, do not provide that level of knowledge and background information about what they sell. The great majority of auction houses sell whatever works of art people bring them, display it all together in the same sale and let the potential buyers figure out what's what. You might see anything from Old Master prints to contemporary abstracts, and from New England coastal scenes to Moroccan landscapes, all up for sale at the same auction.

Auction houses do the best they can, with whatever resources they have on hand, to determine whether the art people consign for sale is authentic and in reasonably good condition. But beyond that, they do not perform the types of in-depth evaluations that private galleries do (such as determining how good the examples are, whether they are typical or atypical of the artists' work, what periods in the artists' developments they represent, whether they are done in the artists' preferred mediums, what condition they're in and so on).

Because auctions accept such a wide range of art, they generally do not present consistent quality the way galleries do. Galleries pick and choose specific pieces for their clientele. Auctions do this to a certain extent, especially the best houses, but most tend to be less selective. Once again, they throw everything together and let the buyers decide what's great, good and not so good. After all, auctions are not in the art-gallery business; they are in the business of selling as much merchandise of all kinds as possible for their consignors within set periods of time.

Auction houses rarely invest money in what they sell. This no-risk situation for the auction houses gives them a special advantage over art galleries, which may at times purchase art outright and, in pretty much all cases, stand behind what they sell in terms of quality, authenticity and significance. Because auction houses sell mainly on consignment, they can take chances and accept marginal items that may or may not do well at their sales. For example, dealers and collectors regularly use the auction option to dispose of second-rate pieces and other types of inferior-quality or problem art that they either can't sell through their galleries or no longer want in their collections. Merchandise that does not sell is simply returned to the consignors, and the auction firms are no worse off for their efforts. In fact, some firms collect fees whether or not the art sells. (Incidentally, some major firms may advance cash on important works of art in attempts to convince certain owners to consign that art to their sales, but that practice involves only a minute percentage of all art sold at auction.)

You have no return or exchange privileges at auction. Unlike buying at galleries, when you buy art at auction, it's yours for keeps. All sales are final. Make sure you like whatever you bid on before you buy it because, if you change your mind, the only way to get your money back is to place it back up for sale and hope for the best.

A most important difference between auction houses and galleries is that the majority of auction houses provide few, if any, guarantees on what they sell. The best houses do offer what amount to limited guarantees of authenticity. Depending on the firm and the country or state they are located in, they may allow you to return merchandise for certain periods of time after it is sold, ranging anywhere from a few days to as long as a few years in exceptional cases. In order for an auction firm to take art back, however, you must conclusively prove, based on expert opinions, that it was not properly represented. When a limited guarantee ends, auctions are no longer legally bound to accept returns, although many established firms still may take them back when buyers present strong enough cases and insist on having their money refunded.

Whenever you attend auctions, familiarise yourself with their policy statements called the 'Conditions of Sale'. You usually see them at the beginning of auction catalogues or posted on auction-house websites. If you can't find them, ask to see them. Read the conditions word for word. Once you become familiar with such conditions, you realise just how cautious you have to be when you buy at auction as opposed to at a gallery. They state exactly what the auction house is responsible for regarding what they sell – which is not too much – and what you are responsible for – which is just about everything.

For example, let's say you are at an auction where the auctioneer states that the next item to go up for bidding is a painting signed 'John Doe'. The auctioneer means exactly what he says – that he is selling a painting signed 'John Doe' – and nothing more. He is not guaranteeing that the painting is by Doe. Maybe it is, maybe it isn't. All he is doing is stating the fact that it happens to have a 'John Doe' signature on it. Are the painting and signature authentic? The auction house does their best to screen their merchandise, but the actual facts are for you and fellow bidders to determine.

The average auction sale is the ultimate arena for the policy 'Let the buyer beware'. Auctions are not like retail art galleries that provide fully documented, fully condition-inspected, fully researched and fully guaranteed products to the public. Never confuse the two.

MISTAKEN BELIEFS THAT PEOPLE HAVE ABOUT AUCTIONS

Some of the reasons why so many art buyers find auctions so attractive are not really valid reasons at all. Clearing up a few commonly held misconceptions will help place auction buying in its proper perspective.

The belief that auctions are where you go to find bargains is not necessarily true. The chances of your getting a bona fide bargain at auction are slim, and the lucky few who tend to make bargain buys are usually highly experienced professionals. First of all, auction houses want everything they sell to sell for as much money as possible. When they receive art on consignment that they suspect might have value, they research it. If they don't have the capacity to research it, they do the next best thing, which is publicise the fact that they have it for sale as widely as possible and do whatever is necessary to catch the attention of buyers who do know how to research it. All they have to do is reach two buyers who know how much the art is worth (which is almost always accomplished with ease), and then let the bidding begin. Add to this the fact that fine-art professionals monitor all significant art auctions around the world in order to make sure that no desirable works of art slip through unnoticed. In the end, virtually all quality pieces end up selling for respectable prices.

Another reason for the lack of bargains is that just about the only person who wants to see art auction cheaply is you, the potential buyer. Everyone else wants to see it sell for as much money as possible. The auctioneer wants high prices because that means more profits and better publicity for the auction house. High prices also mean more business for the auction house because potential consignors are encouraged to consign merchandise. Consignors naturally want to get as much money as possible for what they consign. Collectors who already own works by artists whose art is up for sale at auction want that art to sell high, because strong sales increase the value of the art in their collections. And don't forget the rest of the art community. They want high prices because that indicates a healthy and active art market in general. So, it's you against the world.

In spite of all this, plenty of people continue to shop at auctions for bargains. An ironic consequence of this 'bargain-hunting' is that prices of second-rate works of art periodically rise to ridiculous heights, especially during times when certain types of art or artists get 'hot' or art speculation is rampant. Later, when markets cool down or speculation subsides, these inflated prices drop back or even fall precipitously. As you read in Chapter 20, price run-ups are often due to inexperienced buyers entering the market, 'buying by name', and not possessing the skills necessary to recognise that the art they think they are getting 'so cheaply' is of mediocre quality or problematic in other ways, and not worth the 'bargain prices' they believe they are paying for it.

The belief that auction prices are always less than art gallery prices is not true. Auction art does not always sell at wholesale or below retail. Some art sells for more money at auction than it does anywhere else. In fact, certain art dealers regularly monitor auctions and cash in on the phenomenon by playing to whatever the current auction buying fads or crazes are. They consign a continuing flow of the exact types of art that bidders are inclined to pay strong prices for at any particular auction.

The belief that art is worth what auction houses think it will sell for is not necessarily true. Many auctions either provide estimated selling prices in their sale catalogues or online, or tell you about how much they expect certain items to sell for. Although many such estimates are accurate, some are too high and others are too low. You take your financial life into your own hands when you bid on art based only on auction-house pre-sale estimates.

Why are estimates sometimes too high? There are a number of reasons. An auction house may place an unrealistically high estimate on a certain piece of art as a favour to a client who regularly consigns merchandise, a research error may lead a staff member to overvalue a work of art, the auction house may be fishing for a buyer to pay at or near a deliberately overestimated price and so on.

Why are estimates sometimes too low? Again, this happens for various reasons. Research errors may be to blame. At other times, auctions purposely put low estimates on art in order to attract bidders and increase bidding at their sales. The theory here (which does seem to work) is that once people commit to following and participating in a sale, they are more likely to buy even if they don't get the art at the low prices they thought they would. Also, the lower the reserve prices that consignors place on their art (the least amounts of money that they're willing to sell it for), the lower the esti-mates can be, and the greater the likelihood that the art sells and the auction houses make money.

The belief that no one ever overpays for art at auction is not true. One reason why people overpay is that they mistakenly accept pre-sale estimates as gospel. For example, when two or more bidders believe that unrealistically high estimates are realistic or that the quality of a work of art is better than it actually is, the art sells for more than it's worth. Other reasons why people overpay usually involve their bidding for reasons other than wanting to own art (more about that in the next section).

The belief that only people who know nothing about art attend small-town, offbeat or country auctions is not true. This is a misconception suffered by bargain hunters who fantasise about finding rare art for pennies at backwoods sales. As mentioned above, knowledgeable professionals monitor just about every auction no matter how remote it is. And these days, most auctions conduct their sales online as well as at their facilities. No matter when or where something good comes up for sale, people who know how much it's worth and are willing to pay good money for it somehow manage to find out about it.

WHO BIDS AT AUCTION AND WHY DO THEY BID?

Assuming you know how to evaluate and research a work of art you see at auction, you still have to know what to do next and how to act at the sale itself. A lot more goes on at auction sales, in a psychological sense, than people innocently bidding and buying art. Within the ranks of the bidders, there are many different forces at work. All kinds of people bid on and buy art at auction for all kinds of reasons.

Experienced rational buyers make up the majority of auction bidders and are also the most predictable. Such buyers research whatever art they are interested in buying and bid in an informed, calculated manner. They know exactly what they want and how much they are willing to pay for it. If they get it, fine. If they don't, they wait until next time.

At the other end of the rationality continuum are those few bidders who go completely wild and are victims of what is often described as 'auction fever'. They bid as much for thrills, excitement and victory over the competition as they do for the art itself. For them, nothing quite equals the emotional charge of bidding either online or in the midst of crowded rooms, beating fellow bidders and taking home their 'trophies'. The most excessive among them decide they must own certain items no matter what the cost.

Other, less common types of bidders and bidding styles include the following:

- *People who purposely bid art up in order to inflate the value of art in their own collections or otherwise have interest in seeing it sell higher than lower.* For example, an individual or gallery that owns a lot of art by one artist places a piece of that art for sale at auction and encourages friends or acquaintances to bid it up to a higher price than it has ever sold for before. Under certain circumstances, this practice may be illegal but, either way, the impressive auction result becomes public knowledge, and people who see it without understanding how it came about mistakenly conclude that the artist's work is increasing in value and collectability.
- *People who bid because they find out a rival will be bidding.* These individuals may not even be interested in owning the art or care how much they have to pay for it. All they care about is competing.
- *People who bid on art only when they find out that specific dealers or experienced collectors are bidding on it.* They

respect those dealers or collectors and figure that anything these pros think is worthwhile bidding on must be good. As an aside, dealers and collectors who don't want people watching their every move often counter the problem by bidding online or by phone or by hiring confederates to bid in their place.

- *People who bid to impress spouses, friends, relatives or business associates.* The art is always secondary here.
- *People who bid on art they never intend to own and do so only to see how high they can push up the final selling prices before safely dropping out of the action.* The few bidders who do this are usually skilled auction buyers who know just when to quit and rarely, if ever, get stuck with anything they don't want. They could almost be called shills except that they have no connection to auction houses and do what they do entirely for personal thrills and amusement.

You see, plenty goes on at auction besides the simple straightforward buying of art. People can bid on whatever they want for whatever reason they want to and pay as much as they feel like paying for it. What does this mean for you? You've got to be absolutely confident of your intentions and your knowledge of what you are bidding on before getting involved.

AUCTION PLUS POINTS: WHY BUY ART AT AUCTION?

In spite of all these cautions and warnings, auctions can be great places to buy art. Any experienced auction buyer will tell you this. *If you know what you are doing, and this is a big 'if', you can buy wonderful works of art for reasonable prices at auction.* You can even find bargains if you're really skilled at researching, setting your limits and bidding.

To begin with, auctions sell a significant amount of better-quality art fresh out of estates or private collections. Private sellers do not always have the time, the inclination or the know-how to sell their art through galleries and, as a result, choose the easy auction option. Corporations, businesses, museums, historical societies and other institutions further contribute to the fascinating array of art that auction houses continually offer at their public sales.

Auctions are about the only places where you can compete for art directly with art dealers and other professionals. Auctions are free and open public forums where anyone has the identical opportunity to bid and buy alongside anyone else. No one has any strategic advantages over anyone else like they do in many other buying situations (such as receiving special trade discounts, having early or exclusive buying or viewing privileges and so on).

All potential buyers are treated equally at auction. Private galleries, on the other hand, frequently offer their latest arrivals to their longest-standing and best clients first. They sell plenty of art before the general public ever has a chance to consider it. At a gallery, as a first-time or second-time buyer, you either have to choose from what's left over or wait until you move up in a gallery owner's customer hierarchy before being able to take first pick of the best new arrivals. At auction, you have that pick immediately.

The fact that auction houses sell art 'as is' gives you reason to be cautious in your buying, but the 'as is' situation can also work in your favour. Perfectly good-quality art may be put up for auction poorly framed, with minor damage, dirty or with other easily rectifiable problems. Dealers or other resellers often buy this art at wholesale prices, clean it up, frame it and mark it up to full retail once that's been done. Like dealers, you can also buy these types of art at reduced prices, have it repaired, cleaned and framed yourself, and save money over the extra profit margin you would normally pay galleries or other resellers to do it for you.

The fact that auction houses do not specialise can be viewed as a plus point rather than a drawback. Because auction houses accept a much greater variety of art than galleries do, they provide you with regular opportunities to view different and unusual pieces you would not ordinarily see for sale anywhere else. You can use these opportunities to broaden your general knowledge of art and possibly even expand your art-buying horizons.

Auction houses tend to be more open with respect to supplying provenance than galleries are. Many auction houses will contact consignors at buyers' requests to see whether they mind answering questions or revealing their identities, whether they are willing to provide written statements or other information about the art they consigned and so on. Galleries tend to be more protective about their sources. When private dealers acquire art at bargain prices or are supplied by regularly producing sources, they are especially not interested in naming names.

At auction, you often have a longer time to deliberate over what you see for sale than you do at galleries. Most auction firms announce their sales anywhere from several weeks to a month or more in advance. This gives you ample time to research the art you like and view it repeatedly during the pre-sale period; you can decide how much you really like it, whether you want to own it and how much you are willing to pay for it. Private galleries, on the other hand, may only offer brief options or opportunities to buy, sometimes lasting as little as a day or two, before they resume offering the art to other clients. This sort of pressure situation is never in the buyer's favour.

HOW TO BUY AT AUCTION

Suppose you want to buy art at auction at some point in your art-buying career. First-timers have to start somewhere, and no matter what type of auction you intend to patronise, the learning process is basically the same.

When you're just starting out, stick with established auction houses that have experience selling art. Be wary of travelling auctions, special art auctions conducted by firms that do not regularly handle art, 'bargain', clearance or liquidation auctions, and other out-of-the-ordinary, transient or irregularly held sales. The risks to beginners are simply too great at events like these. Attend offbeat sales without participating in order to broaden your knowledge of what auctions are all about, but as far as actually bidding goes, wait until you've had more experience bidding at established auctions first.

The first step in learning about auctions is to preview online or attend as many sales as you can *without bidding*. Research any art that interests you just as though you were actually going to buy it. Do standard artist and art research, inspect the art's condition, research past selling prices and decide the maximum amounts you would be willing to pay if you were really bidding. Attend the sales themselves or watch them online, feel the excitement, watch what happens, pay attention to how the auctioneers offer the merchandise and how the buyers respond, get accustomed to the rapid pace at which the lots sell, imagine yourself making bids and acclimatise yourself to the pressurised atmosphere of the sales. Once you feel reasonably comfortable and familiar with how auctions progress, you're ready to seriously compete against other bidders and buy art.

An essential rule to follow at any auction where you intend to bid is this: always attend the preview either online or in person, and spend plenty of time studying the art. The preview is the most important part of any sale because it is here that you have a chance to study the art, examine its every detail, ask questions, request detailed images, inspect it for condition or authenticity problems, and decide how much you like it and whether you want to own it. Auction sale previews always take place in advance of auctions, and vary from auction house to auction house in terms of how far in advance of the sale they begin, whether they occur online or in person or both, and how long they last. Anytime you are considering bidding at an auction, make sure you know the dates, times and options for previewing the items in advance of the sale. *Never* bid on or buy art that you have not previewed and researched beforehand.

In any preview situation, study all the art for sale. Even if you don't like a piece, spend at least a little time looking at it and learning about it. This exercise will increase your knowledge of art in general. After you've taken a preliminary look at the offerings, then start focusing on the specific works of art that appeal to you the most.

Carefully study your favourites, request additional images if you are not previewing in person, ask to see close-up details as necessary and so on. The more you look at your choices, the better you get to know them, understand how strongly you feel about owning them, and can assess how they would look on display in your home or place of business. Make sure you like the way they look and that you really want to own them because, once you buy them, they're yours. (You can't take auction art home on approval or take it for a 'test drive' like you can with gallery art.)

Determine the condition of any art you intend to bid on. Look at everything whether you're online or in person. In person, you can turn it over, lift it up, look at the back, look at it under a magnifying glass, do whatever you have to do in order to inspect its every detail. Note whatever problems the art has. (At some auctions, particularly the better ones, you need either permission from the management or staff supervision in order to examine art closely.)

Study all information the auction house provides about the art. This may be an item description in an auction catalogue, online or in some other form. Keep all such information on hand for future reference.

Have an auction staff member or persons in charge of art tell you whatever they know about any art you are interested in. You can do this either in person, by phone or via email. See if the staff member is aware of any condition problems. Ask also if they know where the art came from, whether any documentation accompanies the art, why it was consigned and any other details you might need to evaluate before you place your bids. Find out everything you can. Save any pertinent information for future reference.

Once you've assembled the information, do your research! Find out everything you possibly can about the art and its artists from sources outside the auction house according to the procedures outlined in Part III of this book. Study biographical information about the artists. Search for them online, look at as many examples of their art as possible, learn about their careers, histories and accomplishments, etc. Determine the significance of the art. Evaluate the artists' price structures according to procedures outlined in Chapter 21. As already mentioned, never rely solely on the pre-sale estimates the auction house provides; independently confirm and corroborate any other statements the auction house has made to you either verbally, online or in the sale catalogue.

Based on your research, decide what your maximum bids will be, and *stick with those bids right through to the close of the bidding*. Whether or not the amounts you are willing to bid relate to the auction house estimates or what the art eventually sells for, do not change your mind at the last minute. The moment you reach your limit on any one bid, stop and wait for the next item you're interested in to come up for sale.

Options for bidding vary from auction house to auction house and sale to sale, and include bidding in person, bidding online or bidding by phone. Find out in advance what your bidding options are. If for any reason you do not want to bid yourself because you want to keep your identity secret, you can either ask or hire someone to bid in your place, and provide complete instructions on how you want them to bid. If for any reason you are unsure of what you're bidding on, you can also hire an informed individual to evaluate it, recommend what your highest bid should be, and then bid on your behalf.

No matter how you intend to bid, controlling yourself during bidding is especially important if you are an inexperienced bidder. Novices tend to get carried away at the last moment, throw their research to the wind and bid just to buy something no matter how much they have to pay for it. In the heat of a fast-paced auction sale, a few seconds of indiscretion can cost you dearly. So, don't be upset if you come away empty-handed. You'll find plenty more works of art to bid on at future sales.

If you are nervous about buying at auction and want to work your way into it more gradually, hire a no-conflict resource, such as a dealer or experienced collector who you know, trust and can confide in to assist you at every step of the research and buying process. Examine and discuss the art together, research it and decide what to do based primarily on this experienced individual's professional recommendations. The best auction houses offer consultation services but, even so, hiring independent, unbiased experts makes better sense. Most such professionals perform this service either for a flat fee or for a percentage of the final selling prices, usually ranging between 4 and 10 per cent.

Asking independent professionals for their opinions without paying them can sometimes be hazardous to your bidding. At worst, they can conceivably become your adversaries when they are under no obligation to work on your behalf. For example, your innocent questions may call their attention to a work of art they did not notice initially and would have overlooked entirely if you hadn't asked about it. The individual might decide you're on to something good and end up bidding against you.

Example

Experienced dealers and collectors know to preview and attend all auctions where art they are interested in bidding on is being sold, either in person or online. They are prepared to bid regardless of how high the pre-sale estimates are, how much people expect the art to sell for and how dim prospects seem for getting that art at the prices they're willing to pay. In the auction business, you never know what's going to sell for what until it actually sells.

A friend of mine likes to relate a story about a painting he saw at an auction preview. It had a pre-sale estimate of $20,000 to $40,000. Interest in the picture was strong and the general word among those in the know was that the final selling price was expected to be somewhere between $40,000 and $50,000. Although this collector was willing to bid as high as $30,000, certainly a respectable amount of money, he had pretty much given up any hope of getting the painting. Nevertheless, he decided to attend the sale in person.

When he arrived, he found the auction room nearly empty. Even so, the other works of art were still selling at substantial prices – nothing was selling terribly low. He didn't have high hopes of being the winning bidder on his favourite painting, but now he felt that at least he had an outside chance, hoping that the low attendance was indicative of a general lack of interest in the sale. When the art came up for sale, he sat silently without bidding and prepared to watch it sell for well over $30,000. To his surprise, bidding abruptly stopped at $18,000. He couldn't believe it. He raised his card and got the painting for $19,000 – almost 40 per cent less than what he would have gladly paid and less than half of what the auction house had expected it to sell for.

He hypothesises on his good fortune as follows. Perhaps everyone who was interested in the painting was so sure it would sell high that hardly anyone bothered to bid, follow the sale online or attend in person. Everyone thought everyone else would be bidding on it when, in fact, they had all psyched each other out. The only person who was apparently willing to pay any serious money for it turned out to be him.

Whether his explanation is right or not, such unexpected turns of events happen all the time at auctions. If you see art you like at a preview, never assume it's out of your reach until the final bid is made, and the hammer falls.

A LOOK AHEAD

Online auctions present an entirely different array of research, bidding and buying situations than do traditional auctions. In fact, the approach to bidding and buying online only vaguely resembles that of bidding and buying at a traditional auction-house sale. Chapter 25 focuses on the differences between traditional auctions and online auctions, and discusses how to evaluate online auction descriptions, how to preview merchandise, how to evaluate photographs of merchandise on your computer screen, how to request additional information from sellers and more.

Buying Art at Online Auctions

Online auctions have forever changed the way fine-art buyers and sellers do business, and they are, without a doubt, the wave of the future. In the old days, art dealers and collectors had to physically travel to galleries and auctions in order to see art for sale. Their other search tools included phones, faxes, trade publications, art dealer organisations, museum-collector groups and the like. People with art for sale had few options other than to sell to local galleries, consign to local auctions or hold estate sales. Today, anybody can sell just about anything to anybody else assuming they have access to computers and understand the simple rules of buying and selling at online auctions.

The great majority of art buying at online auctions is fun, easy, cost effective and satisfying. Buyers can locate quality items for sale in faraway places, and sellers can reach more buyers and occasionally sell for higher prices than ever before. The volume of internet auction transactions is steadily on the rise as people have become entirely comfortable with this new way of doing business.

If you're a beginner, though, buying art at online auctions is a risky business, even riskier than buying at traditional auctions such as those discussed in the previous chapter. The nature of this risk, and the major difference between online auctions and traditional auctions, is, without a doubt, that all kinds of people are selling all kinds of art, and unless you really know what you're doing, you can get into all kinds of trouble. If you'll recall from the last chapter, the most important part of the auction buying process is previewing and hopefully seeing the art in person *before* you bid. Accurately assessing art from images on computer screens, especially inferior-quality images, can be challenging even for seasoned professionals.

THE TWO TYPES OF ONLINE AUCTIONS

The two basic types of online auctions are those that are vetted and those that are not vetted. A vetted auction is one where art specialists examine all works of art before they are placed for sale in order to determine whether they meet certain requirements in terms of quality and are properly represented by the sellers, who are usually established dealers, collectors or traditional auction houses. Art that passes this critical inspection is deemed appropriate for auction and is placed up for sale in much the same way that meat or dairy products are inspected, graded and deemed appropriate for sale at your local supermarket. (All art that you see for sale at better auction houses has been vetted.)

Pretty much all established auction houses (and many less established ones), from major international companies to regional and local firms, have their own websites and conduct vetted online sales either on their own sites or through other websites like Liveauctioneers, Artnet, Invaluable and others. Experienced sellers also sell on eBay, but so do private sellers and all kinds of other individuals who are not necessarily that knowledgeable about art.

If you're new to online auctions and would like to try your hand at bidding and buying, shopping at vetted sales either conducted by or under the auspices of established auction houses or auction websites is the best way to start. These sales provide you with modest assurances and protections that, as you will soon see, are lacking at online auctions that are not vetted. At vetted sales, you can be reasonably sure that the art you are bidding on is authentic, properly represented and accurately described. You usually also have access to knowledgeable individuals who can answer your questions.

Online auctions that are not vetted – eBay being the major player – may be fairly described as anarchistic free-for-alls. In this arena, sellers need no art-related experience, references, résumés or qualifications in order to place art up for sale. All they need to know is how to use a computer. For example, any seller can place any item up for sale, no matter what it happens to be and without any prior inspection by specialists, and call it 'art'. To complicate matters further, any seller can call herself a dealer and state that she has a gallery or a shop or has been buying, selling or collecting art for decades. Online bidders who may live hundreds or thousands of miles away from these sellers cannot easily verify this information.

Although the large majority of online sellers are honest and do their best to represent their art properly, naive and inexperienced sellers routinely make mistakes in describing art, and novice buyers who believe that what these sellers state is correct may end up overpaying for those items. For example, prints are called paintings, reproductions are called originals, authorship is attributed without sufficient proof, an item made in the mid-1970s might be described as 'old and rare', and that's only the beginning. At worst, sellers can make the most ordinary, everyday items sound like long lost treasures by peppering their descriptions with superlatives like 'rare', 'important', 'fantastic', 'exquisite', 'beautiful' or 'museum quality' without qualification or regard for accuracy. On any given day, hundreds of thousands of items described as 'art' are for sale on eBay, and thousands of them contain the word 'rare' in either their titles or descriptions. Now, I don't mean to sound sceptical, but I have a hard time believing that this much rare art is simultaneously for sale on eBay, or anywhere else on the planet for that matter.

Another problem with online auctions that are not vetted is that a handful of unscrupulous sellers specialising in fakes, forgeries and misrepresentations reach more unsuspecting buyers with greater ease and anonymity than ever before (learn about their methods in Chapter 18). What's even more amazing is that they can cultivate respectable online presences for themselves through vehicles such as eBay's feedback system while, at the very same time, making spurious claims about their art and victimising innocent buyers for anything from small to significant monetary amounts. All a seller has to do to receive positive feedback and create a positive seller profile is to answer enquiries from potential buyers promptly, make sure that buyers believe that the art they're bidding on is authentic, pack the art securely when shipping it to winning bidders, ship it on time and appropriately respond to all requests for information from potential bidders. For example, buyers who have no idea they've bought bogus art, assuming the transactions have proceeded smoothly and they're satisfied with their purchases, leave the sellers positive feedback.

To complicate matters, buyers who get burned by dishonest sellers are reluctant to leave negative feedback for fear those sellers will leave negative feedback for them in return. Sadly (and amazingly), you can buy problem art from eBay sellers with 100 per cent positive feedback. Just because a seller has perfect feedback is no guarantee that the art they sell is authentic or accurately represented.

Back in the good old days before the internet, sellers almost always had to physically appear in person alongside the art that they had for sale. Regardless of the methods sellers chose to sell their art, buyers almost always knew who those sellers were, what they looked like, what their reputations were, where they lived and how to contact them. Significant works of art rarely changed hands without being inspected and evaluated (or vetted) first-hand by experienced professionals like dealers, traditional auction-house art specialists or appraisers.

Dishonest sellers acquired reputations in their communities for trafficking in questionable works of art. When art dealers and collectors found out who these sellers were, they advised other dealers and collectors in the art community to avoid them. Traditional marketplace safeguards, such as those just mentioned, protected the great majority of art buyers and assured a reasonable level of quality control in the fine-art marketplace. Online auctions that are not vetted, unfortunately, cannot provide these types of checks and balances.

Even though they have rules, warnings and restrictions in place for selling art, that unfortunately does not stop a small percentage of unscrupulous sellers from attempting to take advantage of unsuspecting buyers. The worst offenders can be permanently banned from online auction sites for repeated violations. But catching and banning them is not easy for online auction staff members, and even those sellers who do get banned may take on different identities or find confederates to continue selling their questionable merchandise for them, and be back in business without too much trouble.

To summarise, outside specialists are not required to inspect or evaluate art that sellers place up for sale at non-vetted online auctions. The sellers alone, regardless of their credentials, decide how important their art is and how to describe it to potential buyers. Sellers are not required to support or qualify any subjective or descriptive claims, judgements, embellishments, representations, statements or conclusions that they make about their art. Whatever the seller says, goes.

In spite of these risks and downsides, skilled and experienced buyers still find good-quality works of art at online auctions that are not vetted. Keep in mind that the key phrase in the above sentence is 'skilled and experienced buyers'. The best buyers know the art business, know art, are patient, professional and buy only when they're sure that the art they're bidding on is right in every respect. They ask the right questions, qualify sellers, evaluate merchandise, request additional photos or computer scans when necessary, and assess accuracy of descriptions before ever placing bids. For the more adventurous among you who wish to jump into the non-vetted online auction fray, the following guidelines, custom-tailored to online auctions and regularly followed by experienced online bidders, will help transform you into a skilled bidder, too. But please, newbies – be careful.

- *Read the COMPLETE description of any item on which you are interested in bidding.* Some less scrupulous sellers hide disclaimers deep in their descriptions, including that the art is being sold 'as is', that they have no idea whether it's genuine or not, that all sales are final and so on.
- *Beware of flowery language, subjective statements or personal opinions about how rare, beautiful, special or stunning art is when reading sellers' descriptions.* All you want are the facts, such as what kind of art it is, what its

dimensions are, who the artist is, what its condition is, how old it is and so on. If you have trouble separating out facts from sellers' personal opinions, study art auction catalogues from traditional auction houses, and see how professional auction specialists describe art.

- *Long, detailed biographical information about an artist in an item description does not automatically mean the art is genuine or even that it is by that artist.* In fact, it is not unusual for an item description to ramble on and on about the life of an artist and proceed to state that the art may not be by that artist or that the seller is not sure who it's by.

- *No claims that sellers make about either the value or authenticity of the art they are selling should be taken seriously* unless they either support those claims with proof or are nationally or internationally respected authorities on the art or artists they are selling.

- *Have sellers qualify all claims that they make about their art.* If a painting is described as rare, for example, find out who came to that conclusion, what they based it on and what qualifications they have to make it.

- *Request to see all documentation that a seller says accompanies the art BEFORE you bid, and make sure that they are originals and not photocopies.* This includes appraisals, certificates of authenticity, bills of sale and so on. Never bid on art when the seller refuses to show such documents or says that they will be sent along with the art to the winning bidder only.

- *Beware of art that is 'attributed' to well-known artists.* Sellers often use this word in their item descriptions when, in truth, they are not qualified to attribute art. Only known, respected experts on artists can make attributions and, even then, all 'attributed' means is that they think the art could possibly be by the artist. Three simple questions are generally all that's necessary to determine the strength of an attribution: 'Who made the attribution?' 'What are their qualifications for making this specific attribution?' 'What specific facts about this work form the basis for making this attribution?'

- *Art being offered for sale as 'attributed' to well-known artists is particularly pervasive on online auction websites.* If an auction site has a searchable database (for sold art as well as upcoming sales), searching a seller's name along with the word 'attributed' is generally a good idea. The more matches you get, the more cautious you need to be. If you get large numbers of matches, your best option may be to avoid that seller altogether.

- *Get credentials and contact information from sellers as well as from any other individuals who sellers refer you to for additional information about art that's up for auction.* In order for someone's claims to be taken seriously, they should be known and respected experts in their fields. If they're not experts, consider what they say to be uninformed personal opinion and not much more.

- *Any seller can state that his or her art is a bargain.* Whenever such a claim is made, request concrete proof that this is so, like having them show you previous sales records for comparable works of art. Furthermore, much of the 'bargain' art that's for sale at online auctions is problematic or compromised in one way or another.

- *When sellers state that art similar to the art that they're selling, or art by the same artists, sells for substantial sums of money at galleries or traditional auctions, request complete documentation on those sales including what sold (subject matter, size, condition, age, etc.), how much it sold for, and where, when and under what circumstances it sold.* For example, someone auctioning a 12-inch-tall sculpture online might state that the artist's sculptures sell at auction for as much as $100,000. The $100,000 sales, however, might turn out to be for sculptures that are 20 feet tall, not 12 inches tall, and 12-inch-tall sculptures by that artist only auction for about $1,000 each. (Misleading descriptions like this are common at online auctions.)

- *When items are represented as coming from important estates, wealthy families, major collectors or other exceptional circumstances, request physical proof including names, addresses, dates, receipts, auction records or published news stories relating to these previous owners.* Never accept hearsay as fact, whether it's verbal or you're reading it on your computer screen, and never assume that all items that come from so-called wealthy estates are automatically high quality, authentic or valuable.

- *When a previous owner is stated to be an important collector, find out who they were, what they collected, why they were considered important, where their collections were exhibited and which experts or public records confirm that these statements are true.* You need verifiable names, addresses, dates, places and events from reputable, established sources confirming the existence and significance of the collector. Accept nothing less.

- *Never assume that just because a work of art is signed or otherwise labelled by a particular artist that it is automatically a genuine work by that artist.* All other aspects of that art must also indicate that it is the work of the artist in question. Keep in mind that the signature or label is only one of many aspects that an expert examines when evaluating a work of fine art.

- *Request complete condition reports including locations and extent of all existing damage as well as previous repairs or restorations.* As you read in Chapter 17, condition problems can seriously devalue a work of art.

- *Never bid on or buy art that is described but not pictured online.*
- *Never buy art when the online pictures are fuzzy, too small to study detail, too dark or too light, show reflections or are difficult to view in any other way.* Buying art based only on photographs is tough enough to do even when the photographs are good. If you need to see better-quality or more detailed images, ask for them.
- *Never buy art from sellers who ONLY accept payment in forms of cash such as personal cheques, money orders or wire transfers.* If the art turns out to be problematic in some way, you have little or no recourse to get your money back. If paying by PayPal, make sure the seller has been active on PayPal for a significant period of time, has accepted many PayPal payments, is 'Verified' by PayPal, and that the PayPal account contact information matches that of the auction seller.
- *In addition to pictures of the front of the art, also request scans of the back, top, bottom, sides, signature and any other areas that may yield additional clues about the art.* By looking at the back of a painting, for instance, you can find out information like whether the age of the stretcher bars matches the age of the painting or whether the canvas has been damaged and repaired.
- *Ask for detailed scans or pictures of any areas of works of art for which you have additional questions.*
- *Always check sellers' other online sales, both ongoing and completed.* Watch for repeated use of the same words or phrases in different descriptions. Works of art from different time periods and by different artists rarely share identical characteristics (unless they're part of a very specific collection), and repeated use of the same words can tip you off to potential problems with that art. For example, if a

seller is auctioning twenty paintings and ten of them are described as 'rare' or 'museum quality', either the seller has outstanding taste in art and is extremely fortunate to own so many top-quality examples, or he could be overstating the truth in his descriptions.

- *Be cautious when one seemingly important work of art is listed alongside ordinary everyday items.* For example, if a 'Rare Sixteenth-century Old Master Painting' is being offered along with lots consisting of kids' toys, golf clubs and car tyres, this could be cause for concern.
- *Never assume that art is properly represented just because seller feedback profiles are positive.* As mentioned above, feedback profiles are not necessarily accurate indications of the sellers' integrity, so always perform complete independent research on art that interests you *before* bidding.
- *Get answers to all questions in writing (emails will do), especially relating to authenticity and condition,* before you bid and not after.
- *Make sure you have a money-back guarantee and adequate time to fully inspect (or have outside experts inspect) any art that you purchase.* You need at least one week from the day you receive a work of art to inspect it. Don't buy from sellers who do not allow returns or exchanges.
- *Make sure you have total freedom to select experts to evaluate your art.* Sellers should have no control over who you would like to examine it.
- *Save all email correspondences with sellers.* Also document all phone conversations and other communications you have with sellers as well as with their associates.
- *If you're at all unsure about a work of art, consult an independent expert before you bid, not after.*
- *If a work of art has few or no bids, but the description implies that it's supposed to be special in some way, get an*

outside expert opinion, and exercise caution before bidding. Art that is genuinely exceptional tends to sell for higher prices and have multiple bids.

- *When a work of art's reserve or current high bid is substantially below what comparable works of art sell for on the open market, this could be cause for concern.* The art may be genuine, for instance, but may also be an inferior example of the artist's work. Quality items generally sell for higher prices no matter whether they're for sale at traditional venues or at online auctions.

- *To repeat, not being able to preview the art in person before you bid on it is always a disadvantage.* If the seller of art you see for sale at an online auction is from your area, ask to inspect it in person (many sellers will allow you to do this). Not being able to physically inspect items first is a drawback to online auction buying, unless you're skilled at evaluating art and can draw informed conclusions from images online.

- *Unless you're an experienced dealer or collector or you have access to proprietary information that few people have access to, never assume that you're the only one who spots an online art bargain.* Many thousands of savvy and knowledgeable buyers from all over the world continuously monitor online auctions for all types of antiques, collectibles and fine art.

- *Never accept a seller's invitation to complete an online auction transaction privately, not on the site where the item is listed for sale.* Not only is this against the rules, but you have no protections or guarantees like those provided on the auction website if you decide to go it on your own.

ONLINE BIDDING STRATEGIES

The key to successful online bidding is this: bid the highest amount of money that you're willing to pay for an item, bid that amount as close to the end of the auction as you possibly can and keep your identity secret. Maximising your chances of making the winning bid at an online auction is that simple and no more complicated.

At traditional auctions, you bid incrementally on an item up to your predetermined limit (as you learned in the last chapter), you bid only as long as someone is bidding against you, and the bidding ends when you're the last bidder left standing, no matter how long that takes. You then win the item and the next item in the catalogue comes up for auction.

At online auctions, the bidding paradigm is entirely different. An online auction lasts for a set time period, usually seven to ten days, and the winner is the last bidder who bids the highest amount *before* the close of the sale, that is, before that moment in time when the sale ends. If you place a new high bid that reaches the auction site even a fraction of a second after the sale closes, that bid is not recorded and you do not win the item.

The strategy of bidding high and bidding late is known in online auction parlance as 'sniping' and is a successful strategy for several reasons. First of all, by bidding at or near the close of a sale, you don't give competing bidders time to perform additional research on the item up for sale or to reconsider, for any other reason, whether they should bid any higher than they already have. Second, bidding at the very end prevents 'shill-bidding' or opportunities for sellers to notify friends or accomplices to fraudulently bid against you, not because they want to buy the item, but for the sole purpose of making you pay more for it.

Third, bidding at the end of the sale minimises unwanted competition from what online auction denizens call 'stalkers'. Stalkers are people who either already know or otherwise conclude that you're an experienced dealer or collector by reading your online auction feedback profile and studying the items that you've bid on and won. When they like what they see, they do what they can to monitor your online activities in order to keep track of what you're bidding on. Even though stalkers may not know much about certain items that you're bidding on, they assume from your history that, whatever those items are, they're good quality and you're getting them for reasonable prices.

Keeping your online identity secret not only minimises bidding from stalkers, but also protects you from having to compete with others who might be inclined to bid against you on particular items just because they know who you are. For example, if you use the online nickname of 'artdealer' and bid on art, competing bidders who buy art may assume that, since you're a dealer, any bid you make is at the wholesale level and, even if they outbid you, they'll still be getting good deals. Divulging information about who you are or what you buy, sell or collect is fine as long as you wait until after an auction is over; when you're the high bidder. But reveal personal information only to the seller.

In order to help bidders place bids at the very close of auctions, several software companies have developed and sell special software to make your bids for you. The majority of experienced online bidders still prefer to bid manually, however, without using sniping software. Bidding software works best when auctions end at odd hours or when bidders know they'll be away from their computers, such as in the middle of the night or on weekdays during working hours. Experienced bidders agree, though, that more and more experienced online sellers time their auctions so that they end when most bidders are at home, like on weekend afternoons or during the early evening hours at the beginning of the week. These sellers know how to make it as easy as possible for as many people as possible to bid on their items.

As an aside, online auctions also happen to be good places to do price research. Simply go to databases of completed auction items (you can do this on eBay), type in the names of the artists you're researching as 'keywords' and study the completed sales results. You see not only what types of art collectors value the most, but also what types don't sell well. Keep in mind that searching online auction databases is *never* an adequate substitute for complete art-price research as outlined in Chapter 21.

THE FUTURE OF ONLINE AUCTIONS

The online auction world is pretty much of a free-for-all in a number of respects. The major auction sites continually seek feedback from experienced online art buyers and sellers as well as from specialists in other areas of collectibles, and sites do attempt to minimise and, hopefully, one day, eliminate system abuses. Here's my personal wish list of safeguards that would be nice to see eventually incorporated onto auction websites.

- *Requiring all items with reserves or opening bids over a certain amount (determined by the auction site) to be evaluated and approved by neutral specialists.*
- *Requiring proof of authenticity or indisputable provenance for all items with reserves or opening bids over a certain amount (determined by the auction site).*

- *Placing certain restrictions on the types of subjective claims and personal opinions that sellers are allowed to make about their merchandise.*
- *Requiring documentation for claims of rarity, scarcity or other superlatives.* Documentation could include quotes from standard reference books (with appropriate bibliographic notations), appraisals by qualified specialists or appraisers (with contact information), opinions of qualified experts or authorities (with contact information) or other verifiable forms of concrete factual documentation.
- *Providing or contracting with expert consulting services to answer buyers' questions about auction items either by phone or by email.* Buyers would probably be required to pay modest fees for these services.
- *Having specialists or experts 'police' sales of particular types of fine art and other types of collectibles where abuses of the online auction model are most prevalent.* This would be done in much the same way that law enforcement agencies patrol high-crime areas in major cities – crime is not necessarily eliminated, but it is substantially reduced. Sellers making questionable claims or placing questionable items up for sale would be contacted by experts and either questioned, notified or warned about how they are representing their merchandise.
- *Archiving sales records of all items that sell for over a certain amount (determined by the auction site) so that abusers can be more easily tracked once they're discovered.* When a seller is spotted selling a fake painting, for example, his or her selling history could be examined in order to assess the extent of his or her abuses. In serious cases, legal action could be taken and victims could be notified with greater ease than is now possible.

Example 1

Unless you're an experienced dealer or collector, being able to preview art at auction in person before bidding on it is essential in order to make sure that it has the qualities that you're looking for. Suppose you're shopping for art at an online auction, and you see a nice mountain landscape painting that looks great on your computer screen. In the foreground are several small figures leading horses up a hillside trail. You do your artist research, ask the seller several questions about the condition of the painting, determine that the piece is properly represented, bid on it and win.

It arrives at your home about a week later. You unpack it and hang it, with great anticipation, in a special place that you've prepared for it on your living-room wall. You step back, take a look and immediately notice something strange about one of the horses. You move closer and see that the horse's eye looks like it's crossed, and one hind leg is so poorly painted that it's in a totally unnatural position. Unfortunately, these problems were too small to be noticeable on your computer screen unless someone had tipped you off to them in the first place.

Since the painting was properly represented for sale and you had plenty of time to look at it and ask questions before buying it, you have no justification for returning it. Many buyers have similar tales to tell. So, to repeat, make sure you know what you're buying before you buy it, and if you need better-quality images or detail shots, ask for them.

Example 2

A buyer who bought a painting at an online auction contacted me by email at my website, www.artbusiness.com. He explained that the painting was described as being attributed to a famous artist and, now that he owned it, he wanted it appraised. He sent me scans of the painting attached to an email; I took one look at them and immediately saw that the painting in no way resembled the style of the artist to whom the seller had attributed it. Below are actual statements (in italics) made by the seller, followed by facts about the painting, determined by myself and a nationally recognised authority on the artist, based on scans of the painting that were provided by the seller.

- *Important oil (on canvas) attributed to (name of artist)*: First of all, this painting was so amateurishly executed that it wouldn't even be considered important at Bob's U-Name-It Thrift Shop. Second, when a traditional auction house describes a work of art as being attributed to an artist, this is a serious claim that normally means that, in the best judgement of a recognised expert on the artist, the art may be by the artist either in whole or in part. In this online case, anyone familiar with the artist could instantly tell that the painting in no way resembled the style of the artist, which begs the question, 'What expert made this attribution?'
- *The painting is on the original canvas*: This statement is meaningless. Show me a painting that's not on its original canvas, and I'll show you a pile of paint flakes lying on the ground.
- *The painting is from an important estate*: No information about whose estate this was or why the estate was considered important was provided by the seller.

The buyer paid well over $10,000 for this painting. At best, the painting had a retail value of $500–$1,000. The happy ending is that, with assistance from me and the independent authority on the artist, the buyer contacted the seller, reported the results of the expert analysis and was able to get his money back. He was one of the lucky ones.

A LOOK AHEAD

So far, you've learned how to buy original works of art one at a time. This next and final chapter is about how to build a collection or, in other words, how to relate those individual works of art to each other in such a way that they make a unified statement about your art-buying experiences.

CHAPTER 26

BUILDING A QUALITY ART COLLECTION

There's a big difference between buying art and collecting art. Buying art is more of a random activity based on likes, preferences or attractions at any given moment, while collecting art is more of a purposeful, directed, long-term commitment. In both cases, you buy what you like, but if your goal is to collect art and do it right, you have to master two additional skills. The first is being able to effectively research, evaluate and decide whether to buy whatever works of art attract you. The second is being able to choose each individual work in such a way as to form a meaningful grouping aka a collection.

If you're like most people, you have some sense of how to buy art on a piece-by-piece basis, but may not be all that accomplished at formulating a plan for making multiple acquisitions over time or, in other words, building a collection. You can find art you like just about anywhere you look and in a seemingly endless array of subject matters, mediums and price ranges, but sifting through it all in a systematic manner can be overwhelming and even intimidating. So, how do you decide where to focus and what direction to go in? How do you relate one purchase to the next? How do you organise or group your art together in ways that make sense?

How do you present it? And, most importantly, how do you do all these things well? This is what collecting is all about; it's the ultimate case of controlled, purposeful buying.

Great collectors are often as well known and widely respected as the art they collect. Take the Eli Broad collection, the Barnes collection, the Doris and Donald Fisher collection or the Herbert and Dorothy Vogel collection, just to name a few. Collectors like these are famous because they demonstrate just as much talent in selecting and grouping their art as the artists show in creating it. Likewise, each work of art in a great collection often commands premium attention as well as a premium price not only because it's good, but also because of the company it keeps.

What makes a great collector great is his or her ability to separate out specific works of art from the squillions of pieces already in existence and assemble them in such a way as to increase or advance our understanding of that art in particular or of the history and evolution of art in general. In any mature collection, the whole becomes greater than the sum of its parts; the collector becomes accepted as a respected authority and, in exceptional cases, goes on to set the standards, determine tastes and trends, and influence the future of collecting for all.

I'll give you an example of how this works on a small scale. For years, I was a specialist dealer in rare and out-of-print art books. Many of my customers were art collectors, dealers, curators, libraries and institutions. The best of them spotted art-world trends before the rest of us and requested materials about certain artists or art movements ahead of everyone else. In many cases, when I found what they were looking for, I'd study it myself before selling it to learn why they regarded it as significant, educate myself, and then locate similar materials for anyone who wanted to follow their leads. So, in this instance, those who made the initial requests and purchases introduced me to trends, and influenced the make-up of my stock and the direction of my buying as well as that of other collectors.

Regardless of how you view your collecting, whether serious or recreational, there are techniques you can use to maximise not only the quality and value of your art, but also your own personal enjoyment, appreciation and understanding of that art. Step one is being true to your tastes. This means acknowledging that you like certain types of art regardless of what you think you're supposed to like or what seems to be the current rage. All great collectors share this trait; it's one thing that makes their collections stand out. When personal tastes and preferences are ignored in favour of the status quo, one collection begins to look just like the next. A few people dictate, the masses follow, everyone walks in lock step, and the art you see from collection to collection becomes boring and repetitive.

Collectors who aren't afraid to express themselves yield exactly the opposite results. Take Jim Shaw, for example, the American artist who put together a collection of paintings bought exclusively at second-hand stores and garage sales, often for little more than a few dollars each. His collection ultimately toured the world and was published as a book. Not only were many of us entertained by it, but it also helped to broaden our definition of what could reasonably be considered art. He taught us that interesting-looking art could be found just about anywhere, not only at the major museums or in the best galleries. But he would most likely never have put this collection together if he had chosen to mimic the tastes of others rather than be true to his own.

Regardless of what stage you are at in your buying or collecting, if you have any nagging doubts about what you've acquired so far as well as what you've deliberately avoided, whether you're totally satisfied or you just want to take a moment to see what's new, perhaps suspend your buying for a bit and take a look around. Don't confine yourself to the same old museums, galleries, websites or wherever you've been looking at art. Get out there and see what else is going on at galleries you've never been to, places you've only heard about, and so on.

Explore the less conventional if that's what you're curious about. Look at art you think might attract you, but that you've always steered clear of. Don't be afraid to experiment. You may end up right back where you started, reinforcing your chosen path, but then again, something new and truly unique may thrill you at some point along the way. Periodic reassessments of your tastes are always a good idea. What excites you today could easily bore you tomorrow (and vice versa). A quality collection is always evolving and never static. And, of course, don't forget to hit the internet; when it comes to art, it's a vast and fantastic place. Websites like Instagram and Facebook in particular can be great for searching and discovering pretty much every kind of art imaginable.

While we're on the subject of beating the bushes for art online, perhaps the most revolutionary change between collecting today and yesterday is the level and ease of access that everyone now has to artists. Way back in pre-internet days, collectors were pretty much limited to acquiring art through dealers and galleries but today they can buy from just about anything anywhere, especially directly from artists themselves. Getting a basic art education from professionals like gallery owners is still generally recommended before heading out into the online wilds to explore other options. Social media platforms like Instagram and Facebook as well as numerous blogs, websites and online groups devoted to specific types of art and artists are also places where you can really get up to speed on the art and artists you like the most, and focus on happenings and trends in those areas. But get that education first, before you start buying, because the internet can be a pretty tricky place if you don't know what you're doing.

Regardless of how much you know about what you collect already, always remember that the educational process is an ongoing one. Be an informed buyer. Learn from the pros. Take every opportunity to discuss the fine points of what you're looking at with as many different experts, curators, artists, collectors, gallery personnel and other informed art people as possible. Not only does this improve your ability to separate out the great art from the good from the not so good, but you also learn how to protect yourself against being taken advantage of in the marketplace – which brings us to this next point.

Hand in hand with knowing the art is knowing the marketplace – and this is where many collectors fall short. The great collectors know just about everyone who sells what they collect; they're on top of the market and the market knows them. They're tuned in to the late breaking news and, when something exciting is about to happen, they're usually among the first to find out and act on it. The top collectors go to great lengths to scoop the competition when the best art comes up for sale because it doesn't come up all that often. They also know how to compare and contrast what's available in the marketplace or whatever they get offered in order to assure that something is as good as they're led to believe it is.

What amazes me about art collecting in general is the lack of comparison shopping, range and market-savviness that a significant percentage of art buyers often show. Far too many establish relationships with only one or two dealers, galleries, artists or online resources and rarely if ever stray. This may be a good strategy at the start, especially in terms of getting a basic education, but the danger in continuing this over the long haul is that your overview of the market suffers. If you inadvertently subjugate yourself to the tastes of a very select few, over time your collection becomes less of what you originally intended it to be and more of what a handful of others tell you it should be.

Knowing the marketplace and how to comparison-shop both at galleries and online also prevents you from overpaying. Simply put, Gallery X may offer you a painting for $10,000; you might find a comparable piece online priced at $7,500; and Gallery Y might have one for $6,500. If you only shop at Gallery X and you don't know Gallery Y exists or ignore online options, you waste money. It's also not that unusual to find the same or very similar works of art available from multiple sources at different prices. Due diligence pays dividends when it comes to making sure you know who's selling what before going ahead and buying.

Regarding the art that does make it into your collection, most novice collectors will tell you they buy what they like. That's definitely the best way to buy, but as you gain experience, the reasons why you buy what you like should become increasingly more conscious, detailed, well thought out and purposeful. For example, you might hear an advanced collector say something like, 'Not only do I love this sculpture, but it's also a prime example of the artist's best subject matter from his most productive time period and it fills a major gap in my collection.'

The best collectors show this sense of sureness and direction in their overall plans. And here's where we get into the essence of collecting, of what distinguishes a superior collection from an inferior one. In a superior collection, every piece belongs; nothing is random or arbitrary or out of place. A less experienced collector, on the other hand, may know plenty about each individual piece of art they own, but lack an overall understanding how they relate to one another or even whether they relate to one another at all. You don't want to look around the house one day and wonder, 'What have I been buying all these years? I'm not quite sure. I never really thought about it.'

What an experienced collector essentially does is pose a problem and then illustrate the solution to that problem by piecing together a collection. That way, everything fits and it all makes sense according to the master plan. Take this problem for instance:

What is the history of abstract painting in America? The solution is an art collection consisting of abstract paintings by American artists that date from the early days right up to the present (or from whatever time period the collector is focusing on). You can just as easily narrow the parameters and build the same or similar collections with works of art by artists from any region, locality or time period.

Pose your problem as soon as you can, as soon as you begin to get a decent feel for where your passions and interests lie. Take the randomness out of your buying. Look at what you've got so far in your collection; reflect on what all those individual pieces you like so much have in common and proceed from there. Ask questions like:

- *Why do I like the kinds of art I'm buying?*
- *What about it satisfies me?*
- *Do I like it for the subject matters, what it represents, what it communicates, its originality, the techniques, the colours, the historical aspects, the places where it's made, the lives and personalities of the artists?*

- *Does it make me think about things I've never thought about before?*
- *Does it make me feel a certain way or see things a certain way?*
- *Do I admire its technical characteristics the most?*
- *Do I like it for the concepts, ideas, themes or philosophies it embodies, communicates or stands for?*
- *Does it alter or inform my perspective on some aspect of life?*
- *Does it portray or represent things in ways they've never been represented before?*
- *Do I like that it's old, new, local, foreign, large, small, round, square, whatever?*

Once you begin to identify the common threads, you can refine your buying to zero in on additional pieces that share those characteristics. It's almost like putting together a mission statement or clearly defining and specifying your goals . . . and a collector with a specific mission or goal is always more effective at acquiring art than one who rarely questions why they buy what they do. By the way, if the answers to your questions sound like these – 'I buy what my friends buy; I buy for investment; I buy only the big names; I only buy bargains' – consider returning to square one, determining what kinds of art you really REALLY like, and then starting all over again.

Another essential aspect of good collecting is documenting your art, not only for authentication and ownership purposes, but also in terms of value. You can see best how documentation really pays off in the markets for older art. Suppose, for instance, that two nineteenth-century landscape paintings by John Doe come up for sale at the same time. They're virtually identical in size, quality, condition, subject matter, date painted and other details. The first is described as a 'Rural Landscape' and that's it. The second is documented as being titled '*Looking North from Smith's Point, Maine, September 23rd, 1876*. Exhibited at the National Academy of Design in 1877. Originally purchased for $100 by Robert Bob from ABC Gallery, New York City, 1879. Sold to Mary Miller in 1922 for $500, descended in the Miller family.' Assuming you find both paintings equally appealing, which would you rather own? Which do you suppose will be priced higher and end up selling for more money? The second one, of course. It's like choosing between a mutt and a pedigree. So, keep good records on every single work of art you own; good documentation adds value, sometimes lots of value.

An interesting aspect of the art business is that when art with little or no documentation comes up for sale, experienced sellers at least do their best to make up interesting titles for it. They know that even when little or nothing is known about art, good titles sell better than boring ones or no titles at all.

The point is that good documentation positively impacts not only on monetary value, but also on the ability to personally appreciate, connect with and understand a work of art. If you know nothing about painting, for instance, you can only guess why it was created, what it means, where it's been. If you know its entire history, you can appreciate it far more deeply and on a multitude of levels in addition to the purely visual.

If you're one of those collectors who thinks you'll always remember everything significant about every work of art in your collection and don't need to physically sit down and assemble or record that information, think again. At some point, your collection will become so large, there'll be simply too much to remember. Either that or time will take its toll on your memory and, as the years pass, you'll likely get worse and worse at recalling every single detail about works of art you acquired years or even decades ago.

The good news is you can begin documenting at any time and even from a standing stop. Write down everything you can about the art you own, either from memory or by contacting the original sellers. Include information like the following:

- Any stories sellers tell you specifically relating to the art.
- Details about the purchases including any memorable moments about making them.
- What the art means or what its significance is, either according to the artist or to whoever sold it to you.
- Biographical and career information about the artist.
- How or why or any other interesting information about the way the art was made.
- When it dates from.
- Whether it's ever been exhibited in public, at galleries or institutions, written about or featured, or publicly discussed in any setting or circumstance.

Another distinguishing feature of a superior collection is that it's organised. It has a beginning, middle and an end – just like any good museum exhibition. This goes back to posing the problem and then using the collection to map out the solution. Take the previous example of the 'history of abstract painting in America'. This collection can be organised in many ways including by date, by artist, by style or by location. Or you can get even more specific. Within a topic like this, there are all kinds of subtopics:

- Abstract painting in New York organised by date.
- Abstract painting in America between 1950 and 1970.

- Geometric abstract painting in America.
- Abstract painting in America by immigrant artists.
- Abstract paintings by American artists no larger than 12 by 16 inches.

The more precisely you state your problem, the more focused you become in your collecting. You define what your art looks like, who creates it, where you buy it, how much you pay for it, what underlying ideas or philosophies it expresses and so on. Once that's taken care of, the search is on.

Or you can narrow your area of interest further yet. How about a collection of abstracts painted by American artists that have subject matters or titles relating to oceans or coastlines? The possibilities for formulating and presenting a collection are limited only by your own imagination.

Don't worry about narrowing your interests too far. One of the keys to successful collecting is specialisation. With all the millions and millions of artworks available, attempting to see and learn something about everything is a hopeless task. Stating your interests up front and precisely, as discussed above, is the first step in specialising; making a commitment to stay within those guidelines is the next step.

Many people hesitate to narrow their interests due to a concern that they'll be missing out on something. Not to worry. Keep in mind that you can change collecting directions at any time, and even with the most stringent set of constraints, the amount of art you'll have to choose from will amaze you. This may not seem true at first, but any experienced collector will tell you the more you explore and learn about your chosen field, the more you'll be inundated with art that matches your collecting criteria.

The way to miss out on good art is exactly the opposite – by not specialising. With no in-depth understanding of what you're looking at, you won't be able to make the qualitative judgements necessary to recognise the best examples for your collection. You'll also have difficulty evaluating prices, tracking the latest developments in your field and getting to know the best resources for the art you want to own, and probably end up aimlessly wandering the vast expanses of artland.

Researching your collection is somewhat different from the standard art and artist research techniques that you learned about in Part III. Once you research a work of art and the artist who created it according to Part III guidelines, you then have to evaluate how well that work of art fits into your collection. You want to make sure it relates well to the pieces you already own and hopefully adds qualities that were previously missing from your collection.

Suppose, for example, that you collect views of a particular geographic location from 1850 to the present. An art dealer offers you a scene painted by Murphy McMurphy in 1903. In addition to evaluating the painting on its own merits and researching Murphy McMurphy, you also have to ask yourself questions like the following:

- *Do I already have this particular view in my collection?*
- *Do I already own enough paintings by Murphy McMurphy?*
- *Is this painting better or more detailed than the McMurphy paintings I already own?*
- *Do I already have enough paintings dating from the turn of the century, or am I weak in this time period?*
- *Is McMurphy as good as or better than most of the artists in my collection?*
- *Was McMurphy known for his paintings of this view or subject matter?*
- *Does the painting have any particular characteristics that are currently lacking in my collection?*

- *Was McMurphy one of the first artists to paint the view from this perspective, or did many other artists paint the same view and perspective before he did?*
- *Did McMurphy influence other artists in painting the way he did?*

Evaluating how well a painting fits into your collection can also be more informal or intuitive than the Part III research is. You and fellow collectors who collect art like the type you collect are the ones who make the rules and establish the criteria by which individual pieces are to be judged. Once those criteria are established, however, you should stick with them and consider every potential purchase in those terms before adding it to your collection. By doing so, you stay focused on your goals, and every work of art you buy relates to all other works in your collection.

Do a good, comprehensive job researching and selecting art, and you'll find yourself immersed within your chosen area of collecting to a degree that few casual buyers ever experience. By getting involved, your collecting adventures can literally turn into a love affair with art. You learn more and more about the objects of your desire; each new experience provides you with a deeper and more profound connection to the art and to the artists who create it.

Investment considerations fade into the background. Fame of the artists or the art's trendiness or popularity take a back seat. What your boss or your friends think makes no difference. You are in the process of surrounding yourself with the things you really love, and that's what counts. All accomplished collectors will tell you that this is what happens to them as their collecting progresses. Below are some activities in which dedicated, thorough and involved collectors participate.

- They try their own hands at creating art that looks like the art they collect.
- They become close friends with the artists, experts, scholars and other members of the art community who share similar collecting interests.
- They support charities, philosophies, organisations and causes that relate to their artists or collections in some way.
- They do community-service work related to their collecting.
- They share their collections with local, regional or larger communities by either giving private tours or lending works of art to museums, historical societies or corporations.
- They visit the studios of their favourite artists, watch them create art and learn about how they create it.
- They offer financial support to artists whose work they believe in so those artists can spend more time creating art and less time trying to make ends meet by working at unrelated jobs that don't allow them any contact with art.

When you find yourself doing these sorts of things, you can consider yourself a total collector. Owning fine art is far more than a money, status, fashion or trend issue. It is allowing the greater good of the art world to become an essential part of your existence.

A superior collection addresses every aspect of the problem that the collector initially proposes. Not only is his curiosity satisfied, but so is the curiosity of others who come into contact with his collection. Every piece of art becomes like a piece of a puzzle that, when combined with all other art in the collection, forms a whole that illustrates or proves the point that the collector has set out to make.

Suppose, for example, that a collector decides to explore how contemporary women artists from a particular region portray themselves in their art. He confines his selections to either artist self-portraits or works of art in which the artists place themselves within the compositions. Whenever possible, he also decides to accompany each piece with an explanation from the artist of what his or her portrayal within the art represents.

In order for this collection to be reasonably complete, the art must come from as many contemporary women artists in that region as possible. If he purchases no art by sculptors, for instance, he will have a gap in his collection. In other words, someone could enquire of the collector, 'How do women sculptors portray themselves in their art?' and the collector won't be able to answer by referencing specific pieces in his collection. The types of questions serious collectors continually ask themselves as they build their collections are similar to the following:

- *Can anyone question any aspect of my collection?*
- *Do I adequately solve the problem that I've posed for myself?*
- *Is my collection missing anything?*
- *Am I weak in a certain area?*
- *Do I have too much of one thing and not enough of another?*

Keep considerations such as these in mind as you collect, and you'll maintain the evenness and balance characteristic of a quality collection. You may find yourself selling off certain pieces along the way or buying more in areas that you believed, at one point, were adequately represented. You might even modify your goals or directions at various junctures along the way, but that's all part of the process. A collection is an ever-evolving entity.

Organising your collection is important for several reasons. First, good organisation helps others to understand what you're doing. Second, you can keep track of what you've purchased and fill any gaps with minimal effort. Third, good organisation provides you with a better understanding of what your collection means and how it's evolving. No set rules for organising exist; you decide how to present whatever you've collected.

The easiest way to get the hang of organising is to go to museums. Here you see the work of professional organisers – also known as curators. Museum shows always have starting points; they always have ending points. What happens in between the two is that viewers learn something about that particular type, selection or grouping of art. Depending on the museum or the show, you have printed, oral or recorded guided tours that explain the way each show is organised.

Now, you don't have to go so far as to physically rearrange your house and print up a catalogue. Everything can still be displayed right where it looks its best. But organise it in your mind. Be able to walk someone through and tell them the story of how and why you've come to own all this wonderful art and how it works so well together.

This not only increases their enjoyment, but also reinforces your chosen direction and your future buying. Additional benefits to organising your collection are that you can see where you've been, where you're going, where you have duplication, where you're weak, what you're missing, what no longer makes the grade and what you have to do to resolve any problems. It's not much different from your kids putting together all the baseball or football cards of their favourite teams to complete their collections.

Get a feel for how other collections are organised. See how museums present their permanent collections, for example, as well as how they arrange their temporary exhibitions and travelling shows. The latter two types of collections are especially good to study because they tend to be narrower in focus, usually don't contain that many pieces, and the text, explanations and order of the individual pieces are easier to understand in relation to the whole. Historical societies, local museums, libraries and corporations are also good places to see how collections are arranged. Some of the more common ways that collectors organise their collections are as follows:

- By date.
- By subject matter.
- By geographical region.
- By artist.
- By style.
- By nationality or ethnic group.

Ask yourself questions like those below in order to best organise what you collect:

- *What similarities or differences are apparent in my art?*
- *Can I arrange the pieces in a way that tells a story?*
- *Is any sort of evolutionary or growth process apparent in my art?*
- *What types of changes are consistently evident from one piece to the next?*
- *What arrangement best educates other people about either my values and philosophies or the goals of my collection?*

Experiment with different ways of looking at and organising your art. Many times, the arrangement you eventually settle on does not become apparent until you're well along in your collecting. Keeping organisational considerations at the forefront of your buying keeps you focused.

Regardless of how you approach and assemble your collection, you have to believe in yourself. Buy what you want to buy, and collect what you want to collect. Far too many people deny their own dreams, compromise their tastes, follow the crowd and end up with dull, boring collections. One collection looks just like the next when unimaginative collectors try harder to be correct than they do to collect. This type of buying behaviour is all too often based on fears of being rejected or ridiculed, of not doing what's 'right', of wasting one's money and so on.

In a way, fears like those mentioned above are somewhat justified. When you're true to yourself and you follow your own inner urges, you become vulnerable to harsh judgements by others who see art differently than you do. Your art tells outsiders revealing things about what you like, what you believe in, what your philosophies are, who you like, what you stand for or how your mind works. And revealing yourself like this can be scary.

But the positive results of honest collecting far outweigh the negatives. For one thing, you end up owning art you really love and not art that you feel lukewarm about just because someone else told you to buy it. You call the shots, you direct the show, you have total freedom and control over your actions, and, in the end, you experience a level of freedom that is not easy to come by in this day and age.

The final step in good collecting is not the most delightful one to talk about, but it is among the most necessary, and that is to plan for future owners – whether they be museums, institutions, family members, friends or complete and total strangers. You'd be surprised how many collectors never say a word to anyone and just think everyone automatically knows everything they've been doing all these years. This is never the case! Think about all the people you've met who own family heirlooms they know little or nothing about because no one ever told them. 'That's the painting that hung over the sofa while I was growing up and it belonged to my grandmother. That's all I know.'

The worst possible outcome for a collection occurs when the owner passes away leaving no information about the art, how much it's worth, how to care for it, or how to sell or donate it. Countless works of art have been resold for pennies, given away or even thrown in the trash because the owners kept little or no records and left no instructions on what to do with it. The lesson in all this is that collectors, no matter how large or small their collections, should provide a complete list of options and instructions for those who'll inherit their art. These include names, addresses, phone numbers, procedures, monetary values and all other particulars for selling or donating as well as for dispersal within the family.

By the way, simple appraisals with no further instructions are not enough. In fact, often they create more problems than doing any good. For example, appraisals that are done for insurance or replacement purposes often quote monetary values that are more than the art is reasonably worth in a selling situation. The inheritors fixate on these values, have no idea what they mean, assume that's what they can sell the art for, and end up spending months or years beating their heads against the wall trying to sell it, getting nowhere and maybe even mistakenly concluding that buyers are only out to take advantage.

So, cover all bases by providing insurance or replacement appraisals should your descendants decide to keep the art as well as realistic wholesale or 'fair market value' appraisals should they decide to sell it. And don't forget those instructions – who to call, where to go, what to do. You don't want them at the mercy of whatever names they randomly find on the internet.

If you expect to have any influence over the long-term future of your collection, lay the groundwork starting right now. Educate your family and those close to you about what you own. Instil a love and respect for what you've accomplished and accumulated all these years. Make sure those close to you are aware of your art's value and significance. Make sure they understand how important it is to you. You can't control the ultimate outcome, but at least you can have your say and know you've done your best to collect like a professional.

Example

Not everyone has tons of discretionary capital to spend on art. Below are ideas for interesting and unusual collections that anyone can afford to put together, regardless of their budgets.

- *Everyday objects that people have carved their initials into, made drawings on, painted on or written words or messages on.* Examples could include pieces of old pavement, tree bark, discarded children's toys or old signs and advertisements with graffiti on them.
- *Your own art.* Maybe you've always had a secret desire to become an artist. Even if you've never created a single piece of art in your life and have no idea where to begin, give it a try. You could be surprised at the results.
- *Objects that look like art, but really aren't.* Perhaps you've seen an old bent piece of metal by the side of a road or a driftwood branch washed up on a beach that looked like an original sculpture. Put enough of these items together, and people will understand how you see art in ordinary everyday objects around you.

- *Artist rejects.* This collection would consist of artist mistakes, ideas that didn't work, art that got damaged, items they're throwing out and so on. (The challenging part about assembling this collection would be convincing the artists to give their mistakes to you rather than throw them out.)
- Art by people you know, but who aren't artists. Have your friends, co-workers, relatives and anyone else who means something to you contribute miscellaneous handmade items and objects, whatever they may be, to your collection.

The ultimate secret to forming a gratifying and successful collection is this: be true to yourself, and never be afraid. Now get out there, have some fun, make your mark and master the art of buying art!

MAJOR INTERNATIONAL ART FAIRS

The following art fairs are among the most significant and high-profile events of their kind. In addition to these, numerous other outstanding international, national and regional art fairs continually take place throughout the world. Get to know the art-fair calendar in your area or vicinity, as they provide outstanding opportunities to expose yourself to all kinds of art, all at once, up close and in person.

Art Basel (artbasel.com): According to the website, 'Art Basel stages the world's premier Modern and contemporary art fairs, staged annually in Basel, Miami Beach, and Hong Kong. A driving force in supporting the role that galleries play in nurturing the careers of their artists, Art Basel frequently expands its platforms to include the newest developments in the visual arts.'

Venice Biennale (labiennale.org): According to the website, 'The Venice Biennale has been for over 120 years one of the most prestigious cultural institutions in the world. Established in 1895, the Biennale has an attendance today of over 500,000 visitors at the Art Exhibition. The history of the Venice Biennale dates back from 1895, when the first International

Art Exhibition was organised. In the 1930s new festivals were born: Music, Cinema, and Theatre (the Venice Film Festival in 1932 was the first film festival in history). In 1980 the first Intl. Architecture Exhibition took place, and in 1999 Dance made its debut at the Venice Biennale.' Held during odd years.

TEFAF (tefaf.com): According to the website, 'Established in 1988, TEFAF is widely regarded as the world's pre-eminent fair of art and antiques. We champion the finest quality art from across the ages by creating a community of the world's top art dealers and experts to inspire lovers and buyers of art everywhere.' Held annually in Maastricht and New York.

Frieze (frieze.com): According to the website, 'Frieze was founded in 1991 by Amanda Sharp, Matthew Slotover and Tom Gidley with the launch of *frieze* magazine, a leading magazine of contemporary art and culture. Sharp and Slotover established Frieze London in 2003, one of the world's most influential contemporary art fairs which takes place each October in The Regent's Park, London. In 2012, Frieze launched Frieze New York taking place in May; and Frieze Masters, which coincides with Frieze London in October and is dedicated to art from ancient to modern. In 2016, Frieze launched Frieze Academy, a year-round program of talks and courses.' Held in London and New York.

FIAC – Foire Internationale d'Art Contemporain (fiac.com): According to convention.parisinfo.com, 'The International Contemporary Art Fair or FIAC is one of the major events on the international contemporary art scene. Seasoned collectors and first time visitors come from all over the world to look at and invest in the work of important modern and contemporary artists. This event takes place at the Galeries

Nationales du Grand Palais in Paris and in different Parisian cultural places in Paris, such as the Musée Eugène Delacroix and Place Vendôme.' Held annually in Paris.

VOLTA (voltashow.com): VOLTA 'debuted in 2005 as a collaboration between dealers and friends. The aim was to secure a platform for international galleries beyond young art stalwart Liste and market heavyweight Art Basel. Concerns and aspirations of the exhibiting gallerists have been first and foremost since VOLTA's inception . . . eclectic and dynamic presentations with a strong focus on solo presentations find a stage as refined as at the main fair.' Held annually in Basel and New York.

ARCOmadrid International Contemporary Art Fair (ifema.es/ arcomadrid_06/): According to the website, 'ARCOmadrid . . . is confirmed as a key date for the art market in Spain, and a point of meeting and exchange between Europe and Latin America.' Held annually in Madrid.

Art Miami (artmiamifair.com): According to the website, 'Art Miami maintains a preeminent position in America's contemporary art fair market. With a rich history, it is the original and longest-running contemporary art fair in Miami and continues to receive praise for the variety of unparalleled art that it offers. It is the "can't miss" event for all serious collectors, curators, museum directors and interior designers, providing an intimate look at some of the most important work at the forefront of the international contemporary art movement.' Held annually in Miami.

The Armory Show (thearmoryshow.com): According to the website, 'The Armory Show is New York's premier art fair and a definitive cultural destination for discovering and collecting the world's most important 20th and 21st century artworks. Staged on Piers 92 & 94, one of the city's industrial gems, the fair features presentations by leading international galleries, innovative artist commissions and dynamic public programs. Since its founding in 1994, The Armory Show has served as a nexus for the international art world, inspiring dialogue, discovery and patronage in the visual arts. The Armory Show was founded by four New York gallerists – Colin de Land, Pat Hearn, Matthew Marks and Paul Morris – who sought a platform to present and promote new voices in the visual arts. In its 23 years, The Armory Show has stayed firm to its mission while establishing itself as an unmissable art event set in the heart of New York City and welcoming over 65,000 visitors annually.' Held annually in New York.

Art Dubai (artdubai.ae): According to the website, 'Art Dubai is a leading international art fair and the preeminent platform to interact with art from the Middle East and North Africa.'

EXPO CHICAGO (expochicago.com): International exposition of modern and contemporary art that 'hosts leading art galleries presented alongside one of the highest quality platforms for global contemporary art and culture'.

Paris Photo (parisphoto.com): According to the website, Paris Photo at the Grand Palais in Paris is 'the world's largest international art fair dedicated to the photographic medium'.

INTERNET ART RESOURCES

Note: The following lists are by no means complete but will certainly give you a start in getting acquainted with art on the internet. The internet is a rapidly evolving place, so don't be surprised if over time certain websites substantially change formats, services and ownership, while new contenders enter the fray. The focus of these lists is on more established sites that have achieved some level of recognition within the art community, but there are numerous additional websites offering art for sale online. No matter what kinds of art you buy or collect, keep current with what's happening and always keep an eye out for online resources that focus on your favourite art and artists.

WEBSITES OFFERING ART AT FIXED PRICES

www.saatchiart.com: In addition to offering art from artists worldwide, the site maintains a blog, offers advisory services, includes articles, featured artists and more.

www.artsy.net: Curated website offering art from an international selection of galleries. The site also has information about gallery and museum shows, art fairs, auctions, articles and more.

www.ugallery.com: Original art directly from an international selection of artists for sale at affordable prices.

www.lumas.com: Limited edition photographs from established photographers at affordable prices.

www.1stdibs.com: Secondary market website offering mainly vintage and collectible art, antiques and decorative items from resellers like galleries and dealers.

www.artbrokerage.com: Secondary market website offering art by mainly more commercial artists, for sale by private sellers.

www.absolutearts.com: All-purpose art website featuring works of art from artists worldwide. This website has been online since 1995.

www.artprice.com: Although this website is primarily an auction-record database service, they also offer artworks for sale at fixed prices both in stores and through classified ads.

ALL-PURPOSE ART WEBSITES

www.artnet.com: artnet bills itself as 'The Art World Online' and that pretty well sums up the site. Offerings include links and websites for national and international art galleries, art mainly by established artists for sale at galleries worldwide, art auctions, an art-auction-price database with images (fee-based), an auction notification service (fee-based), art articles and features updated frequently, international art market and market trend coverage, links to international auction houses and much more.

www.artsy.net: According to the website, 'Artsy features the world's leading galleries, museum collections, foundations, artist estates, art fairs, and benefit auctions, all in one place. Our growing database of 500,000 images of art, architecture, and design by 50,000 artists spans historical, modern, and contemporary works, and includes the largest online database of contemporary art.' The site lists over 400,000 artworks for sale, includes news and features, art-show information and more.

www.blouinartinfo.com: Blouin Artinfo provides information on fine and performing arts, museums, auctions, architecture, design and more. The site includes a gallery guide, events notices, news, features, articles, art-market information, an art-price database (fee-based) and more.

www.deviantart.com: An online social network for artists and art enthusiasts with a focus on science fiction, animation, digital art, fantasy art, illustration and more.

www.artcyclopedia.com: Provides basic information about art, artists, art history, art movements, links to museums, images of art, news, articles, information about major museum shows and more.

ARTIST AND ART COMMUNITY WEBSITES

http://www.london-galleries.co.uk: An A–Z of London museum and gallery links.

www.visualartsource.com: Guide to art galleries and museums in the Western USA with particular focus on Los Angeles and Southern California. Includes a calendar of upcoming art events plus articles, reviews and maps to all gallery and museum locations.

www.nyartbeat.com: Guide to art galleries, events and art news in the New York City area, including news, reviews, features, interviews and more.

www.sculpture.org: International Sculpture Center website, and publisher of *Sculpture Magazine*. According to the website, 'The International Sculpture Center (ISC) is a member-supported, non-profit organisation founded in 1960 to champion the creation and understanding of sculpture and its unique, vital contribution to society. Members include sculptors, collectors, patrons, architects, developers, journalists, curators, historians, critics, educators, foundries, galleries, and museums – anyone with an interest in and commitment to the field of sculpture.' Offerings include resources, membership and chapters, portfolios, work for sale, news and events, etc.

www.wetcanvas.com: According to the website, 'WetCanvas. com is the largest forum on the internet for visual artists. Founded in 1998, it's home to over 11 million posts, adding about 4,000+ news posts daily. With over 800,000 members, WetCanvas is a great place to connect with other artists.'

ARTIST AND ART-PRICE RESEARCH DATABASES

The following databases are listed in no particular order and can differ significantly in the numbers of auction sales they archive, the numbers of artists they include and in other particulars. Compare the various services and their offerings in order to find the best one (or ones) for the art you buy or collect.

artsalesindex.artinfo.com: The Blouin Art Sales Index database contains 6 million sales records of works of art by over 500,000 artists sold at auctions from 1922 through to the present at 1,380 auction houses. The site is continually updated as auctions around the world are completed and price results are made public. Monthly and yearly unlimited-search subscription options can be purchased.

www.invaluable.com: According to the website, 'Invaluable is the world's leading online marketplace for fine art, antiques and collectibles. Auction houses, galleries and dealers use Invaluable to deepen relationships with millions of clients around the world, connecting people with the things they love.' The database consists of 58 million auction-price records, 4000 sellers, and data on fine art, decorative art, jewellery, collectibles, furniture and Asian art. Subscription plans range in price from $20 for a basic monthly subscription with limited data success to full-access, professional-level subscriptions priced at $1,995 per year.

www.artnet.com: According to the website, artnet's auction-price database contains 'over 11 million colour-illustrated art-auction records dating back to 1985. We cover more than 1,700 auction houses and 330,000 artists, and every lot is vetted by our team of multilingual specialists. Whether you are appraising a collection, researching an artist's market history, or pricing an artwork for sale, the Price Database will help you determine the value of art.' Subscription options range from $32.50 per day to $1,175 per year.

www.artprice.com: An auction record database consisting of over 30 million indices, econometric analyses and auction records for art; over 620,000 listed artists; information on 36,000 artist signatures, monograms and symbols; 120,000 artist biographies; coverage of 4,500 auction houses in 72 countries; fixed-price art for sale from Artprice stores, and more. Price records are for art sold at auctions held from 1987 to the present. Subscription plans range from $265 to $689 per year.

www.artvalue.com: Free art-auction-price database containing approximately 1.5 million auction records from works of art by 160,000 artists and 900 international auction houses.

www.askart.com: This website states that the auction-record database contains 'millions of auction results since 1987' but is not clear on numbers, and covers over 300,000 artists. Subscription options for individual users range from $14.95 for a twenty-four-hour period of access to $30.95 per month of access.

www.findartinfo.com: Pay art-auction-price database containing information for '438,004 artists – 3,775,766 art prices – 369,594 signatures – 2,269,620 photos of artwork'. You can see very abbreviated auction results at no charge (not much help, but better than nothing); to see complete details, you can pay by day, month or six-month periods. Subscription options range from $4.95 per day to $119.95 per year.

www.gordonsart.com: The LTB Gordonsart, Inc. website offers both photography and print price databases. Subscription options for each database range from $69.95 per month to $299 for the first year ($250 for each additional year).

www.liveauctioneers.com: This is an online auction website, but past sales results can also be searched. Having access to price results is free, but you do have to open an account in order to access them.

www.ebay.com: This is an online auction website, but recent past sales results can also be searched. Price results are free, but you do have to open an account in order to access them.

www.worthpoint.com: An auction-price database of antiques, art and vintage collectibles containing information on over 300 million items (including over 5.1 million works of art) and including over 1.2 billion images. Much of the database consists of archived eBay sales. Subscription options range from $19.99 per month to $539.99 per year.

ONLINE AUCTION SITES

www.liveauctioneers.com: The site is a platform for over 4,000 international auction houses to conduct sales online and offers art from all time periods and from around the world. Search both upcoming auctions as well as price results from past auctions. Since many of the firms conducting auctions on the site are smaller and do not necessarily have art experts on staff, thoroughly researching any items you are interested in bidding on is highly recommended. Make sure you fully understand item description before bidding. If you have any questions, ask. And save all email correspondences with sellers. Pay special attention to the terms and conditions of individual auction houses as well. They vary from auction house to auction house. Understand fully what the auction house is responsible for, and what you are responsible for, before bidding.

www.ebay.com: Anyone can sell art on eBay and that includes sellers who know little or nothing about art. So you have to be extra careful when bidding or buying. Make sure you fully understand any terms and conditions that sellers provide. Fully research any item you are interested in bidding on, make sure you understand item descriptions and verify any claims made by sellers. If you have any questions, ask. Save all email correspondences with sellers. If you know what you're doing, eBay can be a great place to shop. If you are just starting out, eBay can be a risky place to shop.

www.invaluable.com: The site is a platform for over 4,000 international auction houses to conduct sales online and offers art from all time periods and from around the world. Search both upcoming auctions as well as price results from past auctions. Since many of the firms conducting auctions on the site are smaller and do not necessarily have art experts on staff, thoroughly researching any items you are interested in bidding on is highly recommended. Make sure you fully understand the item description before bidding. If you have any questions, ask. And save all email correspondences with sellers. Pay special attention to the terms and conditions of individual auction houses as well. They vary from auction house to auction house. Understand fully what the auction house is responsible for, and what you are responsible for, before bidding.

www.paddle8.com: Paddle8 consists of art, collectibles and technology experts conducting art auctions focused primarily on post-war and contemporary art, prints and multiples, photographs, street art, collectibles and more. Paddle8 specialists curate all auction items. Individual collectors can consign their works to sell either at auction or via private sales. They do not disclose sales results or publish sales in price databases (not necessarily a good thing for either buyers or sellers).

www.artnet.com/auctions: artnet auctions focus primarily on modern and contemporary paintings, prints, photographs and more. All art offered on the site has been evaluated by artnet specialists. Every item description provides comprehensive information about the artwork, including details about provenance, condition and art-market data. artnet sellers guarantee the authenticity of every artwork listed on the site, and all bidders are protected by artnet's Return Policy and Terms of Use.

THE AUTHOR'S WEBSITE

Alan Bamberger's website, www.artbusiness.com, provides current articles, information, art-reference resource reviews and regular updates on art-market conditions for dealers, collectors and artists, and offers a wide range of services including appraisals, seminars, consulting and advising (for buyers, sellers and anyone else with issues involving art), collection development, expert witness testimony and complete comprehensive career consulting for artists. www.artbusiness.com is a consumer-oriented website with no conflicts of interest and prides itself on offering fair, honest and straightforward advice, content and opinions regarding current art-world events, and is dedicated to increasing knowledge and understanding of how the art business works.

THE AUTHOR'S SOCIAL MEDIA PAGES

Alan Bamberger is active on social media. Postings include links to current art-market articles, information and news, commentaries and discussions about significant art and artist issues, art-show and -event reviews and images, photographs of artists and more. You can follow him and keep current on all of that and more here:

https://www.facebook.com/bamberger.alan
https://www.facebook.com/alanbamberger.artbusiness
https://twitter.com/AlanBamberger
https://www.linkedin.com/in/artconsultant/
https://www.instagram.com/alanbamberger/

ART PERIODICALS

You can add yourself to the email lists of a number of the following publications in order to receive regular updates, news stories, event announcements, features, gallery and museum show reviews, and much more.

The American Art Review, www.amartrev.com: Good resource for period American art and artists, and contemporary artists who paint in traditional styles. Loads of dealer advertisements, illustrated reviews of regional museum shows from around the United States, and more.

Apollo, www.apollo-magazine.com: Articles and advertisements related primarily to British and European fine and decorative arts. Contemporary art is also covered.

Art & Antiques, www.artandantiquesmag.com: Coverage includes contemporary art, modern and post-war, outsider and folk art, Old Masters, tribal, antiques, photography, video and more.

Art in America, www.artinamericamagazine.com: Articles and advertisements relating to international contemporary art with the focus on contemporary art in America.

The Art Newspaper, www.theartnewspaper.com: Superior art-world news publication. Worldwide in-depth coverage of galleries, museums, legal issues, collectors, personalities and much more. A must for serious dealers, collectors and professionals. Plenty of great content on the website, some available free, access to their entire article database available for a fee.

Artforum, www.artforum.com: Articles and extensive advertisements relating primarily to domestic and international contemporary and avant-garde art. Good online content includes international exhibition announcements.

ARTnews, www.artnews.com: Articles and advertisements relate primarily to international contemporary art. Good content on the website.

Blouin Art & Auction, Blouin Modern Painting, Blouin Shop, Gallery Guide, www.blouinartinfo.com/subscriptions: Content includes visual arts, art fairs, galleries, auctions, reviews, architecture and design, performing arts, lifestyle, culture and travel. Available in both print and digital formats.

Journal of the Print World, www.journaloftheprintworld.com. Important resource for buying, selling and collecting of prints, drawings and photographs. Contains information about museum and library exhibitions, dealer catalogues, auction reviews, print fairs and more.

The Magazine ANTIQUES, www.themagazineantiques.com: 'Since its inception in 1922, *The Magazine ANTIQUES* has been America's premier publication on the fine and decorative arts, architecture, preservation, and interior design. Each bimonthly issue includes regular columns on current exhibitions, personalities in the field, notes on collecting, book reviews, and more.'

Note: There are numerous additional local, regional, national and international art-related periodicals, especially ones that focus exclusively on specific areas of collecting. Check with art dealers, collectors, art librarians and curators in relevant areas to see which best suit your needs.

ARTIST INDEXES

For those of you researching older antique or period art and artists, not all information about artist careers and accomplishments can be found online. Particularly for more minor or obscure artists, books still come in mighty handy on occasions, especially when it comes to acquiring biographical and career information. Here are some of the more significant such references, both online and in book form:

Art Index (New York: The H. W. Wilson Company, published quarterly). This publication indexes the articles and ads of over 680 art periodicals from around the world, and more than 14,000 art dissertations, and has nearly 218,000 art reproductions. It is extremely comprehensive and can be quite valuable not only in locating information about specific artists, but also in locating illustrations of works by those artists and names of dealers who deal in their art. All major art libraries subscribe to it and it is accessible online for a fee (www.ebscohost.com/academic/art-index).

The Artists of the World: Bio-bibliographical Index A–Z, 12 vols, second revised and enlarged edition (Berlin: Walter de Gruyter, 2002). Indexes and provides basic biographical information on over 730,000 artists (www.degruyter.com/view/serial/35779).

Busse, Joachim, *Internationales Handbuch Aller Maler und Bildhauer Des 19. Jahrhunderts* (Wiesbaden: Busse Kunst Dokumentation, 1977). This important and comprehensive index contains 89,000 entries of nineteenth-century painters and sculptors and is particularly strong on European art.

Caplan, H. H. and Creps, Bob, *Encyclopedia of Artist Signatures, Symbols, and Monograms* (Land O' Lakes: Dealer's Choice Books, 1999). Over 25,000 cross-indexed signature examples of American, European, Australian, Latin American, Russian and Canadian artists. Best signature index.

Castagno, John, *Artists' Signatures*. Database containing over 100,000 examples of signatures by 65,000 artists who worked in a variety of styles and mediums, including American, European, Old Masters, Middle Eastern, African, Latin American, British, Irish and more (www.artistssignatures.com).

Davenport's Art Reference and Price Guide (Phoenix: LTB Gordonsart, 2012). The reference contains over 335,000 entries. Now significantly outdated but it can still come in handy at times. Available as a book or CD-ROM (www.gordonsart.com).

Edwards, Gary, *International Guide to Nineteenth-Century Photographers and Their Works* (Boston: G. K. Hall & Co., 1988). Over 4,000 photographers of all nationalities. Much information taken from dealer and auction catalogues.

Havlice, P. P., *Index to Artistic Biography*, 2 vols (Metuchen: Scarecrow Press, 1973; first supplement, 1981). Good for researching American artists, but lists European artists as well.

Havlice, P. P., *World Painting Index*, 2 vols (Metuchen: Scarecrow Press, 1977; first supplement, 2 vols, 1982). Use this reference whenever you want to locate publications that contain illustrations of art by whatever artists you happen to be researching.

Mallett, D. T., *Mallett's Index of Artists*, 2 vols (New York: Peter Smith, 1948). This index is dated, but still worthwhile to check, especially if you are collecting art by artists who were active before 1950. Strong on American, adequate on European. A number of listings contain obscure information found hardly anywhere else.

McNeil, Barbara, *Artist Biographies Master Index* (Detroit: Gale Research Co., 1986). This index lists not only artists, but also photographers, craftspeople, illustrators, designers, graphic artists and architects. A bit quirky in terms of who's in it, but a worthwhile index to check, especially when you are researching less well-known artists. Strong on American, adequate on European.

Meyer, George H., *Folk Artists Biographical Index* (Detroit: Gale Research Co., 1987). Good to check if you collect American folk art. Lists artists who were active from the seventeenth century to the present. Not necessary to check otherwise.

Palmquist, Peter E. (ed.), *Photographers, A Sourcebook for Historical Research* (Nevada City: Carl Mautz Publishing, 2000). Includes a list of directories of photographers of all time periods and all nationalities, organised by country, and helpful articles and instructions on how to research photographers.

ARTIST ENCYCLOPAEDIAS

For those of you researching antique and period art, not all information about artist careers and accomplishments can be found online. Particularly for more minor or obscure artists, books still come in very handy on occasion, especially when it comes to acquiring biographical and career information. Here are some of the more significant such references:

The Artists of the World: Bio-bibliographical Index A–Z, 12 vols, second revised and enlarged edition (Berlin: Walter de Gruyter, 2002). Contains information on over 730,000 artists. Now available as a database on the De Gruyter Saur website (www.degruyter.com).

Benezit, Emmanuel, *Dictionnaire critique et documentaire des peintres, sculpteurs, desinateurs et graveurs, de tous le temps et tous le pays* (Paris: Librairie Grund, 2006). Now available through Oxford Art Online (www.oxfordartonline.com), the database contains nearly 170,000 artist entries from the 2006 English edition plus revisions and new biographies available exclusively online. You can access Benezit either separately or alongside *Grove Art* (*The Grove Dictionary of Art*) and other Oxford art reference works.

Bihalji-Merin, Oto. *World Encyclopedia of Naive Art* (London: Scala/Philip Wilson, 1985). If you like to buy folk or naive art, this reference is for you. Contains numerous colour illustrations.

Comanducci Dizionario Universale delle Belle Arti, 5 vols (Milan: Luigi Patuzzi Editore, 1970). Essential to check if you like to buy art by modern Italian artists. Contains numerous illustrations (www.comanducci.it).

Creps, Bob, *Biographical Encyclopedia of American Painters, Sculptors & Engravers of the U.S., Colonial to 2002*, 2 vols (Land O' Lakes: Dealer's Choice Books, 2002). Worthwhile reference for American artists of all time periods. Contains numerous signature examples and artist biographical information culled from over 600 reference resources on American art and artists. Also includes data on nearly 5,000 living artists.

Gesualdo, Vincente, *Enciclopedia del Arte en America*, 5 vols (Buenos Aires: Bibliografica Omeba, 1968). This is the encyclopaedia for you if your focus is on period Latin American art and artists. Contains black-and-white illustrations.

The Grove Dictionary of Art, 34 vols (New York: Grove's Dictionaries, Inc., 1999). This resource has been continually updated since it was published and is now accessible online through Oxford Art Online (www.oxfordartonline.com). It covers all forms of the visual arts including painting, sculpture, architecture, graphic arts, decorative arts, photography and more, from prehistory to the present.

Scheen, Pieter A., *Lexicon Nederlandse Beeldende Kunstenaars, 1750–1950*, 2 vols ('s-Gravenhage: Pieter A. Scheen, 1969).

Lists artists who were active in the Netherlands between 1750 and 1950.

Thieme, Ulrich and Becker, Felix, *Allgemeines Lexikon der Bildenden Kunstler*, 37 vols (Leipzig: Seemann, 1908–50). This is among the best and most comprehensive artist encyclopaedias. It lists artists from around the world who were active from the earliest times up through recent years, but is particularly strong on Europeans. Many times, you will find an artist listed here who is listed nowhere else. For information on the latest revised, enlarged edition, visit www.thieme-becker-vollmer.info.

Vollmer, Hans, *Allgemeines Lexicon der Bildenden Kunstler des 20. Jahrhunderts* (Leipzig: Seemann, 1996–7). Check this reference if you collect art by twentieth-century artists. Includes artists from around the world, but is particularly strong on Europeans. For the latest updates and information, visit www.thieme-becker-vollmer.info.

ARTIST DICTIONARIES

As mentioned in Appendix V, not all artist biographical and career information is available online. Especially with more minor or obscure artists whose art only infrequently comes up for sale in the marketplace, books may be the main resources for locating relevant information. This list is by no means complete, but the following specialised dictionaries and directories of artists are certainly worth checking if you find yourself coming up empty-handed elsewhere.

Cederholm, Theresa D., *Afro-American Artists, A Bio-bibliographical Directory* (Boston: Boston Public Library, 1973). Major African-American artist reference.

Cummings, Paul, *Dictionary of Contemporary American Artists* (New York: St Martin's Press, 1994). Good for researching American artists who began their careers after 1950.

Falk, Peter H., *Who Was Who in American Art*, 3 vols (Madison: Sound View Press, 1999). This is a superior single reference for researching American artists who were active at any time from the last quarter of the nineteenth century to 1975. It is primarily a condensation of artist listings from a series of books published between those years called *American Art Annuals* and the first four volumes of another series called *Who's Who in American*

Art, but numerous other references on American art and artists were consulted. Contains a few signature examplese.

Groce, George C. and Wallace, David H., *The New York Historical Society's Dictionary of Artists in America, 1564–1860* (New Haven: Yale University Press, 1957). This is the best single reference for researching American artists who were active at any time before 1860.

Johnson, J. and Greutzner, A., *The Dictionary of British Artists, 1880–1940* (Woodbridge: Antique Collectors' Club, 1984). The title of this book is self-explanatory.

Krantz, Les, *American Artists, an Illustrated Survey of Leading Contemporary Americans* (New York: Facts on File Publications, 1985). Best for researching American artists who began their careers after 1950. Each listing contains descriptive statements about the artist's art in addition to the usual biographical data. The book is also illustrated.

Lester, Patrick D., *Biographical Directory of Native American Painters* (Tulsa: Sir Publications, 1995). Best reference for Native American artists.

Mackay, James, *Dictionary of Sculptors in Bronze* (Woodbridge: Antique Collectors Club, 1977). Biographical information on 8,500 sculptors primarily from the eighteenth to the early twentieth centuries.

Milner, John, *A Dictionary of Russian and Soviet Artists, 1420–1970* (Woodbridge: Antique Collectors Club, 1993). Best quick reference on the subject. Contains illustrations.

Naylor, Colin, *Contemporary Artists* (Chicago: St James Press, 1989). This dictionary is recommended for researching contemporary artists from around the world. Most useful when researching artists who began their careers after 1950.

Opitz, Glenn B., *Dictionary of American Sculptors, 18th Century to the Present* (Poughkeepsie: Apollo, 1984). If you collect American sculpture, this book is an absolute necessity. Has illustrations at the rear of the book.

Opitz, Glenn B., *Mantle Fielding's Dictionary of American Painters, Sculptors & Engravers* (Poughkeepsie: Apollo, 1986). This book was once a standard art-business reference, but has since been superseded by more specialised and comprehensive references. Still good to check, though. Primarily covers American artists who were active before 1940.

Petteys, Chris, *Dictionary of Women Artists* (Boston: G. K. Hall, 1985). This extremely well-researched dictionary contains information about women artists from around the world who were active before 1900. It also has a great bibliography.

Wood, Christopher, *The Dictionary of Victorian Painters* (Woodbridge: Antique Collectors Club, 1981). Lists British artists who were active between 1837 and 1901. Contains about 500 illustrations that cover the full scope of Victorian painting. Excellent reference.

Zellman, Michael D., *300 Years of American Art*, 2 vols (Secaucus: Wellfleet Press, 1987). This dictionary lists over 800 American painters and covers the time period from the late seventeenth to the mid-twentieth centuries. Artist listings are comprehensive. Each contains at least one colour illustration, many also contain market information which, unfortunately, is well outdated. This is one of the best and most unique American art-reference books ever published.

ART ANNUALS AND DIRECTORIES

For those of you researching antique and period art, not everything you need in terms of acquiring information about artist careers and accomplishments can be found online. Particularly for more minor or obscure artists, books still come in very useful on occasion, especially when it comes to acquiring biographical and career information. Here are some of the more significant such references, both in book and online formats:

American Art Annual, 33 vols (Washington, DC: American Federation of Arts, 1898–1936). This is an excellent source of information about American artists who were active during this time period. Many major art libraries have the entire set of AAAs in their reference sections.

Art in America Annual Guide (www.artguide.pro). This extensive guide is now available online. Contains thousands of listings of art galleries, museums, non-profits, consultants and more. The focus is on contemporary American art, but it also includes information about a number of resources for period American art collectors.

International Directory of Arts (Berlin: De Gruyter Saur, 2016), www.degruyter.com. The current edition is available online and includes approximately 150,000 entries including museums and public galleries, universities, academies, schools, associations, fairs, galleries, auctioneers, art restorers, art publishers, art journals, art booksellers and more. This reference is extremely comprehensive and the closest thing to an almanac of the art world.

Official Museum Directory (www.officialmuseumdirectory. com): 'The authority for reliable museum data. Published in partnership with The American Alliance of Museums . . . the one-stop source for museum professionals, students, library patrons, and researchers who need comprehensive information on those institutions committed to celebrating and preserving the world's culture, art, music, nature, and history. This valuable reference is vital for all types of professionals working in this field, including curators, finance managers, educators, and suppliers. With accurate and frequently updated listings that provide operating hours, admission prices, exhibit information, and other essential details.'

Who's Who in American Art (New Providence: Marquis Who's Who, 1936; currently in its 36th edition for the year 2016), www.marquiswhoswho.com. This is a good basic source of information about American artists who have been active at any time between 1936 and the present. The more recent editions also list art curators, historians, librarians, writers, critics, gallery/museum administrators and other art-related professionals.

Significant Auction Houses

Altermann Galleries, 345 Camino Del Monte, Santa Fe, NM 87501, USA
Tel. +1 855 945 0448, www.altermann.com

Artcurial, 7 Rond-Point des Champs-Élysées, F-75008 Paris, France
Tel. +33 1 42 99 20 20, https://www.artcurial.com/en/artcurial

Bonhams, 101 New Bond St, Mayfair, London W1S 1SR, UK
Tel. +44 (0)20 7447 7447, www.bonhams.com

Bukowskis, 126 30 Hägersten, Stockholm, Sweden
Tel. +46 8 614 08 00, https://www.bukowskis.com/en

Christie's, 8 King Street, St James's, London SW1Y 6QT, UK
Tel. +44 (0)20 7839 2869, www.christies.com

Dorotheum, Palais Dorotheum, 1010 Wien, Dorotheergasse 17, Austria
Tel. +43 1 515 60 0, https://www.dorotheum.com/en.html

William Doyle Galleries, 175 East 87th St, New York, NY 10128, USA
Tel. +1 212 427 2730, www.doyle.com

Du Mouchelles, 409 East Jefferson Ave., Detroit, MI 48226, USA
Tel. +1 313 963 6255, www.dumouchelles.com

Eldred's Auctioneers, 1483 Route 6A, Box 796, East Dennis, MA 02641, USA
Tel. +1 508 385 3116, www.eldreds.com

Samuel T. Freeman and Co., 1808 Chestnut St, Philadelphia, PA 19103, USA
Tel. +1 215 563 9275, www.freemansauction.com

Heritage Auctions, 3500 Maple Ave., 17th Floor, Dallas, TX 75219, USA
Tel. +1 877 437 4284, www.ha.com

Leslie Hindman Auctioneers, 122 North Aberdeen St, Chicago, IL 60607, USA
Tel. +1 312 280 1212, www.lesliehindman.com

James D. Julia Auctioneer, Route 203, Skowhegan Road, Fairfield, ME 04937, USA
Tel. +1 207 453 7125, www.jamesdjulia.com

Ketterer Kunst, Joseph-Wild-Str. 18, 81829 Munich, Germany
Tel. +49 89 55 244 0, http://www.kettererkunst.com

Koller, Hardturmstrasse 102, CH 8031 Zürich, Switzerland
Tel. +41 44 445 63 63, https://www.kollerauktionen.ch/en/home.htm

Lempertz, Neumarkt 3, 50667 Cologne, Germany
Tel. +49 221 925729 0, https://www.lempertz.com/en.html

John Moran Auctioneers, 7145 East Walnut Ave., Monrovia,
CA 91016, USA
Tel. +1 626 793 1833, www.johnmoran.com

Neal Auction Company, 4038 Magazine St, New Orleans,
LA, USA
Tel. +1 800 467 5329, www.nealauction.com

Phillips, 30 Berkeley Square, London W1J 6EX, UK
+44 (0)20 7318 4010, www.phillips.com

Skinner Inc., 63 Park Plaza, Boston, MA 02116, USA
Tel. +1 617 350 5400, www.skinnerinc.com

Sotheby's, 34–35 New Bond Street, London W1A 2AA, UK
Tel. +44 (0)20 7293 5000, http://www.sothebys.com

Tajan, 37 rue des Mathurins, 75008 Paris, France
Tel. +33 1 53 30 30 30, https://www.tajan.com/en

Swann Galleries, 104 East 25th St #6, New York, NY 10010, USA
Tel. +1 212 254 4710, www.swanngalleries.com

Adam A. Weschler and Son, 40 West Gude Drive, Rockville,
MD 20850, USA
Tel. +1 202 628 1281, www.weschlers.com

A good basic international auction house directory is maintained by artnet at www.artnet.com/auction-houses/directory. Some of the major art-price database websites listed in Appendix II also maintain comprehensive lists of international auction houses, and you can search for auction companies in your area online.

APPRAISER ASSOCIATIONS

Note: There are no UK or EU specialist appraiser membership organisations. For valuation questions, you might try contacting relevant specialists at auction houses listed in Appendix VIII, or relevant galleries and specialists through dealer associations listed in Appendix X.

International Fine Art Appraisers, 478 West Broadway New York, NY 10012, USA
Tel: +1 212 475 0622 Fax: +1 212 475 5709 www.ifaacertified.com

International Society of Appraisers, 225 West Wacker Drive, Suite 650, Chicago, IL 60606, USA
Tel: +1 312 981 6778 Fax: +1 312 265 2908 www.isa-appraisers.org

American Society of Appraisers, 11107 Sunset Hills Rd, Suite 310 Reston, VA 20170, USA
Tel: +1 703 478 2228 Fax: +1 703 742 8471 www.appraisers.org

Appraisers Association of America, 212 West 35th St, 11th Fl. So., New York, NY 10001, USA
Tel: +1 212 889 5404 Fax: +1 212 889 5503 www.appraisersassoc.org

Association of Online Appraisers, Inc., 1612 Shookstown Rd, Frederick, MD 21702, USA
Tel: +1 301 228 2279 www.aoaonline.org

When choosing an appraiser, the most important questions to ask are whether they specialise in appraising art – particularly the kinds of art that you own– and how much experience they have and how long they've been appraising it. Which associations they belong to or how long they've belonged are also important, but what's most important is that they have experience appraising the types of art that you own.

ART DEALER ASSOCIATIONS

The Society of London Art Dealers
CK International House, 1–6 Yarmouth Place, Mayfair,
London W1J 7BU, UK
Tel: +44 (0)20 3617 0531 www.slad.org.uk

LAPADA, Association of Art & Antiques Dealers
535 King's Road, London SW10 0SZ, UK
Tel: +44 (0)20 7823 3511 lapada.org

Federation of European Art Galleries Association
c/o Galerie De Zwarte Panter, Hoogstraat 70-72, B-2000,
Antwerp, Belgium
Tel: +32 32 34 92 93 www.europeangalleries.org

Art and Antique Dealers League of America, Inc.
PO Box 2066, Lenox Hill Station New York, NY 10021, USA
Tel: +1 212 879 7558 Fax: +1 212 772 7197 www.aadla.com

Art Dealers Association of America
205 Lexington Ave. #901, New York, NY 10016, USA
Tel: +1 212.488.5550 www.artdealers.org

Association of International Photography Art Dealers
2025 M Street, NW, Washington, DC 20036, USA
Tel: +1 202 367 1158 www.aipad.com

Fine Art Dealers Association
9663 Santa Monica Blvd, Suite 316, Beverly Hills, CA
90210, USA
Tel: +1 310 659 9888 www.fada.org

International Fine Print Dealers Association
250 W. 26th St, Suite 405, New York, NY 10001, USA
Tel: +1 212 674 6095 Fax: +1 212 674 6783 www.ifpda.org

National Antique and Art Dealers Association of America
220 East 57th St, New York, NY 10022, USA
www.naadaa.org

Private Art Dealers Association
P.O. Box 872 Lenox Hill Station, New York, NY 10021, USA
Tel: +1 917 200 8167 www.pada.net

ART REFERENCE BOOKSELLERS

Thomas Heneage Art Books
42 Duke Street, St James's, London SW1Y 6DJ, UK
Tel: +44 (0)20 7930 9223, www.heneage.com

Sims Reed
43A Duke Street, St James's, London SW1Y 6DD, UK
Tel: +44 (0)20 7930 5566 www.simsreed.com

Marcus Campbell Art Books
43 Holland Street, London SE1 9JR, UK
Tel: +44 (0)20 7261 0111, www.marcuscampbell.co.uk

Art Base, Gabelsbergerstr. 15, 97318 Kitzingen, Germany
Tel: +49 9321 268855, http://artbase-books.de

Arcana: Books on the Arts
8675 Washington Blvd, Culver City, CA 90232, USA
Tel: +1 310 458 1499 www.arcanabooks.com

Hennessey + Ingalls
300 S. Santa Fe Ave., Los Angeles, CA 90013, USA
Tel: +1 213 437 2130 Fax: +1 213 437 2134 www.hennessey-ingalls.com

Ursus Books Ltd
981 Madison Ave., New York, NY 10021, USA
Tel: +1 212 772 8787 www.ursusbooks.com

Note: For out-of-print, hard-to-find and rare art-book titles, visit the International League of Antiquarian Booksellers (www.ilab.org) or the Antiquarian Booksellers Association of America (www.abaa.org) and search their membership directories for booksellers specialising in the types of art that you like to buy. If you know the title and/or author of the book you're looking for, you can also search international online databases of new, used, rare and out-of-print books like www.addall.com, www.bookfinder.com, www.abebooks.com or www.alibris.com.

ONLINE ARTIST RESEARCH: TIPS AND TECHNIQUES

Knowing how to research an artist online is necessary for a number of reasons. Those reasons include finding out price information, comparison shopping, finding out where else art by the artist may be available for sale, locating biographical information, determining how desirable an artist's art might be in the marketplace, evaluating the artist's overall online presence, and in order to confirm or corroborate what sellers tell you about the art.

- *Begin by searching the artist's name to see all search results.* The results may include galleries or dealers showing or representing the artist; the artist's website; websites, blogs or pages dedicated to the artist; articles, reviews or features on the artist; art for sale; videos of the artist; the artist's social media pages, etc.

- *If another person turns out to have the same name as the artist, subtract select keywords from your search in order to remove all results containing those words.* Do this by placing a minus in front of each word. For example, if your search also shows results for a musician with the same name, add keyword/minus sign combinations to the artist's name like '-music' or '-musician' or '-discography' or '-song' in order to eliminate all search results containing those words. Soon you will have mainly results for the artist.

- *Pages from Pinterest often clog search results with irrelevant images or links that have no research value.* When this is a problem, add the keyword and minus sign '-pinterest' to your search in order to eliminate results from that website.
- *To locate price information for an artist:* search the artist's name along with keywords like 'price' or 'sold' or 'for sale'. When the artist is from another country, also searching those terms in the language of that country may yield additional results.
- *To locate auction-price information for an artist:* search the artist's name along with the keywords 'auction' and 'price'.
- *To locate biographical or career information:* search the artist's name along with terms like 'biography', 'bio', 'CV' or 'résumé'.
- *To see whether anyone (dealers, collectors, galleries, etc.) is interested in acquiring works of art by the artist:* search the artist's name along with the word 'wanted' or the phrase 'wanted to buy'. Positive results for this search generally give an idea of the strength of the market for the artist. You don't really want to contact any of these individuals or businesses, but simply make a note of them.
- *To search a particular type of art by the artist:* search the artist's name along with keywords like 'painting', 'sculpture', 'limited edition' or 'photograph' in order to narrow results to those specific types of art.
- *To search a specific limited edition print, search the artist's name along with the title of that print.* If you get confusing results, put quotes around the title. Titles may vary or a print may have more than one title, especially when the artist is from another country. Often searching the title in

the language of the artist's home country yields the best results.

- *Google image searches often yield interesting search results as well.* To do an image search, type images.google.com into the search bar and click the camera icon at the right of the search field. This will show you an option to either upload an image from your computer or paste in the URL of that image if the image is already online. Results may include pages where the art is for sale, collections that own the art if it's a limited edition print, past auction sales results, similar works of art by the artist, etc. Image searches are usually worth doing.

- *To search prices for a particular type of art by the artist:* search the artist's name along with the relevant keyword combinations like 'painting' and 'price', 'sculpture' and 'price', etc.

- *Search major social media platforms to see whether the artist maintains pages, or whether individuals or galleries maintain pages or post on the artist's behalf.*

INDEX